Fund Palestine Exploration

Our work in Palestine

1865

Fund Palestine Exploration

Our work in Palestine
1865

ISBN/EAN: 9783337282660

Printed in Europe, USA, Canada, Australia, Japan

Cover: Foto ©Andreas Hilbeck / pixelio.de

More available books at **www.hansebooks.com**

OUR WORK IN PALESTINE;

BEING

AN ACCOUNT OF THE DIFFERENT EXPEDITIONS SENT OUT TO THE HOLY LAND

BY THE

Committee of the Palestine Exploration Fund

SINCE THE

ESTABLISHMENT OF THE FUND IN 1865.

ISSUED BY THE COMMITTEE.

TORONTO:
ADAM, STEVENSON, & CO.

1873.

PREFACE.

THIS book is designed as a full answer to the question often asked, "What have you done in Palestine?" It is intended to tell what we have done up to the present date, why we have done it, and what we propose to do in future. Thus—as everybody has not read the works of Messrs. Robinson, George Williams, Lewin, Fergusson, and Captain Wilson—it has been thought advisable to give, as briefly as possible, some account of Palestine knowledge previous to our work; to re-tell the story of the City; to select some of the historical evidence, without comment, as to the sites; and to give the rival theories, before showing what Captain Warren has done in Jerusalem.

The accounts of the expeditions of Captain Wilson, Captain Anderson, that of Captain War-

ren's country work, that of Professor Palmer
and Mr. Tyrwhitt Drake, are here for the first
time collected together from their letters and
reports. The Sinai Survey does not belong to
us, but is introduced here, as without it Professor
Palmer's story would be incomplete. The survey of Palestine—a work which will, we hope,
prove of inestimable benefit to the students of
the Bible—is now in progress, and asks for your
support. And whatever you read in the following pages is, remember, but an instalment of
what we have to do. As is explained in another
place—*we have not done yet.*

9, PALL MALL EAST, S.W., OCT., 1872.

TABLE OF CONTENTS.

"LOOK UNTO THE ROCK WHENCE YE ARE HEWN, AND TO THE HOLE OF THE PIT WHENCE YE ARE DIGGED."—ISAIAH, LI. I.

CHAPTER I.

THE EXPLORATION OF PALESTINE.

PALESTINE* is a name which in the Authorized Version is applied only to Philistia, and not to the rest of the country at all. As such it is used by Milton, when he speaks of "that twice battered God of Palestine." The country is spoken of in the Bible by more than one name. It is called the Land of Canaan, as opposed to the Land of Gilead, lying on the opposite side of

* See, for the best *résumé* of the subject, Smith's "Dictionary of the Bible," article "Palestine," by Mr. George Grove.

B

the river Jordan; the Land of the Hebrews (Genesis, xl. 15 only); the Land of the Hittites (Josh., i. 4); the Land of Israel (1 Samuel, xiii. 19, &c.) during the Monarchy. In Hosea it is the Land of Jehovah; in Zechariah it is the Holy Land; in Daniel the Glorious Land; in Amos it is the Land of the Amorite; while sometimes it is simply "the Land." Between the Captivity and the time of our Lord, the name Judæa had extended itself over the whole country; and in 2 Esdras, xv. 31, it is called the Land of Zion.

The name of Palestine was given to the whole country after the Christian era. Ptolemy (A.D. 161) calls it Palæstina. Later on it was divided into Palæstina Prima, Secunda, and Tertia.

The name by which it was known during the middle ages was "Terra Sancta," the Holy Land.

The whole country is no larger than the Principality of Wales—viz., 140 miles long and 40 in average breadth. Small as this theatre of the most stupendous drama in the world's history is, it has never to this day been scientifically or even superficially explored. From end to end are ruins. There are ruins which the Israelites found when first they dispossessed the Canaanites; ruins which date from their own two monarchies; ruins of that long period between Nehemiah and Herod; ruins Herodian; ruins Roman, but post Herodian; ruins Christian; ruins Saracenic; ruins Christian, of later date; and ruins Mohammedan. On every hill-top is a heap, on every hillside is a mound. No traveller, even if there were one found totally ignorant of the Bible and its histories, could put foot upon the soil without perceiving at once that it is a land of ancient story. What that long story is we know. What we want to do—the reason for which we exist—is so to clear up our geographical and archæological knowledge of the country as to make its history intelligible to its readers. It is not too much to say, that the first clear grasp of Palestine geography is like a revelation: it makes that light which was dark; it shows us as men and women those who were before puppets; it makes their actions intelligible which were before obscure, or even fantastic. You will see, as we go on, how we have done this in some cases, and how we hope to do it for all.

The country consists of plains, hills, and torrent beds. A range of hills extends from the Lebanon southwards, having on either side, east and west, a belt of lowland, to which access is gained by the ravines (*fiumaras*, as Captain Burton calls them), the *wadies* which, dry in summer, carry down the winter rains to the plains below. To know this country intimately, to be able to describe its peculiarities, and to illustrate by its present condition the narrative of the Old and New Testament, is the aim of every earnest student of the Bible, and more especially of those who, by assuming the duties and responsibilities of teachers, may influence the young so powerfully to feel either repugnance or love to the Sacred Books.

Of the authorities from which this knowledge can be obtained, we have, first of all, Josephus, a writer who, with many faults, has yet a priceless value. He knew his own country, probably, as few Jews of his time knew it; for he had studied its capabilities as a general as well as its story as a student. It is true that he exaggerates from time to time—whenever, that is, he is not checked by the stern facts of Roman engineers; but in all cases, save where the national glory is concerned, he appears to be entirely trustworthy.

There comes next the *Onomasticon*, which is the translation and the expansion by Jerome of a tract by Eusebius.

The early travellers in Palestine often left notes of their journey, itineraries, description of the sacred sites, &c. Among them are the Bourdeaux Pilgrim, A.D. 330; Bishop Arculf, A.D. 700; Willibald, A.D. 720; Bernard the Wise, A.D. 867; Sæwulf, A.D. 1103; Benjamin of Tudela, A.D. 1163, and others. See "Early Travels in Palestine" (Bohn's Antiquarian Library, 1848).

The next geographical work is to be found in the very curious Peutingerianæ Tabulæ, which are a map of the whole Roman Empire at a date fixed, by a most ingenious and exhaustive argument in the first edition, at the year 393 A.D. The tables were found in the year 1753 in the library of Vienna, and published, with a treatise on their date and value, in that year. They have never been published in England at all, and the map of Palestine here printed will be new to most of our readers. Its chief value is in the roads, which are accurately laid down, with the distances. One of these roads was actually found in the Desert of Tîh, by Professor Palmer and Mr. Tyrwhitt Drake, just as it is laid down here. Curious illustrations of the change of names may be gathered from the map. The name of Ælia Capitolina still holds its own, but the world is now Christian; and we are reminded that it was called formerly Jerusalem. Cæsarea Philippi, formerly Paneas (now Banias), is now losing its later name, and appears as Cæsarea Paneas. The old Bethshean, which has now regained its name and is called Beisan, still retains the Greek name of Scythopolis. Neapolis (now Nablous) stands over the site of Shechem. Tyre, Sidon, Beyrout, are there; and in the north our modern Baalbec, under its Greek name of Heliopolis, the City of the Sun.

We come next to Mohammedan books. Of these, the two best known are the works of Edrisi and Mejr ed Deen. The account of Jerusalem during the twelfth century by the former is given in Mr. Williams's "Holy City," vol. i., appendix ii. Side by side with this he gives an anonymous account, called the "Norman Chronicle," written after the conquest of the city by Saladin. In the same appendix will also be found an account of the Haram Area by Mejr ed Deen. Abulfeda also, about 1300, wrote his description of Syria, which has been translated. There is no doubt that further research in Arabic literature will yield much valuable infor-

mation. We come next to modern books on
Palestine. Their name is legion. We may mention, before modern travellers revolutionized our
previous notions on the subject, two principal
writers. Quaresmius' "Terræ Sanctæ Eluci-
datio" was published in 1639; and it contains
general dissertations, with five books of peregri-
nations through the Holy Land, historical accounts, and attempts at identification. Here also
are given all the Latin traditions of every site.

Reland's "Palæstina ex Monumentis Veteri-
bus illustrata" contains everything that was
known or could be gathered from travellers and
writers down to his own time.

It was not till the present century that travel in
Palestine changed its form from the enthusiasm of
pilgrimage to the colder spirit which belongs to
research. Seetzen was the first. In the years
1805 to 1807 he travelled to the east and west
of the Jordan, being the first to visit the Hauran,
the Ghor, and the mountains of ʿAjlun. He
travelled completely round the Dead Sea borders,
exploring the east side a second time. He was
employed by the Oriental Museum at Gotha, to
collect antiquities and natural objects.

It was about this time that, stimulated no
doubt by the accounts sent home from Seetzen,
a small body of Englishmen formed themselves
into the "Palestine Exploration Society." Of
their labours, and of the means which they had
at their disposal, we have not been able to find
any trace, except in one thin folio volume of

travels. Probably the disturbed state of Europe at the time prevented any successful appeal for funds; and the Committee, disheartened at their ill-fortune, allowed the project to be deferred till a more fitting opportunity—that is to say, for sixty years.

Burckhardt, whose travels were published in 1822, is chiefly remarkable for his labours in the Trans-Jordanic regions. He was the first to visit the Leja, being sent out by an English society, and made a very full description of regions which were then entirely unknown.

At the same time, Messrs. Irby and Mangles were visiting the Holy Land, and especially the country of Moab.

But the first real impulse, because the first successful impulse, towards scientific examination of the Holy Land is due to the American traveller, Dr. Robinson. He it was who first conceived the idea of making a work on Biblical Geography, to be based, not on the accounts of others, but on his own observations and discoveries. He fitted himself for his ambitious undertaking by the special studies of fifteen years, mastering the whole literature of the subject, and, above all, clearing the way for his own researches by noticing the deficiencies and weak points of his predecessors. He went, therefore, *knowing what to look for* and what had been already found. His first journey was in 1838, his second in 1852. On each occasion he had the good fortune to be accompanied by his

fellow-countryman, Dr. Eli Smith, a master of
the Arabic language, and a keen and careful
observer.   Both travellers were gifted with that
calm and sober common sense necessary, above
all things, in a country where enthusiasm so often
endangers accuracy, and a man perfectly and
entirely truthful and honest sees what he wishes
to see.   Dr. Robinson seems first to have recognized that most important aid to Biblical
identification, the modern Arabic names, and his
work (first edition) contains a very valuable list
of names, chiefly collected by Dr. Eli Smith.
Dr. Robinson, starting with the broad canon
"that all ecclesiastical tradition respecting the
sacred places in and round Jerusalem and
throughout Palestine is of no value, except so
far as it is supported by circumstances known
to us from the Scriptures or from other contemporary history," was the first (except the
German bookseller, Korte, of the eighteenth century) to impugn the accuracy of the traditional
sites.   We shall not go into the question here
of his theories, and his reconstruction of the old
city, on which he has had both followers and
opponents.   Let it, however, be distinctly remembered that Dr. Robinson is the *first* of
scientific travellers.   His travels took him over
a very large extent of ground, covering a large
part of the whole country from Sinai north, and
his books are still, after thirty years, the most
valuable works which we possess on the geography of Palestine.

His principal opponent, as regards the genuineness of the sacred sites, is the Rev. George Williams, to whom we refer in many places farther on. Mr. Williams's work, entitled "The Holy City," published in 1843, remains a monument of erudition and research. No writer on Palestine, probably, has approached his subject with a deeper love and reverence for it than is everywhere shown by Mr. Williams. No writer, certainly, has more laboriously collected information and evidence. He is supported in those of his arguments which rest upon architectural points by the authority of Professor Willis, a name of the greatest possible weight in ecclesiastical architecture. The book, which is by no means intended to be entirely controversial, gives the history of the city from the earliest to modern times, with special reference to that obscure period of its ecclesiastical history between the foundation of our faith and the conquest of the country by the Caliph Omar. It is greatly to be wished that this work should be republished in a form more adapted to general use, and with Mr. Williams's opinions, as modified or strengthened by the recent discoveries.

In 1848, Lieutenant Lynch and his party went down the Jordan, in two open boats, from the Lake of Galilee to the Dead Sea. The latter they thoroughly surveyed and sounded. The official report of this journey has become the standard authority upon this most curious and remarkable feature of Palestine.

Other American books, more recently published, have maintained the reputation of American explorers. Among them may be mentioned especially, Dr. Thomson's "The Land and the Book," which added largely to our knowledge of Biblical localities, and assisted in popularizing the illustrations of the Bible from the natural scenery and history of the Holy Land, and from the manners and customs of the present inhabitants; Dr. Barclay's "City of the Great King" (1858); Mr. Osborne's "Palestine, Past and Present;" and Professor Hackett's "Illustrations of Scripture." Besides these, there have been issued in America, from time to time, a large number of papers, journals, and reports, upon the same fruitful theme. France has been represented by the Count de Vogüé (with his travelling companion, Mr. Waddington); M. de Saulcy's "Voyage autour de la Mer Morte" (1853), and "La Terre Sainte;" M. Renan's work in Phœnicia; M. Lartet's geological researches; M. Clermont Ganneau, and others. Germany has Schwarz's "Sepher Tebuoth," translated into English, and published in Philadelphia under the title of "A Descriptive Geography of Palestine;" Tobler's "Topographie von Jerusalem und Seine Umgebungen" (1854); and other works, especially valuable to those who cannot find time or are otherwise unable to refer to originals; and Ritter's "Die Vergleichende Erd Kunde, &c.," of which great geographical work six volumes are devoted to Sinai, the Holy Land, and Syria.

Lieutenant Van de Velde, of the Dutch navy, has produced the best map yet published of Palestine, accompanied by his "Syria and Palestine" (2 vols., 1854), and his "Memoire" (1858), which gives elevations, latitudes, longitudes, and much valuable information.

Among more recent travellers may be mentioned the Dean of Westminster, whose "Sinai and Palestine" is the most widely known of recent books on the subject; the Rev. Dr. Porter, the Rev. Canon Tristram, Captain Burton, the Rev. H. Bonar, Herr Wetzstein, and many others.

The foundation of the Palestine Exploration Fund, whose original prospectus is added as a note to this chapter, is due mainly to the exertions of Mr. George Grove, one of the most laborious and zealous contributors to "Smith's Bible Dictionary." The compilation of these volumes, while it collected together the most able and competent men for a work so much wanted, and gave the world for the first time a digest of all the knowledge in their hands up to that date, revealed a state of ignorance in many branches which struck the writers with something akin to shame. It seemed to them, as it seems now, that while we, as a people, pride ourselves, and justly, on being the greatest lovers and the most earnest students of the Bible in the world; while our children's minds are steeped in the history of the Old and New Testaments; while those illus-

trations go the deepest into our hearts which
are founded on the Bible; while no language
touches us so keenly as the grand, sonorous
language of the Bible; while every incident in the
Bible is familiar to us; while we love it and
reverence it so much that we believe nothing can
be a greater boon to those savage races over
which GOD has placed us as masters than to give
them the Bible—with all this love, all this reverence, all this desire to make others participate
in our own blessings, the land remains unknown
and unexplored. Turn over the pages of the
"Dictionary," read the notices of the "fenced
towns" and ancient cities: their sites are unknown,
uncertain, only guessed at. Go, if you will, to
Jerusalem. As you watch the pilgrims kneeling
at the Holy Sepulchre, you cannot be moved like
the rest, because you know that some have said
it cannot be here at all, but is where the Moslems
have built their Dome of the Rock. But here,
again, there is no certainty; because another has
called it the site of the tomb of Alexander
Jannæus. Where was the Temple? Where was
the Altar? Was it here? Was it there? We
know nothing for certain, till we can prove it
by excavation. Where were the Tombs of the
Kings? Where was David buried? We know
not. Where was the inner wall, behind which the
Jews made their last and most desperate stand
against the legions of Titus? We know not.
Unless we agree to accept tradition, and stifle
the voice of criticism, we know nothing certainly.

And yet, when we do know, with what fulness of light the history comes in upon us! "Here," says Captain Anderson, "we can trace exactly the adventurous journey of King Saul, when, the night before his death, he sought counsel of the Witch of Endor." And so, too, Dean Stanley, standing at the head of the mountain pass of Bethhoron, could see in imagination the flying hordes of Canaanites overtaken by the driving storm of sleet and hail, while the leader of the Israelites stood at the head of the valley and watched the enemy flee. It is by such realization, even at second-hand, that faith is strengthened and reverence increased.

To help every one who cares to read the Bible intelligently, to lead those who care for it little to care for it much, to give light to dark places, to make things hard become things easy, to narrow the bounds of controversy—these are some of the aims of the Palestine Exploration Fund.

NOTE.

(FROM THE ORIGINAL PROSPECTUS OF 1865.)

No country should be of so much interest to us as that in which the documents of our Faith were written, and the momentous events they describe enacted. At the same time, no country more urgently requires illustration. The face of the landscape, the climate, the productions, the manners, dress, and modes of life of its inhabitants differ in so many material respects from those of the western world, that without an accurate knowledge of

them it is not too much to say the outward form and
complexion of the events and much of the significance of
the records must remain more or less obscure. Even to
a casual traveller in the Holy Land the Bible becomes, in
its form, and therefore to some extent in its substance, a
new book. Many an allusion which hitherto had no
meaning, or had lain unnoticed, starts into prominence
and throws a light over a whole passage. It is not to be
expected that the modes of life and manners of the ancient
Israelites will be revealed by any discovery of monuments
in the same fulness that those of the Egyptians and
Assyrians have been. But, still, information of value cannot fail to be obtained in the process. Much would be
gained by obtaining an accurate map of the country; by
settling disputed points of topography; by identifying
ancient towns of Holy Writ with the modern villages
which are their successors; by bringing to light the
remains of so many races and generations which must lie
concealed under the accumulation of rubbish and ruins
on which those villages stand; by ascertaining the course
of the ancient roads; by the discovery of coins, inscriptions, and other relics—in short, by doing at leisure and
systematically that which has hitherto been entirely
neglected, or done only in a fragmentary manner by the
occasional unassisted efforts of hurried and inexperienced
travellers. Who can doubt that if the same intelligence,
zeal, knowledge, and outlay were applied to the exploration of Palestine that have recently been brought to bear
on Halicarnassus, Carthage, Cyrene—places without a
single sacred association, and with little bearing on the
Bible—the result would be a great accession to our
knowledge of the successive inhabitants of Syria—
Canaanite, Israelite, Roman?

Hitherto the opportunity for such systematic research has been wanting. It appears now to have arrived. The visit of H.R.H. the Prince of Wales to the Mosque at Hebron has broken down the bar which for centuries obstructed the entrance of Christians to that most venerable of the sanctuaries of Palestine; and may be said to have thrown open the whole of Syria to Christian research.

The survey of Jerusalem at present in progress under the direction of Captain Wilson, R.E.—a survey supported by the private liberality of a single person—has shown how much may be done, with tact, temper, and opportunity, without arousing the opposition of the authorities or inhabitants. Recent letters of Sir H. James and others in the *Times* have borne testimony to the remarkable fitness of Captain Wilson for such undertakings, and have pointed out other places where explorations might be advantageously carried on.

It is therefore proposed to raise a fund to be applied to the purposes of investigating the Holy Land by employing competent persons to examine the following points:—

1. *Archæology.*—Jerusalem alone would furnish an ample field in this department. What is above ground will be accurately known when the present survey is completed; but below the surface hardly anything has yet been discovered. The Tombs of the Kings on Mount Zion—the course of the Tyropœon Valley—the real extent of the Temple enclosure—the site of the Tower of Antonia —of the Palace of Herod—of Ophel—of the Pool of Bethesda—the position of the towers of Hippicus and Psephinus—the spring and conduit of Hezekiah—are all awaiting excavation; and it is not too much to anticipate that every foot in depth of the "sixty feet of rubbish" on

which the city stands will yield interesting and important materials for the archæologist or the numismatist.

Beyond the Holy City the country is full of sites which cannot fail amply to repay examination. Of these a few only may be enumerated:—Mount Gerizim, possibly the Moriah of Abraham's sacrifice, certainly the Holy Place of the Samaritans, containing the stones which they allege to have been brought up by Israel from the bed of the Jordan—the Valley of Shechem, the earliest settlement of Jacob in the Holy Land, with his well, and the tomb of Joseph—Samaria, with the traditional tombs of John the Baptist and others, and with the extensive remains of Herod's edifices—the splendid Roman cities along the coast, Cæsarea of Herod and St. Paul—Antipatris—the once-renowned harbours of Jamnia and Gaza—the mounds and other remains of Jiljilieh, probably the Gilgal which contained the great College of Prophets in the days of Elijah and Elisha—the Fortress and Palace of Herod at Jebel Fureidis—the tombs (probably those of Joshua) at Tibneh—the mounds at Jericho—the numerous remains in the valley of the Jordan—Bethshean, one of the most ancient cities of Palestine, with remarkable remains of Roman, and perhaps still earlier, date—Jezreel, the capital of Ahab and Jezebel—the Assyrian mound, called Tel es Salhiyeh, near Damascus, &c., &c.

2. *Manners and Customs.*—A work is urgently required which shall do for the Holy Land what Mr. Lane's "Modern Egyptians" has done for Egypt—describe in a systematic and exhaustive order, with clear and exact minuteness, the manners, habits, rites, and language of the present inhabitants, with engravings intended, like his, "not to embellish the pages, but to explain the text." Many of the ancient and peculiar customs of Palestine are fast vanish-

ing before the increasing tide of Western manners, and in a short time the exact meaning of many things which find their correspondences in the Bible will have perished. There are frequent references to these things in the books of travellers, and they have recently formed the subject of more than one entire work; but nothing sufficiently accurate or systematic has been done. It can only be accomplished by the lengthened residence of a thoroughly competent person.

3. *Topography.*—Of the coast-line of Palestine we now possess an accurate map in the recent Admiralty charts. What is wanted is a survey which, when we advance inland, should give the position of the principal points throughout the country with equal accuracy. If these were fixed, the intermediate spots and the smaller places could be filled in with comparative ease and certainty. In connection with the topography is the accurate ascertainment of the levels of the various points. The elevation of Jerusalem and the depression of the Dead Sea are already provided for by the liberality of the Royal Society and the Royal Geographical Society; but the level of the Sea of Galilee (on which depends our knowledge of the true fall of the Jordan) is still uncertain within no less than 300 ft.—as are other spots of almost equal moment.

The course of the ancient roads, and their coincidence with the modern tracks, has never been examined with the attention it deserves, considering its importance in the investigation of the history.

The principle on which the modern territorial boundaries are drawn, and the towns and villages allotted between one district and another, would probably throw light on the course of boundaries between the tribes and the distribution of the villages, which form the most puz-

C

zling point in the otherwise clear specification of the Book
of Joshua.

4. *Geology.*—Of this we are in ignorance of almost
every detail. The valley of the Jordan and basin of the
Dead Sea is, geologically, one of the most remarkable
on the earth's surface. To use the words of Sir Roderick
Murchison, "it is the key to the whole of the geology of
the district." Its Biblical interest is equally great. To
name but one point. The decision of the question whether any volcanic changes have occurred round the margin
of the lake within the historical period, may throw a new
aspect over the whole narrative of the destruction of
Sodom and Gomorrah.

5. *Natural Sciences—Botany, Zoology, Meteorology.*—
These are at present but very imperfectly known, while
the recent investigations of Mr. Tristram, limited as they
necessarily were, show that researches are likely to furnish results of no common scientific interest. Naturalist
after naturalist will devote himself for years to the forests
of South America, or the rivers of Africa. Why should
we not have some of the same energy and ability applied
to the correct description of the lilies and cedars, the
lions, eagles, foxes, and ravens of the Holy Land?

It will perhaps be said that many of the points above
enumerated have been already examined—that Robinson,
Stanley, Rosen, and others have done much in the department of topography—that Hooker, and more recently
Tristram, have reported on the botany—that Roth and
Tristram have brought home shells, fish, birds, and eggs—
that the researches of M. Lartet on the geology of the
Dead Sea, and those of the Duc de Luynes, De Vogüé,
and De Saulcy on archæology, are on the eve of publication. This is true; but without intending to detract from

the usefulness or the credit of the labours of these eminent
men, it is sufficient to observe that their researches have
been partial and isolated, and their results, in too many
cases, discrepant with each other. What is now proposed
is an expedition composed of thoroughly competent persons in each branch of research, with perfect command of
funds and time, and with all possible appliances and facili-
ties, who should produce a report on Palestine which
might be accepted by all parties as a trustworthy and
thoroughly satisfactory document.

CHAPTER II.

THE MODERN CITY.

To describe the City of Jerusalem as it now exists would seem to be repeating an oft-told tale. Travellers, it will be said, have done so over and over again, till the very school children are familiar with the stones of the city, its aspect from the Mount of Olives, and the ruins over which the modern houses are built. This is true; but most of the travellers have described the city as it appeared to them during a short stay of two or three weeks at most. And amid all the modern books of travel in Palestine which have appeared so plentifully during the last thirty years, it seems to us that there are very few which have given a faithful and com-

PLAN OF JERUSALEM

plete account of the city as it is. Among these may be mentioned Robinson's "Biblical Researches in Palestine," the Rev. George Williams's invaluable work on "The Holy City," and the "Notes" to the Ordnance Survey, written by Captain Wilson. The costly nature of the last-named publication puts it out of the reach of most, and the two preceding works have for some time been out of print. Let us, then, with Captain Wilson's map before us, take a preliminary walk round and through the city. It may safely be premised that, except to those who have already studied the question—and for those we do not write—many points, without which neither the work nor the views of the Palestine Exploration Fund would be intelligible, will be cleared up as we go along.

The position of Jerusalem, as must always be borne in mind, is that of a mountain city. From the Mediterranean Sea on the one hand, and the Dead Sea and Valley of the Jordan on the other, there is a steady ascent to the city. It stands 2,500 ft. above the level of the Mediterranean, and 3,700 ft. above that of the Dead Sea. Moreover, it is built on that mountain ridge, the backbone of Palestine, which runs through the country from north to south. At the same time, there are no cliffs, or what may be called hill scenery, around the city; and the first impressions of the traveller are generally those of disappointment at the smallness of the hills and the tameness of the landscape. As we shall see farther on, the ancient aspect of the city must have been far more picturesque than at present, from the depth of those ravines which are now choked up with the rubbish of twenty sieges.

The city is built on a plateau of tertiary limestone. The geological character of the country, viewed as a whole, is described ("Ordnance Survey Notes," p. 3) as consisting of tertiary and cretaceous strata, in the following series:—

1. The nummulitic limestone, dipping 17 deg. to the N.N.W., and composed of soft white limestone, with bands of flint and fossils, locally known as "Cakooli."

2. Hard siliceous chalk, with bands of flints, containing fossils, called "Missæ."

3. A white soft limestone (or chalk), called "Malaki."

4. Pink and white strata of indurated chalk, containing the pink "Santa Croce" marble.

In the immediate neighbourhood of Jerusalem the strata have been greatly denuded, leaving large detached areas of the several rocks described above. In a section from the Mount of Olives to the Mount of Evil Council, across the valley of the Kedron, about half a mile south of Jerusalem, we find that the Cakooli forms the summits of the mountains, and has a thickness of 291 ft.; that the Missæ has on each side of the ravine a thickness of 71 ft.; that the Malaki is 40 ft. thick; and that the Santa Croce marble occupies the bottom of the ravine, but the thickness of it could not be ascertained.

It is clear to the most superficial observer that the city is built on two hills, one of which, Zion, is considerably higher than the other, Moriah. In fact, where the city now stands two tongues of land project southwards, separated by a valley, now nearly filled up (the valley of the Tyropœon), dipping respectively into the valley of Hinnom on the west and the valley of the Kedron on the east—the Tyropœon running south, and joining the two larger valleys just above their point of junction. The west wall of the modern city, without any doubt, follows the old line of wall from the south-west corner to the Jaffa Gate. It is built on the edge of the ravine; and though now there is a considerable accumulation of rubbish, it is still so deep and difficult of ascent as to be a formidable assistance to the fortification; while there are yet to be seen old escarpments of rock by means of which the natural advantages of the position were improved upon. The modern wall is massive and well built. It is the work, in its reconstructed form, of Suleiman the Magnificent, and was mostly built in the year 1512. On the north side the city is protected by a ditch, partly cut in the rock. Just where the western wall bends in a north-west direction, and before we come to the Jaffa Gate, stands the citadel, Al Kala. Accurate sketches and measurements of this fortress, most important from the topographical point of view, have been made by Captain Wilson. It consists of a group of buildings, including, besides soldiers' and officers' quarters, the saluting battery and four towers; three of these are evidently of modern date, though they may stand on sites of more ancient towers. Their masonry is composed of portions of arch stones, shafts of columns, &c., mixed with better dressed stones; but the fourth, known as the Tower of David, is very different. It is an oblong building, 68 ft. long by 58 ft. broad. Its construction is very singular. It has an escarp of masonry sloping to a ditch; round the top of this is what is known as a *berm* or *chemin des rondes* (see "Ordnance Survey Notes," plate xix. 3); upon this is a solid mass of masonry, into which no entrance or appearance of any entrance could be found: this is 29 ft. high. Above this the tower is built, the actual tower, which consists of several chambers and a cistern. The lower part of the masonry is very fine, and resembles that at the well-known Wailing Place in its dressing, having, however, a larger marginal-draft. This tower is at the north-east angle of the citadel. The smaller one at the north-west angle also contains a cistern.

Close to the citadel is the Jaffa Gate, Bab el Khalil (Gate of the Friend—*i.e.*, of Hebron). It consists of a massive square tower, and is the only gate on the west side of the city. The wall from the gate to the north-west angle shows signs of being built upon a more ancient one. A great quantity of rubbish lies without the wall.

At the north-west angle is the so-called Kala't

al Jalûd, or Castle of Goliath. Here the ground
(2,581 ft. above the sea level) is higher than at
any other point, and a fine view may be obtained
of the whole city. The ruins were sketched and
measured by Captain Wilson (see "Ordnance
Survey Notes," p. 73, and plate xxvii.). Within
the castle is a vaulted chamber of modern date.
Breaking through the floor, Captain Wilson found
three chambers beneath it, nearly filled with rubbish, in which two piers, constructed of large stones
with marginal drafts, were discovered. These
the discoverer considered to be more ancient
than the rest of the building, to which he is not
disposed to assign a more remote date than the
Crusading times. But he does not consider his
own excavations at all exhaustive at this spot.

The wall now turns to the east, and runs in a
direction north-east as far as the Damascus
Gate (Bab el 'Amud, the Gate of the Column).
The wall is evidently a reconstruction, built on
the foundation of an older one, with all sorts of
material. At the Damascus Gate itself, lying in
a depression of the ground, are two towers, also
a reconstruction. Beyond the Damascus Gate
the wall crosses the Royal Caverns.

Jerusalem, as is well known, is honeycombed
with excavated caves, natural caverns, cisterns
cut in the rock, subterranean passages, and aqueducts. In its underground chambers and catacombs it is richer than any known city—Rome,
Constantinople, Paris, Kief, or any other. The
catacombs of Rome, Kief, and Paris appear to

have been originally designed for the most part
as places of burial; those of Constantinople were
uniformly constructed for the purpose of water
supply.   In Jerusalem the excavated chambers
and caves were for three purposes.   Some of
them, especially the Bahr el Khebir, were for the
supply of water; some, those outside the city,
were for burial places; while of those *under* the
city, the vast caverns known as the Royal Quarries were actually used as quarries for the stone
used in building. The entrance to them is by an
opening so low that it is necessary to stoop; but
the height rapidly increases.   The evidences of
the place having been used as a quarry are very
plain and numerous—the cuttings, about 4 or 5 in.
wide, still remaining; and on the left-hand side
of each cutting may be observed a little hollow
formed at the corner, into which a wick and oil
may have been placed.   The quarries extend, so
far as was ascertained when measurements were
taken, to about 200 yards in a south-easterly
direction; they are about 100 yards wide.   But
considerable additions must be made to these
measurements, owing to quite recent discoveries
by Mr. Schick.

Between the Damascus Gate and the north-
east angle is the Gate of Herod, called by the
natives Bab ez Zahiré (Gate of Splendour).   It
is now walled up.

We come next to the north-east angle, where
the wall bends southward and runs along the
western slope of the valley of the Kedron.   The

wall above ground seems built on to the Haram wall at its north-east angle. About 200 ft. north of that angle is the Gate of St. Stephen, called by the natives Bab Sitty Mariam, the Gate of Lady Mary. A road leads from it across the valley, here of no very great depth, to the Mount of Olives; and so on to Jericho.

Omitting the Haram Area for the present, let us complete our round of the walls by passing at once to the south wall, abutting on the wall of the Haram at the Double Gate. Nothing distinctive is remarked about this wall, which is modern, and following a comparatively modern line. Two gates are in the southern portion, that called Bab el Maghâribé, the Gate of the Westerns (the word is the same as that from which we get the word *Morocco*), and by the Franks, the Dung Gate; and the Gate of Zion, called Bab el Neby Daûd, Gate of the Prophet David.

The town itself covers an area of 209·5 acres, of which 35 are occupied by the Haram esh Shereef. The remaining space is divided into different quarters: the Christian quarter, including the part occupied by the Armenians, taking up the western half; the Mohammedans have the north-east portion; the Jews the south-east. The whole population of the city is now about 16,000. The circumference is very nearly two and a quarter miles, while the extent of the city— small as it is, it now seems too large for the population—may be illustrated by the fact that it would very nearly occupy the space included

between Oxford-street and Piccadilly on the
north and south, and Park-lane and Bond-street
on the east and west.

To the Christian pilgrims, who yearly flock
to the city in thousands, the chief object of interest has always been the Church of the Holy
Sepulchre. The historical account of this building will be found below. A detailed account of
the building may be read in Williams's "Holy
City," and in the "Ordnance Survey Notes."
Also, farther on, will be found enumerated the
principal traditions and legends connected with
the place. The church itself was very much
damaged by the great fire which nearly destroyed it on the night of October 12, 1808;
though there are conflicting statements as to the
extent of damage effected. The work of reconstruction was commenced as soon after the fire
as permission could be obtained, and the church
as it now stands was consecrated in 1810, the
architect having been a Greek named Com-
menes.

The so-called Holy Sepulchre, which was not
injured by the fire, lies within a small chapel,
26 ft. long by 18 ft. broad, built of the Santa
Croce marble. The interior of this building is
divided into two chapels; the eastern one being
known as the Angel Chapel, and the western
one being the Sepulchre itself. In the Angel
Chapel is shown what is called a portion of the
stone rolled away from the Sepulchre—only the
Armenians claim to have possession of the real

stone, and say that this is only a forgery. On either side of the entrance are holes through which the imposture known as the Holy Fire is given out every year.

A long, low doorway leads to the Sepulchre itself, the western chapel. It is very small, being only 6 ft. by 7 ft., or 42 square feet in area, of which space 19 square feet are taken up by the marble slab shown as the Tomb of our Lord. The slab is cracked through the centre, and is much worn by the lips of adoring pilgrims. The chapel—marble-cased throughout, so that no rock is anywhere visible—is lit by forty-three lamps, always burning.

Before proceeding to describe the Haram esh Shereef itself, let us first mention other points of interest which bear upon the great questions at issue.

Connected with the water supply (see 2 Chronicles, xxxii. 30; 2 Kings, xx. 20; Ecclesiasticus, xlviii. 17; Nehemiah, ii. 13, 14, &c., &c.), the city is supplied mainly by cisterns, either built in rubbish and cemented, or cut in the rock. Some of them are very large. An opening was first made in the hard Missæ rock; on arriving at the softer Malaki, the chamber was here excavated to as large a size as was wanted, with a roof of the native rock. Some of the cisterns are retort-shaped. There are also several open pools in the city, including the Pool of Bathsheba, now filled in; the Pool of Hezekiah; and the great Birket Israil—the so-called Pool of

Bethesda. Outside the city are, especially, the two pools known as Birket Mamilla (Upper Pool of Gihon), and Birket es Sultan (Lower Pool of Gihon). These are in a dilapidated state ; but water is still found in the former. Tradition— probable in this instance—identifies them with the narrative in Isaiah, vii. and xxxvii., and 2 Chron. xxxii. 30. One of them may be, also, the Dragon Well of Nehemiah, ii. 13.

To the south of the city lie the three very important sources—the Fountain of the Virgin, the Pool of Siloam, and Bîr Eyub (the Pool of Joab). The first of these is an intermittent fountain. The recurrence of the flow is very irregular, occurring sometimes two or three times a day, sometimes only once in two or three days. Dr. Robinson thinks the pool may be the ancient Bethesda. Others identify it with the King's Pool (Nehemiah, ii. 14, 15). It is certainly that called by Josephus the *Reservoir of Solomon*. The second is below this, connected by a subterranean passage, 2 ft. wide, and from 3 ft. to 15 ft. high, along which Captain Warren made his way. This pool is, apparently, only mentioned three times in Scripture—viz., Isaiah, viii. 6; Nehemiah, iii. 15; John, ix. 7. The very ancient pool Bîr Eyub lies down in the valley. It is now a deep well, with a small building over it, where troughs are placed for the reception of the water when drawn. Its great importance is in the fact that tradition identifies it with En Rogel, the spring just below Jerusalem which marked the boundary line between Judah and Benjamin. Others, however, identify the Fountain of the Virgin with the En Rogel. The arguments for both sites may be read in the "Bible Dictionary," vol. i., p. 556.

The ancient aqueducts by which the old city was supplied, in part at least, are fully described by Captain Wilson in the "Ordnance Survey Notes." Three of these came from "Solomon's Pools," of which one—the low level aqueduct—is thirteen miles long.

On the southern slope of Mount Zion stands the "Cœnaculum." It is a building of modern date, constructed over a crypt, supposed by Captain Wilson to be of the Crusading period. Here the Mohammedans keep a large sarcophagus of rough stone, covered with green satin tapestry, and call it the Tomb of David. This is, of course, only a cenotaph; and the tradition itself can only be traced back for seven hundred years. The tomb of David is said to lie in a cavern beneath this. We know that it was on Mount Zion—" he was buried in the City of David ;" his tomb is " between Siloah and the house of the mighty men"—*i.e.*, the guard house (Nehemiah, iii. 16). It became the general burial place of the Kings of Judah. Its position was known down to the destruction of the city by Titus. That event, which confused the knowledge of all the sacred sites, occasioned the loss of this; and the Tomb of David has been variously fixed at half a mile from Zion, on the side of Olivet, and on Mount

Moriah. For the legends connected with the place, see chap. v.

In a city of such extensive antiquity as Jerusalem, and where the people have always reverenced the resting-places of their dead, the extent of space occupied by the tombs will be expected to be very great. All round the Holy City lie these memorials of the past—Jewish, Roman, Christian, and Mohammedan tombs being all alike represented on the slopes of the valleys. Among them are the so-called tombs of Absalom, Zachariah, St. James, and Jehoshaphat, all of which are of comparatively modern architecture. About half a mile beyond the city, up the valley of the Kedron, lies the very curious collection of tombs called the Tombs of the Kings, a full description of which has been given by M. de Saulcy. Sarcophagi in marble, richly carved with flowers and wreaths, were found here, and carried off to the Louvre by M. de Saulcy, under the impression that he had found the tomb and sarcophagus of David. The tomb may possibly have been that of the illustrious convert, Queen Helena, as is argued by Thrupp. One of the most curious things connected with it is the machinery by which the sepulchre was closed. It consisted of a round stone, rolled before the entrance. The stone was found by M. de Saulcy in its proper place. The contrivance was such that the sepulchre could only be opened or closed by means of a lever, and to use the lever it was necessary to gain access to a certain secret corridor usually kept covered up.

It may be remarked here that there are two kinds of tombs in Palestine chiefly met with, the rock-hewn and the masonry tombs. Specimens of the latter have been examined and described by Captain Wilson (see "Quarterly Statement," Palestine Exploration Fund, p. 66, First Series). The bodies were laid in the tomb either with or without a sarcophagus. In the tombs are sometimes found small rectangular excavations, apparently for the purposes of treasure. The tombs are generally closed by a stone door, turning on sockets, hinges, &c. The apparatus found by M. de Saulcy for closing the tomb by means of a round stone rolled over the entrance was not always of so complicated a kind as that used in the Tomb of the Kings; it could only be used in the case of very wealthy and distinguished persons, who could afford the great expense and labour of the contrivance.

CHAPTER III.

THE HARAM ESH SHEREEF.

WE have reserved, in our hasty walk round and through Jerusalem, the Haram Area —the "Noble Sanctuary"—for the last. Let us, with a copy of the Ordnance Survey map before us, examine this, the most sacred of all holy places, as it is also the most ancient. On this Area was the threshing floor of Araunah the Jebusite, where the Angel of the Lord appeared to David; here was the altar set up by David; here the Temples of Solomon, Zerubbabel, and Herod; here, perhaps, the Palace of Solomon. Here was the great fortress Antonia, built by Herod where Baris had been; here is the Mosque, more sacred than any other to the Mohammedans, except that

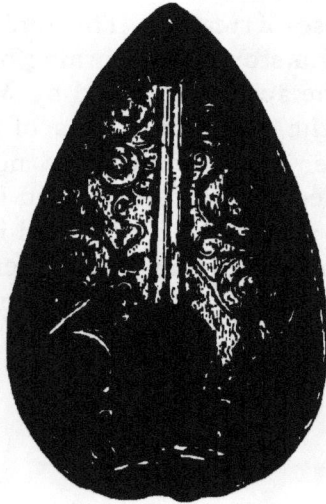

of Mecca. About this place are gathered the legends of Jew, Christian, and Moslem; but, above all, it was loved by the Jews themselves. This holy hill was more to them than even Rome's citadel to the Romans; more than the Acropolis to the Athenians. It represented at once their religion, their history, their country. All their memories of glory and disaster, of honour and of disgrace, were gathered together on the hill of the Temple. With what passionate love they regarded it, with what desperate tenacity they could defend it, the history of Titus's siege is enough to show us by itself. And we have more than Josephus —we have the soul of the Psalmist poured out in love and admiration of the city and the Sanctuary; we have the prophets taking the holy place as an illustration of the New Heaven and the New Earth; we have our Lord Himself rejoicing over the glorious prospect that lay beneath Him as He stood upon the Mount of Olives; and we have to this day the form of lamentation kept up by the Jews, when, once a week, they go to kiss the sacred stones, and weep outside the precincts they may not enter. Every stone of this Area, desecrated as it has been by conquerors, polluted with blood — as when Titus's men murdered the starving Jews on that day when the Holy of Holies was burned, or when Godfrey and Tancred rode up to their horses' knees in the blood of the Saracens—has its sacred association; and, in the uncertainty that attends the Christian

D 2

sites, the modern pilgrim turns to this spot as, alone among holy places, without dispute or contradiction. For here was Mount Moriah; here stood the Temple.

Until very recently, Christians, as well as Jews, were forbidden to enter the Haram Area at all. They could sketch the place from the Mount of Olives, and look at it from the roofs of one or two houses; but death was threatened to any who entered, and insult was certain to any who approached too near. It was in the year 1833 that Messrs. Catherwood, Arundale, and Bonomi first got in, and, under pretext of carrying out necessary repairs, made certain sketches and measurements, which for a long time served as the only reliable authority. But the Ordnance Survey has, of course, superseded all previous imperfect descriptions and details. It is from the Ordnance Survey map that our illustration has been reduced, with the addition of Captain Warren's excavations, which will be described in their proper place. The Area is now open to all travellers who are willing to pay a small fee.

The Haram esh Shereef is enclosed by a massive wall, running very nearly all round it, and standing 50 to 60 ft. above the present surface of the ground. The masonry of this wall presents several marked and very important differences of work. These, as we shall shortly see, may be divided into five. The stones are thus prepared :—
In the first instance they are dressed square on

the upper and under surface and at the two ends: the dressing is in many cases so true that a knife cannot be inserted between the two stones. They are placed one above the other, each stone being set half an inch to an inch farther back, so that the wall is not perpendicular, but stands at a slight angle—the great advantage being that buttresses and other supports are not needed. No mortar or cement has been used. The faces are dressed with what is known as a "marginal draft"—*i.e.*, the central portion of the stone projects from a marginal cutting of 2 in. to 4 in., or even more, broad. The projecting face is left rough in what appear to be the oldest portions, and is smoothed in others. This marginal drafted masonry is found all round the Haram Area below ground, and in a few places—especially at the Jews' Wailing Place—above. It has been called the Jewish bevel, and may be seen at Hebron, at the Palace of Hyrcanus (now Arak el Emir), in the foundation of the wall encircling the Temple at Hebron, and in many old buildings in Jerusalem. It has been seen also on the tomb of Cyrus at Passargadæ.

There are altogether five distinct kinds of masonry, denoting, *perhaps*, five distinct periods of workmanship in the Haram wall:—

1. Marginal drafted masonry with a rough face, found chiefly along the eastern wall (see the account of the excavations there).

2. Marginal drafted masonry with a smooth face, found chiefly along the western wall.

3. Ashlar of large stones with smooth faces, without marginal drafts.

4. Ashlar of small stones, without marginal drafts.

5. Common rubble masonry.

The average height of the older stones is 3 ft. 3 in. to 6 ft. Their length varies considerably. The longest stone is 38 ft. 9 in. long.

Come with us from the north-east angle, and let us journey round the walls, before we attempt to describe the interior. We begin with a corner tower, 83½ ft. long. Here there are above ground five perfect courses left of the marginal drafted stones; and were it not for the irregularity of their jointing, there would be no doubt that the stones are *in situ*. Between the north-east angle and the Golden Gateway, a distance of 373 ft., the wall is a modern construction out of old materials, containing several very large stones, one of these being as much as 18 ft. long. The Golden Gate itself, which M. de Vogüé maintains to have been an ancient gate long before the present building, comes next. It is said by Mr. Fergusson to be of late Roman date, probably of the time of Constantine.

The masonry from the Golden Gateway to the south-east angle is very clearly of modern date. Large stones are met with, and fragments of pillars and columns are built in. On one of these Mohammed will take his seat, it is believed, at the Day of Judgment. At the south-east angle the ground sinks, and shows sixteen courses of the marginal drafted masonry, above which the rubble masonry stands in so tottering a condition, says Captain Wilson, that it looks as if a touch would bring it down. The eastern wall is 1,530 ft. long, and there are 1,018 ft. between the Golden Gate and the south-east angle—a measurement which will be found important. We shall see, also, farther on, how our description of this great eastern wall, which we give here from the Ordnance Survey and other sources, has been modified by Captain Warren's discoveries. It must be borne in mind that all along the base of the eastern wall lie tombs, the presence of which renders excavation extremely difficult.

Turning the corner, we find ourselves at the south wall. This is built overlooking that lower tongue of Moriah which was called Ophla, or Mount Ophel, where Captain Warren made some of his most important discoveries. The southern wall is chiefly remarkable for its three gates. Of these, the Single Gateway is apparently the most modern. It is a pointed gate, whose sill is lower than that of the other two. It is now closed up. The Triple Gate consists of three circular arches, now built up with small masonry. Its arches are semi-circular, with a space of 13 ft., and are 25 ft. high. M. de Vogüé found that the sides of the arches, like those of the Golden Gateway, were monoliths. These formed the opening to a large subterranean avenue or passage, which led up to the platform. Under the gateway are three very curious passages, first discovered by M. de Saulcy, and afterwards examined by Captain Wilson and Captain Warren.

Where the modern city wall abuts upon the Haram wall we come upon the "Huldah," or Double Gateway. This is the most remarkable, in many ways, of all the gates. It is 42 ft. wide, divided by a rectangular pier 8 ft. broad and 14 ft. deep. The central pier and the eastern and western jambs are all built of marginal drafted stones. Within is a subterranean passage leading up to the Haram Area. There is also a curious single column, 21 ft. high and 6½ ft. in diameter—a monolith—which, according to Mr. Fergusson, cannot be later than the time of Herod.

The south wall is altogether 922 ft. long. The south-east angle is not a right angle, but the south-west angle is exactly square.

The western wall is for a great portion of its length built against by houses, and therefore it has been found impossible to examine it with the same care as the rest. At 39 ft. north of this angle is the famous Robinson's Arch—i.e., a row of projecting stones, showing that here an arch must once have stood. Captain Wilson estimated the span at 45 ft., and endeavoured to find the pier. In this he was not successful, although his estimate was mainly correct. Higher up is the Bab el Maghâribé, or Gate of the Moors, which does not appear to be of great antiquity. Above this is the Wailing Place. Captain Wilson thinks,

judging from the coarseness of the jointing, that
the stones at this place—the most perfect specimens of the marginal draft—may not, as generally supposed, be *in situ*. Along this wall are
as many as eight gates to the Haram, but most
of distinctly modern construction.

The barracks form the northern boundary for
some distance. They are built on the rock,
which has an escarpment of 23 ft. on the south
side of the barracks, and another of 8 to 10 ft. on
the northern side. Between the barracks and
the Pool of Bethesda, or Birket Israil, the wall
and rock cannot be seen for the accumulation of
buildings on the same level as the Haram. The
Pool itself is 360 ft. long, 130 broad, and 75
deep; the bottom being encumbered with deep
rubbish. On the east side are two high arched
passages, which run east and west for more than
100 ft., and are choked up with filth and rubbish.
Between the western end of the Birket Israil and
the Valley of the Kedron is the wall of the city.
Here, as will be seen farther on, Captain Warren
made discoveries of the highest interest and importance.

Leaving the walls, let us proceed to the interior.
The Haram Area is undoubtedly the most beautiful spot in the whole city. In the midst of it
rises the great Dome of the Rock—most splendid
of Syrian buildings. Its grassy surface is covered
with cypresses, olives, and marble fountains; and
the platform on which the Dome stands is enriched by arches, cupolas, and graven pulpits.

This great enclosure consists of rock, made
ground, and rubbish. The configuration of the
rock, and the filling in of the broken parts may
be fairly illustrated by taking an inverted saucer
and placing an oblong upon it, less in either
breadth or length than the diameter of the saucer.
One corner should cut the saucer where its depression commences. We should thus have one
corner at the highest level or edge (the north-west
corner), and three other corners at the lowest.
These three corners have been either filled in
with made earth, or been built up by means of
vaults. For it is not impossible that vaults,
which are known to exist at one angle, will be
found at the others also; because the difficulty
and trouble of filling up depths so great over
an extent so vast would have been very much
greater than that of building sustaining vaults.
At the north-east angle, rock has been cut
away so as to lower the ground, and the filling
in of the eastern side to bring all to the same
level has been evidently done at a later period
than the construction of the present Golden
Gate, modern as this may be, because the gate is
26 ft. below the present level. But, M. de Vogüé
maintains the antiquity of the gate; it is by no
means improbable that the ancient gate level
should have been preserved when a new gate
was constructed. Then the question arises, for
what purpose was an ancient gate existing there?
It could not lead into the valley, because it stands
30 or 40 ft. above the rock. We have no hint

that here was a bridge across the valley. In more modern times, when the accumulation of ages had raised the level of the slope, or when an embankment had been built, the gateway probably opened upon a level road.

The celebrated Dome of the Rock, the history of which, as given by the Arabic historians, is given in a subsequent chapter, can only be properly described by an architect. A full account of it may be read in Mr. Williams's "Holy City," Mr. Fergusson's "Jerusalem," and Captain Wilson's "Ordnance Survey Notes."

It is an eight-sided building, each side being 67 ft. long, and is ornamented by seven windows on each side. The interior has two cloisters, separated by an octagonal course of piers and columns; within this, again, another circle of four great piers and twelve Corinthian columns, which support the great Dome. This stands immediately over the projecting sacred rock, which rises 4 ft. $9\frac{1}{2}$ in. above the marble pavement at its highest point, and 1 ft. at its lowest. It bears the marks of chiselling; but at what date and for what purpose no one knows. Beneath it is a cave, which is entered by a flight of steps at the south-east. This cave is about 24 ft. broad by nearly the same long, though the side at the entrance is not square. It covers an area of nearly 500 square feet, and has an average height of 6 ft. The sides are covered with plaster and whitewash, so that it is impossible to see the rock. The floor is paved with

marble; and there is in the centre a small slab of
marble, covering what is called by the Moslems
the Bir el Arwah, or Well of Spirits.   This slab
is never lifted.   The Mohammedans believe that
it is the Gate of Paradise.   In the roof the rock
is pierced with a round hole, like those sometimes found in cisterns and rock-cut quarries.

The Dome of the Rock is not a mosque properly so called, and has never been so regarded
by the Mohammedans.   The Mosque proper of
the whole sacred enclosure, called the Musjid, is
the El Aksa, standing at the south-west angle.
This great building, about which controversy has
been very keen, is by some said to be the Basilica
of Justinian, by others the Mosque of Abdelmelck.
The Count de Vogüé, for instance, thinks there
can be no doubt of its having been originally a
Christian structure.   But the hands of successive
restorers and repairers have greatly modified and
altered the original aspect of the structure.   Supposing the opinion of the learned French explorer
to be correct, we must remember that, after ex-
periencing the ravages of the Persians, it passed
through the hands of Saracen and Crusader, and
then reverted again to the Mohammedan, in
whose possession it has ever since been.   The
Crusaders assigned the building to the Templars
on their establishment.   They resided here, and
called it Palatium Solomonis, or Templum Solomonis, to distinguish it from the Dome, which
they always called Templum Domini.

The known cisterns with which the Haram

Area was supplied with water have been all examined and measured by Captain Wilson and Captain Warren. Those who have had the opportunity this summer of visiting Mr. Simpson's collection of pictures, called "Underground Jerusalem," will remember his striking drawing of the "Great Sea." But the whole of this vast area is honeycombed with excavations and reservoirs, and the connection of one with the other, if such connection exists, by subterranean channels cut in the rock, is by no means thoroughly ascertained.

In the south-east corner of the Haram are the very curious vaults known as the Stables of Solomon. In their present condition they are a reconstruction, built up of old materials. De Vogüé maintains that the vaults are of Arab workmanship, standing, however, where older vaults stood before them. They are approached by a hole broken through the crown of one of the arches near the Mosque, called the "Cradle of the Lord Jesus."

In making the rapid and very imperfect sketch of the city and its sacred places in this and the preceding chapter, we have not endeavoured to convey an idea of the actual aspect of the city, which would be foreign to our purpose, but to point out those spots round which legend and tradition have gathered, and those points which are important as helping to solve the great problems attempted by the Palestine Exploration Fund. What these problems are, and

how their solution was attempted, we cannot
state intelligibly till we have still further cleared
the ground by giving the leading facts in the
history of the city, the historical evidence, and
some of the legends and traditions which have
grown up. But thus much may be premised.
The destruction of the Temple, and the expul-
sion of the Jews from the city, followed, as it
was, at an interval of sixty years, by the bloody
and disastrous siege when Bar Cochebas had
usurped power, resulted in more than the destruction of the sacred buildings—in the loss
of the actual sites. Tradition—how old it is
not always possible to ascertain—has certainly
pointed out all of them with confidence; but
the moment scientific investigation began the
authority of tradition was assailed. We are
no longer—perhaps it is not altogether a gain
—of the same temper as those earnest and
simple pilgrims who were wont to worship in
undoubting faith at every shrine which a monk,
credulous himself, pointed out as the scene of
some act in the holy history. We no longer behold, with unsuspecting eyes, the spot where our
Lord was scourged; and where He suffered we no
longer pray, like the pilgrims of the tenth century, for death to strike us swiftly, even while we
stand upon soil so sacred. The cold breath of
doubt has dispelled the modern traveller's enthusiasm; nothing seems real, nothing unques-
tioned, within the narrow limits of the modern
walls. Even in the Haram Area itself, the Area

of the Temple, where surely one would expect the most perfect certainty, the conflicting controversies shift the Temple from one 'spot to another, till we are certain of nothing, save that somewhere here Solomon and Herod built, and Titus destroyed.

The preceding, therefore, may be taken as merely an introductory description of the city as it is seen by the modern traveller, with some few of Captain Wilson's measurements and discoveries, carrying us down to the period when Captain Warren commenced his excavations.

CHAPTER IV.

HISTORY OF JERUSALEM.

LET us recapitulate in as few words as possible the history of Jerusalem, from the earliest times to the present. The first thought of one who reads the story of the city is that it has suffered from siege and war more frequently than any other city of the world. And this not only because, in ancient as in later times, it was a sacred city, fought over by contending religions, but because its position was always one of the very greatest importance. "Who gains Paris," said Louis XI., "gains France." Much more was that true of Jerusalem, the central

point of all the patriotism, pride, and religion of
the Jews. It has been finely observed by Mr.
Grove (article on Jerusalem in Smith's "Bible
Dictionary"), that whereas the last mention
of Jerusalem in the Bible is contained in the
solemn warnings of Christ that the city shall be
compassed with enemies, so the first mention is
that of Judges (i. 8), when the children of Judah
fought against it, took it, smote it with the edge
of the sword, and set the city on fire. That
was its *first* siege, about 1400 B.C., so that its
history begins 700 years before Rome was
founded, and even then the city is already built.
Probably, of course, it was then only a rudely
fortified mountain post. It has been identified
by some with Cadytis, a town described by He-
rodotus as a large city of Syria, almost as large
as Sardis; and an attempt has been also made to
identify the place with that called Kedesh, the
capital city of the Khatti or Hittites, taken by
the Egyptian, Sethee I., about the year 1320 B.C.
Such identifications, although they would greatly
confirm the Bible narrative could they be clearly
established, must always be too fanciful to bear
serious investigation.

The city, which could not be taken, remained
in the occupation of the Jebusites until it was reduced by David; the lower city falling at once,
the citadel being taken by assault (2 Samuel, v.
6—10, and 1 Chronicles, xii. 23—39). The date
of this, the *second* siege of Jerusalem, is given at
about 1046 B.C. David built a wall and a palace,

E

and commenced the "Royal Garden." His
sepulchre was placed on Mount Zion.

Solomon's buildings in Jerusalem comprised
not only the great Temple, but also his own
palace and a stronger wall round the city. He
further took care of the roads which led to the
city.

Some years after his death, Shishak, King of
Egypt, invaded Judah, and advanced to Jerusalem, which threw open its gates (2 Chronicles,
xii. 9, and 1 Kings, xiv. 25, 26). On this occasion—which may be fairly called the *third* siege,
although no resistance was made—the splendid
treasures which Solomon had accumulated, and
the costly decorations of the Temple, were all
carried away. The splendour of the Temple
was, however, restored by Asa, after his victory
over Zerah the Cushite (*circa* 940 B.C.) (2 Chronicles, xv. 10—15). But ten years later, Asa
was obliged to strip the Temple again, in order
to bribe Benhadad (2 Chronicles, xvi.).

The *fourth* siege took place under Jehoram (2
Chronicles, xxi. 16), who began his reign about
887 B.C. This time the royal palace was sacked,
and all its treasure, together with that of the
Temple, carried away. It is reasonable to suppose, as we hear of repeated pillage of the
treasures of the Temple, that these were speedily
replaced—at least, in part—by the offerings of
the faithful and the care of the priests. Thus,
a few years after the sack of the city in Jehoram's siege, we hear of the treasures of the Temple

being taken away by the sons of Athaliah, and removed to the Temple of Baal (2 Chronicles,. xxiv. 7).

The *fifth* siege was by a King of Israel—Jehoash, who broke down 400 cubits of the northern part of the wall, rode through the Temple in triumph, and pillaged the treasures of the Temple and the royal palace (2 Kings, xiv. 13, 14). This is the first time that any portion of the wall was injured.

Under the reign of Uzziah the walls were rebuilt and strengthened. The city was also further fortified by the addition of towers furnished with some kind of *balistæ*, for the hurling of stones at an enemy. A great earthquake shook the city during this reign, which made a breach. in the Temple, and caused a landslip in the hill at En Rogel, beneath which the royal gardens. were buried.

The *sixth* siege of the city was by Rezin, King. of Syria, and Pekah, King of Israel, against. Ahaz. The city this time appears to have held. out, although Ahaz suffered a disastrous defeat (2. Chronicles, xxviii. 6—8), for there is no mention of any sack or pillage either in the Bible or in Josephus. Against so formidable a coalition, the strength of the small kingdom of Judah was quite inadequate, and Ahaz had recourse to the Assyrians. Then a period of great shame and disgrace came upon Jerusalem—the Sanctuary being polluted by idolatrous worship, and the treasures of the Temple being stripped from it and sent to Tiglath Pileser (2 Chronicles, xxix. 6, 7).

A revival of true religion took place under Hezekiah, who made this movement a national one, and by so doing ensured for himself the firm support of the people, when, fourteen years later, the *seventh* siege of the city took place by the Assyrians (2 Chronicles, xxxii.). The city escaped conquest, but at the sacrifice of its treasures. Perhaps it was never regularly invested by the Assyrians, the story of whose invasion and its termination is too well known for repetition here.

Under Manasseh there was again—if not a siege, which is uncertain — another time of national disaster, when the King was taken prisoner and carried to Babylon. We know how affliction turned him back to the true religion, and led him to spend the rest of his life in an attempted atonement for the past. He was a great builder in the city. He built a wall (2 Chronicles, xxxiii. 14) "without the city of David, on the west side of Gihon, in the valley, even to the entering in at the fish gate, and compassed about Ophel, and raised it up a very great height." Jotham had begun the works at Ophel, and it is not impossible that the great wall found there by Captain Warren may actually contain portions of Manasseh's work.

In the reign of Josiah, the Book of the Law was found by Hilkiah in the House of the Lord (2 Chronicles, xxxiv. 14).

Under Jehoiakim the city was taken (*eighth* siege) by Nebuchadnezzar, and the Temple partly pillaged (2 Chronicles, xxxvi. 7).

Under his successor, Jehoiachin, another siege (the *ninth*) took place, when the Temple and city were despoiled of all the remaining treasures, and the King, with all the royal establishment, the princes, the chief warriors, and the artificers, in all 10,000 men, were carried off to Babylon.

The *tenth* siege was in the following reign, that of Zedekiah. It was the longest and the most disastrous that had yet befallen the city. For eighteen months Jerusalem held out in spite of pestilence and famine. It was taken by effecting a breach in the northern wall. Then it was that the Temple was finally stripped and burned, that the royal palace was destroyed, the walls broken down, the city itself overthrown. Then, taking with them all the important people, and leaving none but a few peasants to till the ground, the Assyrians left the city to desolation and solitude. This was about 586 B.C. Fasts are still kept up among the Jews to commemorate the events of this disastrous year. For fifty years the ruins lay untouched—not unvisited, because the site of the Sanctuary was the resort of pilgrims, who came to weep over it, as their descendants do to this day.

When the people came back, 42,360 in all, they brought with them the vessels of the old Temple. The foundations were laid amid the tears of the old and the shouts of the young; and in spite of opposition and delay, the work went on, until, after years of labour, it was finally completed and dedicated in the sixth year of Darius, B.C. 516.

There follows next a period of fifty-eight years about which little is known. We come then to the arrival of Ezra, with a caravan of priests, Levites, Nethinims, or servants of the Temple, and laymen; amounting to 1,777 souls in all. The next eleven years were occupied in religious reforms. All this time, though the city had been slowly growing again, the walls were lying as the Assyrians had left them. It was on the arrival of Nehemiah (B.C. 445), 140 years after the great destruction, that the walls began to be rebuilt. By the united exertions of the whole populace, the work was completed in fifty-two days. The wall thus rebuilt was that of the city of Jerusalem, as well as that of the city of David.

For twelve years after this the city was ruled by Nehemiah. For some time after the death of Nehemiah, the history of the city is the history of the high priests and the disputes over the office. Joshua, for instance, who was intriguing for the post with the Persian general, was murdered in the Temple by his brother Johanan. He, in his turn, had two sons, of whom one became high priest of the Samaritan Temple in Gerizim, when that was built by Sanballat, his father-in-law. It was during the priesthood of his brother Jaddua that the visit of

Alexander the Great occurred. According to
the story, Jaddua had been warned by a dream
how to avert the anger of the King, who was
marching from Tyre upon Jerusalem. In accordance with his dream, he waited till the
Macedonians were near the city; and then, clad
in robes of hyacinth and gold, he led a long
train of priests and citizens to meet the King.
Within sight of the Temple, Alexander—to the
astonishment of his followers—did reverence to
the holy name on the tiara of the high priest,
declaring that he had seen the God whom Jaddua
represented, in a vision at Dium, encouraging
him to cross over to Asia. He then visited
Jerusalem and offered sacrifice there, heard the
prophecies of Daniel which foretold his victories,
and conferred important privileges upon the
people. Whether the story be true or not, the
fact remains that the Jews did enjoy important
privileges from this time.

Ten years later, however, the *eleventh* siege
took place, by Ptolemy Soter—the city falling
into his hands on account of the refusal of the
Jews to fight on the Sabbath day. The account
given by Josephus is very short, and contains no
details of the siege. Ptolemy took with him into
Egypt a great number of Jews, both of Jerusalem and Samaria, chiefly, it would seem, out of
admiration of their character for fidelity in the
observation of oaths and covenants. The Samaritans and Jews quarrelled in Egypt as to the
place whither their offerings should be sent.

For the successor to Ptolemy Soter, Philadel-
phus (B.C. 285), the Septuagint version was made.*
It was at this time also that a family arose who
became able to dispute the power of that of the
high priest. · This was effected by Joseph, the
nephew of Onias II., the high priest. He became
farmer of the revenues of the whole of Syria—
an office which speedily gave him immense
wealth. From him came the family of Hyrcanus.

Then came more disasters. Jerusalem was
taken (*twelfth* siege) by Antiochus the Great, in
B.C. 203. In B.C. 199 it was taken again *(thirteenth* siege) by Scopas, the Alexandrian general, who left a garrison in the place. But in the
following year the Jews opened their gates themselves to Antiochus, and helped him to reduce
the Egyptian garrison. For this service, Antiochus conferred certain presents and privileges
on the city, and affirmed the sacredness of the
Temple from the intrusion of strangers. Meantime, the process of "Grecizing" had been making
rapid headway; and under the influence of
Greek manners, Greek customs, Greek sports,
neglect of the law and religion had become universal. Quarrels arose between the high priest and
his brother; and although Antiochus Epiphanes

---

* "The Greek version of the Old Testament known by
this name is, like the Nile, *fontium qui celat origines.*
The causes which produced it, the number and names of
the translators, the times at which different portions were
translated, are all uncertain."—*Dr. Selwyn, in the " Bible
Dictionary."*

entered the city in B.C. 172 in great amity and
much pomp, he returned, two years afterwards, to
punish the unhappy city for seditions caused by
the ambitions of two men, and plundered the
Sanctuary of all its valuable contents. Nor was
this all; for two years afterwards the King
came with a large army, with the design of ex-
terminating the people altogether. He got possession of the city by a stratagem, says Josephus,
who, perhaps, confuses two campaigns. On this
occasion—we may call it the *fourteenth* siege—
the whole city was pillaged, about ten thousand
captives taken, the city walls destroyed, the
finest buildings burned, the altar defiled by the
sacrifice of swine, the Jews forbidden the practice
of their religion, and cruelly tormented, and
the books of the law destroyed wherever they
could be found. Since the taking of the city by
the Assyrians, five hundred years before, no such
terrible calamity had befallen the people.

This was in the year 168 B.C. A garrison of
Macedonians occupied the citadel which overlooked the Temple.

Then began that glorious and successful revolt
of the Maccabees, the history of which does not
belong to this place. On their at last coming
up to Jerusalem they found the sacred precincts
deserted, and the area of the Temple—on whose
altar still lay the remains of the last desecrating
sacrifice—overgrown with weeds and brushwood.
They restored the Sanctuary as best they could;
and after holding a feast of dedication, they

strengthened themselves in the Temple, and
made it into a fortress.   In B.C. 162, Judas, after
sustaining a defeat from Antiochus, was besieged
(*fifteenth* siege) in his sacred stronghold.   Terms
were made by which the Jews were permitted to
reside and practise their religion.   But the walls
were partially destroyed.

These were, however, quickly repaired, and
after the death of Judas, in 161, Jonathan greatly
strengthened the fortifications of the city.   The
repairs were fully authorized by Demetrius, who
gave the privilege of sanctuary to the Temple,
and endowed it with the revenues of Ptole-
mais.

Taking advantage of these favourable circumstances, Jonathan began the attack of the Acra,
still occupied by the Macedonian garrison.   The
investment of the fortress lasted three years,
during which Jonathan was killed, and his place
taken by his brother Simon.   After the garrison
had capitulated from want of food, three years
were occupied in levelling the hill of the Acra, so
as to make it lower than the Temple hill beside it.
This done, the fort of Baris, afterwards Antonia,
was built in the north of the Temple.   Simon
was murdered in 135 B.C., and his son John
Hyrcanus was besieged in Jerusalem (*sixteenth*
siege) by Antiochus Sidetes, King of Syria.   The
siege was raised by John making terms with
Antiochus.   He paid a subsidy—to obtain which
he opened the sepulchre of David and took 3,000
talents out of it—and gave hostages.

John Hyrcanus was succeeded by his son, Aristobulus, king as well as high priest; and he, after a year of office, by his brother, Alexander Jannæus, B.C. 105. The tomb of Alexander Jannæus was situated outside the north wall of the Temple. It was in his reign that the dissensions began between the Pharisees and Sadducees. After his death, his son Hyrcanus became high priest, and Aristobulus had the command of the army. The quarrels of the two brothers led to the *seventeenth* siege, B.C. 65, which was raised by the interference of Scaurus, one of Pompey's lieutenants. The party of Aristobulus held the Temple, however, and refused to submit; whereupon Pompey regularly besieged it, putting a garrison into the strong places of the upper city.* This may be called the *eighteenth* siege. The Temple was only reduced by Pompey taking advantage of the Sabbath rest to move his machines. Of the defenders, 12,000 were slain. This was in the year 63 B.C. Pompey contented himself with examining the sacred treasures and the Holy of Holies, and refrained from plunder. Hyrcanus was confirmed in the high priesthood. He continued to reside at Jerusalem, ruling with the aid of Antipater the Idumean, father of Herod.

In B.C. 40, the city was taken by sudden

---

* Mr. Grove calls attention to the fact that as "Baris" is not mentioned, it was then but a small and unimportant fortress attached to the Temple.

assault by Antigonus, son of Aristobulus, with the assistance of a Parthian army.

Next year, B.C. 39, Herod appeared before the city, with the title of King of Judea, and a large force of Romans, and began the *nineteenth* siege of the city. He took it after five months, and began his long and chequered reign.

His principal additions to the buildings of the city were, at first, his own palace and the completion of the fortress of Antonia, where the old Baris stood. But his great work was the rebuilding of the Temple. He announced his intention in the year 19, and spent two years in making preparations. The Holy House itself—*i.e.*, the Porch, the Sanctuary, and the Holy of Holies—was completed in a year and a half. And in the year 9 B.C., eight years after the commencement of the building, the whole Temple was finished.

Herod died B.C. 4 (*i.e.*, a few months after the birth of Christ). It does not belong to our limits to trace the troublous history of the next seventy years, which includes the life of our Lord, or to show how fanaticism, blind zeal, ignorance, ambition, and the most ardent patriotism, all united to bring upon Jerusalem the fulfilment of our Lord's prophecies, and her utter desolation.

The siege of Titus was the *twentieth* in our history. When, at length, the conquest was completed, a garrison consisting of the Tenth Legion was left behind to carry on the work of desolation; and for fifty years the city disappears from history.

The hopeless struggle of the Jews against their conquerors, which continued to be carried on in Egypt and elsewhere, left the city undisturbed in its ruins, till the last desperate attack under Bar Cochebas (A.D. 132—135). Under this leader they acquired possession of their city, pulled down Hadrian's Temple to Jupiter, which had been built on the site of the Temple, and attempted to restore the latter (see Mr. Lewin's "Probable Sites of the Jewish Temple").

Then came the *twenty-first* siege, of which we know nothing, except that the struggle was so desperate, after the fall of Jerusalem, at Bether, where the last stand was made, that Hadrian, in announcing to the Senate the conclusion of the war, refrained from the usual congratulatory phrase.

After this, the policy of the Romans was to obliterate every trace of the city. This they endeavoured to do by planting a colony of legionaries in the ruins, by building a temple to Jupiter Capitolinus on the site of the Temple, by prohibiting the Jews from visiting the city, and by changing its name to that of Ælia Capitolina. They also built a theatre and market places, and erected a statue to Hadrian on the site of the Holy of Holies.

The history of the city enters now upon a new phase. The old sites were either forgotten or remembered only by tradition; the name of the old city, except among the Jews, has passed so entirely out of men's minds, that once when a Christian

convert, in a time of persecution, proclaimed himself a native of Jerusalem—meaning the heavenly
Jerusalem—the judge ordered him to the torture,
because he pretended citizenship of a place which
did not exist. For two hundred years no Jews were
allowed to come into the city, and then only once
a-year were permitted to weep over the ruins.
It is an extremely important point to remember
that there is this complete gap, or rather series
of gaps, in the history of the city. First, there
are fifty years, after the siege of Titus, of complete silence; then a brief note in history of another bloody siege, during the revolt of Bar
Cochebas; then two hundred years, while the
city was Roman.

At the same time, we must remember that, by
the evidence of the Bordeaux Pilgrim, A.D. 333,
and of St. Jerome, the position of the Temple was
never forgotten either by Jews or Christians; so
that, could it be clearly ascertained where the inhabitants of Jerusalem placed it at this date, we
should have little need of further controversy.
Moreover, there was an unbroken line of Christian
bishops.

The following theory is advanced by Mr. Lewin
in his "Probable Sites:"—When Diocletian ab-
dicated the imperial crown and retired to
Spalatro, he built there a Temple to Jupiter.
It stood near the centre of a rectangular platform; it was octagonal in form, and of the
Corinthian order; it had a vault under it; it was
approached by a golden gate, built in the wall of

the outer platform. When Maximinus Deza obtained, for his share of the empire, Syria, Egypt, and Palestine, he erected over the image of Jupiter, in the Temple Area of Jerusalem, a temple modelled after that erected by Diocletian at Spalatro. If this story is authentic, the Temple of Maximinus would be octagonal, of the Corinthian order, would be near the centre of a rectangular platform, and would have a golden gateway in the eastern outer wall—would resemble, in fact, in every particular except the dome and other modern additions, the Dome of the Rock as it stands at present.

Then we come to Constantine, an account of whose buildings at Jerusalem is given by Eusebius. Suffice it here to say that he built a great Basilica on the spot where the Cross was found, east of the site of the Holy Sepulchre, which he ornamented with great care and magnificence.

Julian gave permission (A.D. 362) to the Jews to rebuild the Temple. The attempt was rendered abortive by flames which issued from the ruins and destroyed the work of the labourers. No historical fact seems better established than this, whatever may have been the cause of the flames, which have been variously assigned to miraculous influence, to an explosion of gas, and to the agency of the Christians.

And now began the first waves of that great-tide of pilgrimages which, at its highest flood, brought with it the crusading armies and the kingdom of Jerusalem. Year after year the pilgrims flocked along the beaten roads, peaceful enough in these centuries, which led from west to east. All Syria was full of monasteries, nunneries, and hermitages; and Palestine was entirely given over into the hands of the Church. More building went on in Jerusalem. In 529, Justinian built his magnificent Basilica, some of the remains of which may possibly be found in the Mosque el Aksa. Churches, cemeteries, and hospices for pilgrims were erected in and without the city, and for more than 400 years Jerusalem was free from the horrors of war. Then its repose was rudely disturbed, for Chosroes, the Persian, swept through the country from end to end, took the city—it was the *twenty-second* siege—massacred thousands of the monks, destroyed the Church of the Holy Sepulchre, and carried off the sacred relic of the Christians, the wood of the true Cross. Heraclius, fourteen years later, entered the city at the head of a grand triumphal procession, bearing with him the Cross recovered from the Persians. He found the church already partly restored.

But nine years later there came another and a more terrible enemy than the Persian, in the shape of the Caliph Omar, at the head of his Mohammedan army. The city held out for four months, and then capitulated on easy and honourable terms. This was the *twenty-third* siege. Omar cleared away the filth and rubbish which covered the site of the Temple, and erected an oratory there, which was afterwards converted

into a great mosque; and the Masjid of Jerusalem
became, next to that of Mecca, the most sacred
place in the world to the Mohammedans.   For
the building of the mosque by Abd el Melek, see
chap. vi.   The Christians had a comparatively
easy time until the accession of the Caliph El
Hakim, by whom they were persecuted, and their
Church of the Sepulchre entirely destroyed.   It
had been previously either quite destroyed or
partially (*circa* 980) during the persecution of the
Christians after the victories of Zimisces (see
Besant and Palmer's " Jerusalem," p. 97).

The contests of rival parties among the Moslems brought evil days upon the city.   It was
pillaged by Afses in 1077; it was besieged (the
twenty-fourth siege) by Afdal, vizier of the Caliph
of Egypt in 1098; and in 1099 was again besieged and taken (the *twenty-fifth* siege) by the
army of the First Crusade.

The events of the Christian kingdom must be
passed over here.   It must be remarked, however,
that they seem to have respected all the places
to which tradition had assigned any sacred association.   Thus, the Dome of the Rock was kept
up as a Church, under the name of the Templum
Domini, from the tradition that it stood on the
site of Herod's Temple; while the Jami el Aksa
assigned to the Templars was called Templum
Solomonis, or Palatium Solomonis, from a tradition that it was Solomon's Palace.   A great
many buildings still remain which date from
their brief occupation of the city, less than a

hundred years in duration. The most important among them is, perhaps, the remains of the buildings erected by the Knights Hospitallers, in what is now called the Muristan, close to the Church of the Sepulchre (see "Quarterly Statement," Palestine Exploration Fund, July, 1872).

In 1187 the city was taken by Saladin, after a siege of seven weeks (the *twenty-sixth* siege).

In 1219 the walls were destroyed, and all the fortifications except the "Tower of David." This was when it was ceded to the Emperor Frederick, on the temporary restoration of the kingdom of Jerusalem.

In 1244 the city underwent its last and *twenty-seventh* siege, at the hands of the wild Kharezmian hordes, who plundered the city, and slaughtered the priests and monks.

The present walls were built by Suleiman the Magnificent, in the year 1542.

Such, briefly and baldly told, is the chronicle of Jerusalem from the earliest to the present time. It is told here, not as a new story, but in order that by its light the work of Captain Warren may be the better appreciated. Let it be remembered, when this is read, that we have to do, not with the ruins of one city, but of many. Jerusalem is builded, according to the prophecy of Jeremiah, on her own heap. There was a city there before the time of David. The second city may be called that of Solomon—from B.C. 1000 to B.C. 597, a space of four hundred years. We have next the city of Nehemiah, which

lasted for, say three hundred years, and gave
place to a more magnificent and Græcised city
which gradually grew up in the stormy period of
Herod and his immediate predecessors. This
city, destroyed by Titus, A.D. 70, was followed,
after an interval of complete ruin, by a purely
Roman city of the later empire, which lasted
till the time of the Mohammedans. The Christian city of Godfrey and the Baldwins may be
called the seventh city; and the modern city—
the result of six hundred years of Moslem rule—
may fairly be called the eighth.

Rubbish and *débris* cover every foot of the
ground, save where the rock crops up at intervals.
The rubbish is the wreck of all these cities, piled
one above the other. If we examine it, we have
to determine, at every step, among the ruins of
which city we are standing. Solomon, Nehemiah, Herod, Hadrian, Constantine, Omar,
Godfrey, Saladin, Suleiman—each in turn represents a city. It has been the task of the Fund
to dig down to the rock itself, and lay bare the
secrets of each in succession. When the hand
of destruction has fallen so heavily and so frequently, what wonder if little has been found to
illustrate the cities of the first three names?
—what astonishment that so much has been
preserved?

CHAPTER V.

LEGENDS AND TRADITIONS.

LIKE the moss clinging to the stones of an old ruin, and growing yearly deeper and wider spread, are the legends which grow up and cling to an old city. And the soil is most especially favourable to the growth of legends when, as in the case of Jerusalem, sites are held in great reverence, and two or more religions converge to the same place.

The traditions of Jerusalem are thus of three kinds. These are—the Jewish legends, chiefly found in the Talmud; the Christian—which, again, may be subdivided into præ- and post-Crusading times, or may be parcelled out among the different churches, Greek, Latin, Armenian, Coptic, which divide the Christian community; and, lastly, there are the Mohammedan traditions.

Jerusalem, say the Talmudists, is the centre of the earth. Near the Holy City was created Adam. It was near the city, but not on its site, that the first blood was spilt. The body of Adam, taken by Noah into the Ark, was by him distributed among his sons; Shem, receiving the head, gave it to his son Melchizedek, by whom it was buried in Jerusalem, on the hill called Golgotha. The city itself was founded by Melchizedek. It was on the rock of Moriah that Abraham prepared to offer up Isaac. And when the days of exile are concluded, Jerusalem will be again the capital of the new and more glorious kingdom, and the site of the new and more glorious Temple.

The Mohammedan legends cluster mostly round the Haram Area. The rock itself is said to be suspended in the air. It was from here that Mohammed made his ascent to the seventh Heaven: they show his footprint still; and, close beside it, the handprint of the angel Gabriel, who seized the rock, and prevented it from rising with the prophet. Here is the tomb of Solomon; here are pomegranates made by the hand of David —according to the Talmud, he was an armourer by trade—the saddle of the Prophet's mule, El Burak; in another place is a mosque where they show the ring to which El Burak was fastened while Mohammed was away on his journey to Heaven. There are also the footprint of Enoch,

the praying-place of Solomon, of David, of the
prophets. And in the Mosque el Aksa they
show the tombs of the sons of Aaron, the footprint of Jesus, the praying-places of John and
Zechariah, and the mosques of the Forty Martyrs.

One or two of the legends are evidently connected with traditions which preserve some germs
of history. For instance, it is reported that a
Mohammedan on a certain occasion dropped his
bucket into the cistern now called the Well of
the Leaf. On descending to recover it, he found
himself in a delicious garden. Here he plucked
a leaf, and, hastening back, begged his friends to
go with him. His story was disbelieved, till the
freshness of the leaf, together with a prophecy of
Mohammed, was adduced as proof of its truth.
Now, it is by no means improbable that the
Royal Gardens lay beneath the southern wall;
and there may have been formerly a connection
between this cistern and the gardens, the knowledge of which by degrees shaped itself into the
legend as we find it now.

The Christians vie with the Mohammedans in
collecting together in one spot all kinds of sacred
sites. Let us enumerate a few of those pointed
out in the Church of the Holy Sepulchre. Here
are shown (all within the precincts of the church)
—the stone where our Lord's body lay for the
anointing with oil, the place where the Virgin
stood while this was being done, the Holy
Sepulchre itself, and the Chapel of the Angel;
the place where Christ appeared to Mary Mag-

dalene, and that where He appeared to the Virgin;
the pillar of Flagellation; the prison of Christ;
the centre of the earth; the place where the Cross
was found; the place where the Cross was recognized; the Chapel of the Mocking; the tomb of
Melchizedek; the rent in the rock; the place
where the Cross was fixed; a piece of the rock
of Calvary; the seat on which our Lord sat when
he was crowned; and the tombs of Joseph and ·
Nicodemus.   It is noticeable that the old legend
of the burial-place of Adam is also kept up by
the Chapel of Adam.   It is stated that the blood
from the Cross, falling upon the skull of Adam,
recalled him to life again.   The story shows how
ignorance may pervert a simple religious belief by
taking it in a literal sense.

In other parts of the city similar legends
abound.   There is no incident in the Bible, however trifling, connected with Jerusalem, whose site
is not fixed by the authority of tradition.   Here
is the place where St. Stephen was stoned ; here
the building which holds within its walls the tomb
of David, the scene of the Last Supper, that of
the day of Pentecost, and the place where the
Virgin Mary died.   You may be shown the
Palace of Caiaphas; the spot where Peter denied
his Master, that where he hid himself in remorse;
the place where the cock crew; the place where
the Virgin was born, where her father was buried
the scene of the Ascension; the Via Dolorosa,
with its eight stations, a quite modern invention,
unknown to the Crusaders; the house of Dives,

even the stones which *might have cried out* if
the disciples had held their peace (St. Luke, xix.
40).

The great period of the invention of these pious
legends, which began very early, was that between
the building of Constantine's great Basilica in
front of the Holy Sepulchre, and the taking of
the city by the Saracens. It must be remembered
that for four hundred years the city and country
enjoyed a profound tranquillity, being disturbed
only by occasional incursions of the lawless
Bedawin, who were easily repulsed. From end
to end of the country it swarmed with hermitages,
ascetics, and monasteries. There was no valley
where monk or hermit was not found. Pious
women and holy men were the inhabitants of the
country. There appears to have been none of the
mediæval abuses of monasticism: the piety of
the monks and nuns, from what we can gather,
was real and unfeigned. So also was their credulity; so, too, their ignorance, which must have
been deep beyond all belief. That they did not
invent sacred sites may very well be believed,
without any stretch of charity; that they found
them, identified them by some slight marks which
they considered proofs, and then fervently believed
in them, may be assumed to have been the real
process followed. Thus, a stone with two holes
is found. What can this be but the two holes in
which our Lord's feet were placed while waiting
His crucifixion? When this process had gone on
for four centuries, there came a rude interruption

in the shape of the Saracen conquest.   But even
then the Christians were not disturbed in their
peaceful possession, nor did any active persecution
harass them till the mad Hakeem destroyed their
Church of the Sepulchre.   Tradition, therefore,
like a stream, flowed onward, gathering more
strength the longer it grew.   Only the *invention*
of new sites received its first great check when
the Caliph Omar marched into the city.   Nor
was it renewed until, five hundred years later, the
Crusaders turned out the Saracens, and the whole
process began over again.

As a natural result of this long series of invention, identification, and credulity, we are driven
from one absurd tradition to another, until we are
fain to ask whether anything is true or not; and
perhaps many a modern traveller has gone too
far in denying the authenticity of all tradition.
On the other hand, there are not wanting stalwart
defenders of tradition.   Chateaubriand argues
with great force the improbability that the important sites of the Christian History should ever
be lost.   The Rev. George Williams takes the
same side; and the names of those who hold the
traditional sites are at least as distinguished as
those who have attacked them.

The legends of the Crusading period are not
concerned with the fixing of new sites so much
as with the strengthening of the old by dreams
and visions.   Everybody had dreams, which seem
to have come when wanted; in most cases, doubtless, the effect of a heated imagination and a

monotonous life on a brain fatigued with fasting
and prayer. Sometimes, however, we find a
story belonging apparently to an earlier age—
such, for instance, as that related by Benjamin
of Tudela:—

"On Mount Zion are the sepulchres of the
house of David, and those of the kings who
reigned after him. In consequence of the following circumstance, however, this place is at present
hardly to be recognized. Fifteen years ago, one
of the walls of the place of worship on Mount
Zion fell down, and the patriarch commanded the
priest to repair it. He ordered stones to be taken
from the original wall of Zion for that purpose,
and twenty workmen were hired at stated wages,
who broke stones from the very foundation of
the walls of Zion. Two of these labourers, who
were intimate friends, upon a certain day treated
each other, and repaired to their work after their
friendly meal. The overseer accused them of
dilatoriness, but they answered that they would
still perform their day's work, and would employ
thereupon the time while their fellow-labourers
were at meals. They then continued to break
out stones, until, happening to meet with one
which formed the mouth of a cavern, they agreed
to enter it in search of treasure, and they proceeded until they reached a large hall, supported
by pillars of marble, encrusted with gold and
silver, and before which stood a table, with a
golden sceptre and crown. This was the sepulchre of David, King of Israel, to the left of which

they saw that of Solomon in a similar state, and
so on the sepulchres of all the Kings of Judah,
who were buried there. They further saw chests
locked up, the contents of which nobody knew,
and were on the point of entering the hall, when
a blast of wind like a storm issued forth from the
mouth of the cavern so strong that it threw them
down almost lifeless to the ground. There they
lay until evening, when another wind rushed forth,
from which they heard a voice like that of a man
calling aloud, 'Get up, and go forth from this
place.' The men rushed out full of fear, and
proceeded to the patriarch to report what had
happened to them. This ecclesiastic summoned
into his presence R. Abraham el Constantini, a
pious ascetic, one of the mourners of the downfall
of Jerusalem, and caused the two labourers to
repeat what they had previously reported. R.
Abraham thereupon informed the patriarch that
they had discovered the sepulchres of the house
of David and of the Kings of Judah. The following morning the labourers were sent for again,
but they were found stretched on their beds and
still full of fear; they declared that they would
not attempt to go on again to the cave, as it was
not God's will to discover it to any one. The
patriarch ordered the place to be walled up, so
as to hide it effectually from every one unto the
present day. The above-mentioned R. Abraham
told me all this."

CHAPTER VI.

THE PROBLEMS STATED.

NOW that the ground is cleared, and we know—
first, what is the present condition, plan, and aspect of the modern city; secondly, what are the leading traditions which attach to different sites within and without its walls; and lastly, what .are the main facts which constitute the history of the city, and have led to the present state of its buildings—it will be well, before advancing another step, to state in a very few words what points we have to decide, and what problems we wish to settle. It would seem that in so small a space, with ground so clearly marked, with so much history to help us, that nothing could be so easy as to put the finger on any site or place in Jerusalem. Doubtless, if we follow tradition, nothing would be easier; but, as we have seen, the stream of tradition, never very clear under the most favourable circumstances, has been

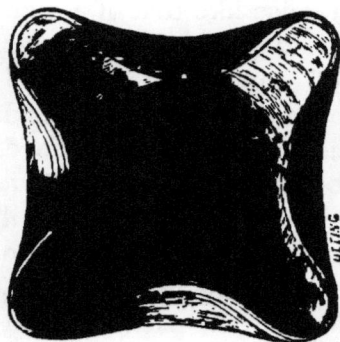

troubled by a succession of faiths, each bringing its own contribution of confusion; and, in the anxiety to identify, the false has been mixed with the true, the incredible with the credible, old legends have been passed over to new, until the difficulty of extrication has become, without the aid of excavation, absolutely insurmountable.

The position of the Temple, that of the fortress of Antonia, that of the Tombs of the Kings, that of the Church of the Holy Sepulchre, are all disputed. The course of the wells is disputed; the ruinous places—such as the Pool of Bethesda; En Rogel; the Pool of Hezekiah; the great Towers of Hippicus, Phasaelus, and Mariamne; the Tomb of Helena—are all disputed. Most wonderful of all, the site of Mount Zion itself is disputed. Directly a traveller—Dr. Robinson was the first in this century, though he was anticipated by the old traveller, Korte—begins to examine into the traditional sites, he finds himself faced by difficulties so overwhelming, and contradictions apparently so insuperable, that often he feels himself compelled to abandon the site altogether, and to make a new theory to suit his own interpretations.

Quot viatores, tot sententiæ. And now the multiplication of theories, as we shall see further on, proves as perplexing as the unblushing confidence of tradition.

Let us for instance take one single site to illustrate our difficulties. Where was the Tomb of the Kings? Eleven kings of Judah and one

priest, Jehoiada, were buried in this sepulchre.
It was on Zion. It was known in the time of
Hyrcanus and of Herod, who opened it, and
took treasure from the tomb of David. It is now
entirely lost. To recover this sepulchre would
be to fix, without a doubt, the position of Zion
and the city of David. In all these uncertain-
ties we seem to have nothing to rest upon—until
we come to the excavations of Captain Warren—
except two or three facts acknowledged by all the
world. The western wall of the city ran, as it runs
now, along the edge of the valley; the Temple
stood somewhere in the Haram Area; the fortress of Antonia was near the Temple. Any
attempt to fix the sites, with even tolerable accuracy, is attended with a necessary amount of
conjecture, hypothesis, and unproved conclusions
that make the theory at best a stop-gap until
something better can be found.

We read the Bible, and picture to ourselves
the streets, the temples, the walls, and towers of
Jerusalem. These are present to the imagination of childhood, and remain with us till we
think the city is as familiar to us as London.
But it is a city of imagination—we know nothing
certain about it. While we say, here is Zion,
here the Church of the Holy Sepulchre, the
theorist calls us from the spot and shows us
another Zion, another Church of the Sepulchre;
so that in the midst of counsellors there is confusion. Now, surely, to bring a history home
with clearness to the mind, it is absolutely neces-

sary to have a map, plan, or sketch of the places
where the events took place.

The work before the Committee of the Fund,
as regards Jerusalem, was, therefore, briefly
this: we proposed nothing less than the abso-
lute identification of every sacred site. To
put an end to controversy, to draw an accurate
map of the ancient city, and to make the sacred
history capable of such illustration as only maps
can give, is our ambitious design. How far we
have succeeded will be presently seen. Now,
there are one or two points which, once settled,
will prove of the greatest help in bringing about
an entire solution of the question. The most
important of these are the Tombs of the Kings,
the course of the Second Wall, and the site of
the Temple. From the first we can get the real
Zion; from the second we can at least decide
whether the present Church of the Holy Sepulchre is in a possible position; and the third is,
of course, an all-important point. There are but
four ways of arriving at a satisfactory answer.
First, by actual measurement and a careful survey of the modern city. This has been done,
through the liberality of Lady Burdett Coutts,
by Captain Wilson. Secondly, by a study of
the general history of the city which we have
just gone through, and then of those passages
from the contemporary records and the descriptions of pilgrims which bear upon the sites.
Some of these we shall give immediately.
Thirdly, by a study of the architecture of the

ruins which remain. This has been done by
Mr. George Williams and Professor Willis (Wil-
liams's "Holy City"), by the Count de Vogüé
("Temple de Jerusalem"), by Mr. Fergusson
("Jerusalem," and certain articles in Smith's
"Biblical Dictionary"), and by others.

But then, these methods having been all
adopted by the different writers, there results
from the reasoning of each a different conclusion.
There remains only the last method—that of
excavation. This was reserved for the Palestine
Exploration Fund, through their indefatigable
officer, Captain Warren. It has been admitted
by the holders of the better known theories—
Mr. Williams, Mr. Fergusson, and Mr. Lewin—
that excavation alone will remove doubt and put
an end to controversy. The secrets of the past
lay buried beneath the surface of the present,
waiting for him who should be able to pluck
them from their hiding place and give them back
to the world.

What Captain Warren did we now propose
to tell; only—if our readers are not already
wearied with preliminaries—let us first give the
most important historical evidence, and the
three theories referred to. It will be carefully
understood that we hold, as a body, no theory
whatever, and that we abstain from forming any
conclusions as to Captain Warren's work. In
chap. ix. will be found, like a bundle of children's bricks, out of which they are to construct
a puzzle-house, the materials—so far as we have

yet gone—for reconstruction. The reader may fit them in to each theory in turn; and although he may be led to form a conclusion in his own mind, we would urge upon him to remember *that we have not done yet.*

CHAPTER VII.

THE HISTORICAL EVIDENCE.

THE Bible, teeming as it is with references to Jerusalem, nowhere gives an account of the city or of the Temple. In Ezekiel's vision (chap. 41—43) we have, it is true, an exact description, with measurements. But the application of the description to any theory is exceedingly difficult. Josephus, on the other hand, is quite clear and distinct, provided certain data are first established. After the taking of the city by Titus, the accounts of Jerusalem are for some centuries very few and

meagre; nor are there any full and complete accounts till we come to those published in Mr. Williams's "Holy City"—first, from the French of the twelfth century; second, from the geography of Edrisi, of the same date; and thirdly, from that of Mejr-ed-deen, of the tenth.

Other help has been derived from the chronicles of pilgrims. In order to guide the reader in studying the full importance of Captain Warren's researches, we give the principal passages which have been gathered by Mr. Williams, Mr. Fergusson, and others from original sources. They should be read with constant reference to the plan of the Haram Area.

And first, Josephus.

(1.) Antiq., viii. 3, sec. 9:—

"When Solomon had filled up great valleys with earth, and had elevated the ground 400 cubits, he made it to be on a level with the top of the mountain on which the Temple was built; and by this means the outermost temple which was exposed to the air was even with the Temple itself."

(2.) Wars, i. 21, sec. 1.

"Herod accordingly, at an incalculable expense, and in a style of unsurpassed magnificence, in the fifteenth year of his reign, restored the Temple, and breasted up with a wall the area around it, so as to enlarge it to twice its former extent. An evidence of its sumptuousness were the ample colonnades around the holy place, and the fort on its northern side. The colonnades he reared from the foundation; the fort, in nothing inferior to a palace, he repaired at an immense cost, and called it Antonia, in honour of Antony."

(3.) Wars, v. 5, sec. 1.—

"The Temple, as I have said, was seated on a strong hill. Originally the level space on its summit scarcely sufficed for the Sanctuary and the altar, the ground about being abrupt and steep; but King Solomon, who built the Sanctuary, having completely walled up the eastern side, a colonnade was built upon the embankment; on the other side the Sanctuary remained exposed. In process of time, however, as people were constantly adding to the embankment, the hill became level and broader. They also threw down the northern wall, and enclosed as much ground as the circuit of the Temple at large subsequently occupied. After having surrounded the hill from the base with a triple wall, and accomplished a work which surpassed all expectation, they built the upper boundary walls and the lower court of the Temple. The lowest part of the latter they built up from a depth of 300 cubits, and in some places more. The entire depth of the foundations, however, was not discernible; for, with a view to level the streets of the town, they filled up the ravines to a considerable extent. There were stones used in the building which measured 40 cubits."

"The entire circuit of the cloisters, including the Antonia, measured six furlongs"—Book v., chap. 5.

(4.) Antiq., xx. 9, sec. 7.—

"They persuaded Agrippa to rebuild the eastern cloisters. These cloisters belonged to the outer court, and were situated in a deep valley, and had walls that reached 400 cubits (in length), and were built of square and very white stones; the length of each of which stones was 20 cubits, and their height six cubits. This was the work of King Solomon, who first of all built the entire Temple. But King Agrippa, who had the care of the Temple committed to him by Claudius Cæsar, considering that it is easy to demolish any building, but hard to build it up again, and that it was particularly hard to do it to these cloisters, which would require a considerable time and great sums of money, denied the petitioners their request in this matter."

The full description of Josephus, which should be read very carefully, and with the help of the map of Jerusalem and that of the Haram Area, will be found in "Wars of the Jews," book v., chap. 4. There is also a vague and brief description of the city by Tacitus (Hist., v. 10—12); but he speaks only from the accounts given by others, and not from personal knowledge.

We come next to the evidence after the Christian era. The Temple being now destroyed, and the writers mostly Christian, it is natural that their evidence chiefly bears upon what to them was of far greater importance than the site of the Temple—viz., the Sepulchre of our Lord.

Let us hastily run through the principal points.

Eusebius, a contemporary authority, gives us a long account, of which the following is an abridgment.

Constantine, taking down a temple to Venus which had been, according to tradition, built on the site of the Holy Sepulchre, and clearing the earth, found a tomb, cut in the rock, still remaining. His workmen immediately concluded that this could be no other than the tomb of our Lord. "He beautified it with rare columns, and profusely enriched it with the most splendid decorations." In front of it, or round about it, he made a level place. "On the side opposite to the Sepulchre, which was the eastern side, the church itself was erected"—*i.e.*, on the eastern side of the level place in front of the Sepulchre. This church, the Basilica of the Martyrion, is the only church mentioned by Eusebius at all. It will be observed that he speaks of it as *the church.* In front of the church is an open market place. It is not at all clear, therefore, from this account that any church was built by Constantine *over* the Sepulchre.

While the buildings of Constantine were in process of erection, there came from Bourdeaux a certain pilgrim to Jerusalem, whose name has not been preserved. He wrote an itinerary, with a description of the city. In it occurs the following remarkable passage:—

"Within, inside the Zion Wall, is seen the place where David had his palace, and (where were) seven synagogues which once were there,

but one only remains (standing), for the rest
were ploughed up and sowed over, as Isaiah the
prophet hath said. Thence, in order to go outside
the wall, for those going to the Neapolitan gate,
on the right hand, down in the valley, are walls
where was the house of Pontius Pilate. There
our Lord was heard before He suffered. But on
the left hand is the hill of Golgotha, where
the Lord was crucified. Thence, about a stone's
throw, is the crypt where His body was placed,
and (from which) He rose again on the third day.
There, lately, by order of Constantine, a Basilica
has been built—that is, a church of wonderful
beauty," &c., &c., &c.

An anonymous description of the Holy Places,
apparently of about the same date, has been published by Dr. Tobler from a work in the British
Museum. It contains the following passage:—
"Not far from the place is a stone, at which every
year the Jews come, and, after anointing it and
weeping over it, go away with lamentation. Here
is the house of Hezekiah, King of Judah, whose
life the Lord prolonged for fifteen years. Then
comes the house of Caiaphas, at a column at
which Christ was bound, scourged, and struck.
At (or near) the Neapolitan Gate is the Prætorium
of Pilate, where Christ was judged by the chief
priests. Not far off is Golgotha, or the place of
Calvary," &c.

It is necessary to observe here that these passages would settle at once the question as to the
site of the Sepulchre could the controversialists

agree as to the Neapolitan Gate. If it is the gate through which passed the road leading to Neapolis (Nâblûs)—the present Damascus Gate—as would at first sight appear, the present site is certainly that of Constantine. But Mr. Fergusson maintains that it is the gate of the New City, in which case the clue is lost.

We pass over three hundred years, and come to Bishop Arculf. He went on a pilgrimage about the year 690. On his way back to his bishopric in France, a tempest drove his ship northwards, and wrecked him on one of the islands of the Hebrides. He was received and entertained hospitably by Adamnanus, Abbot of Iona, and spent the winter in telling and re-telling to the monks his travels and adventures in the East. Adamnanus wrote down, either from his dictation or from remembrance, his description, and drew a plan of the church, which has come down to us. It is manifest, from his description and that of other writers who follow him, that if Eusebius is correct in placing no church over the Sepulchre, but only a circle of pillars round it, building must have gone on after Constantine, and an actual church built over the tomb.

"The Church of the Holy Sepulchre," says Arculf, "is supported by twelve stone columns of extraordinary magnitude. In the middle space is a round grotto (tegurium) cut in the rock itself, about a foot and a half higher than a man of full stature, in which nine men could stand

and pray. The entrance of the grotto is on the east side. On the north side, within, is the tomb of our Lord, hewn out of the rock, seven feet in length, and raised three feet above the floor."

And in another place:—"In that famous place where was formerly the splendidly built Temple, in the neighbourhood of the eastern wall, the Saracens have erected a quadrangular house of prayer . . . . which house is able to contain three thousand men at once."

As regards the buildings in the Haram Area, the Arabic account of them has been fully given, for the first time, by Professor E. H. Palmer (Besant and Palmer's "Jerusalem"). It amounts, briefly, to this. When the Caliph Omar took Jerusalem, he found the Masjid (place of adoration) of David covered up and defiled with all kinds of filth and rubbish. This systematic pollution of the place had been going on for many centuries; and we learn from Eutychius, that "when Helena, the mother of Constantine, had built churches in Jerusalem, the site of the rock and its neighbourhood had been laid waste and so left. But the Christians heaped dirt upon the rock; so that there was a large dunghill over it." Omar built a mosque of timber in the Masjid. It must be remembered that the word Masjid el Aksa is always used for the whole of the Haram Area. Abd el Melek (A.D. 684) erected the buildings which now stand in the Haram Area, including the Dome of the Rock, the Dome of the Chain, the Mosque (Jami) el Aksa, and the oratories.

The Kubbet es Sakhra, or Dome of the Rock, is not a mosque, and was never intended for one. It is a domed edifice, intended to mark a spot to which traditions cling. In form it is identical with a Moslem *weli*, or saint's tomb. Professor Palmer insists that the Arabic accounts of the buildings are as clear and distinct as would be one now of the building of St. Paul's by Sir Christopher Wren. On the other hand, nothing in these accounts appears inconsistent with the building on old foundations, or with pillars, &c. which had belonged to older structures.

To sum up the historical evidence :—

Ezekiel, in his vision, seems to describe the actual measurements of the Temple. Josephus gives a detailed account of Jerusalem as it stood in his own day. Eusebius describes the buildings of Constantine. A contemporary Christian describes the city at the same period. Various pilgrims, from time to time, have narrated their travels and described the sites. The Mohammedans have preserved several accounts of the city, as old as the tenth and twelfth centuries. We have accurate accounts from the crusading period downwards. The great Christian builders were Constantine and Justinian. The great Roman builders were Hadrian, and, according to Mr. Lewin, Maximinus Deza.

All the buildings in the Haram Area, according to Mohammedan historians, are due to Abd el Melek and his successors.

We are now ready to advance another stage,

and to give, in a very few words, the leading theories on the sacred sites. It will of course be remembered that the conclusions we shall quote are all derived from the amount of knowledge, of which we have given a condensation, possessed by the world before Captain Warren's researches commenced.

CHAPTER VIII.

THE RIVAL THEORIES.

THE rival theories which have been brought before us from time to time may be briefly stated. Up to the time of Dr. Robinson, there was little attempt to question any tradi- ·tional site; though Korte, the German bookseller, who visited Jerusalem a hundred and fifty years ago, called attention to the impossibility of the traditions being all true.

According to Dr. Robinson, who, so far as the Temple Area is concerned, is followed by Messrs. Kraft, Barclay, Kiepert, and Porter, the Temple of Herod occupied the whole southern portion of the Haram enclosure —a space of about 925 ft. Dr. Robinson thinks there can be no doubt that the present site of the Holy Sepulchre is the same as that chosen by Constantine for the Basilica.

Mr. Williams thinks that the southern portion is mainly the work of Justinian, the site of whose great church, described by Procopius, he con-

siders to be that now occupied by the Mosque el
Aksa. In the latter opinion he is followed by
the Count de Vogüé and others, who see in the
architecture proofs of the mosque having been
originally a Christian structure. Mr. Williams
also thinks the traditional site of the Holy
Sepulchre the true one; arguing that, considering
the unbroken succession of Christian bishops, and
the very short time during which the Christians
were probably out of the city, it is extremely unlikely that the knowledge of the site of Christ's
Sepulchre should ever have been forgotten.
Chateaubriand took a similar line in his "Itine-
raire." Mr. Williams's course of the second wall
may be put down as nearly the same as that in
Captain Warren's plan. His third wall, however
takes a much larger area.

According to Sir Henry James, the Count de
Vogüé, and M. de Saulcy, the Temple occupied
the whole of the Haram Area, Antonia being
joined on at the north-west angle, perhaps projecting a little into the outer court. Messrs.
Tobler and others suppose a Temple of about
600 ft. a side, nearly coincident with the present
platform.

Mr. Fergusson considers that the Temple stood
in the south-west corner. According to him, the
eastern wall was an addition of Agrippa, the cave
under the Holy Rock was the Lord's Sepulchre,
the site of which was perfectly well known to the
Christians at the time of Constantine; and the
Dome of the Rock, altered and added to by the

Mohammedans, is substantially as it now stands
a church built by Constantine over the tomb.
Antonia, he places just north of the Temple—*i.e.*,
close to Wilson's Arch.   The Mosque el Aksa
is the work of Abd el Melek.   As for the present
Church of the Holy Sepulchre, it was originally ?
church built by the Christians in imitation
their real church, when they had been forbiden
to enter it any longer; and the traditions attaching
to the old church were bodily removed, partly by
fraud, partly by ignorance, to the new site.   He
further places the second wall in such a position
that the present church must have been *inside*
it.   For his views on other points—the population of Jerusalem, the strength of Titus's army,
the position of Zion, that of the minor sites—we
refer the reader to his two books on the subject,
and to his articles in Smith's "Bible Dictionary,"
where they are set forth and explained in full.
It may be stated that his arguments are based
mainly upon architectural evidence, and that
having formed his opinion as to the date of the
Kubbet es Sakhra, by examining the style of the
building, he has proceeded to fortify himself by
the historical evidence.

As regards his position of the Temple, Mr.
Lewin and Mr. Thrupp agree with him.   But
Mr. Lewin totally disagrees with him as to the
Dome of the Rock.   He admits that the building
is of the date which Mr. Fergusson assigns to it,
but contends that it was built by Maximinus
Deza, one of the successors of Diocletian, in imi-

RECONSTRUCTION OF THE TEMPLE.

ACCORDING TO
WILLIAMS, FERGUSSON, PORTER & LEWIN.

Williams

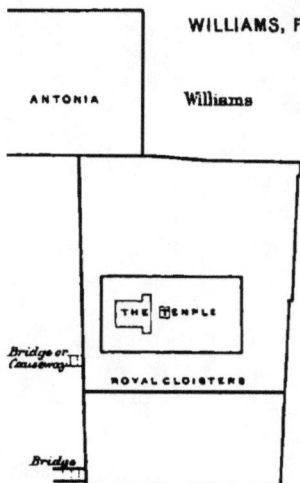

Fergusson

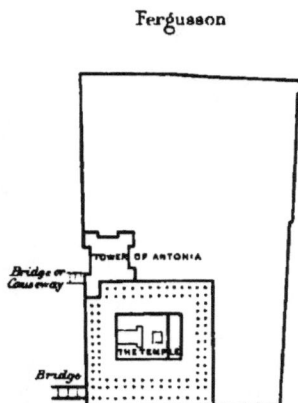

Porter

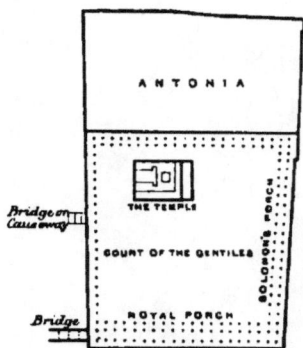

Lewin

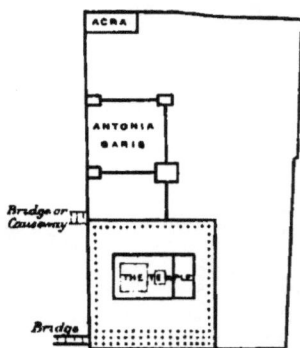

SCALES.

tation of the temple which Diocletian built at Spalatro, the ruins of which still stand. Further, he thinks that the cave in the rock was the tomb of Alexander Jannæus. Antonia he would separate from the Temple by cloisters, and the Palace of Solomon he would place just south of the Haram wall at the western end. So far for modern controversialists. The voice of tradition places the Temple of Herod, the second wall, the Holy Sepulchre, Zion, where Mr. Williams places them. Further on we shall give Captain Warren's own conclusions.

The accompanying illustration will give, better than any lengthened description, the different arrangement of the Haram Area proposed by Dr. Porter (who agrees with Dr. Robinson), Mr. Williams, Mr. Lewin, and Mr. Fergusson.

We have now, then, cleared the way for Captain Warren. We have told what the city is now, what and where are its ruins, what traditions attach to them, what is actually known, and what is conjectured. We have also sketched out, as fully as our space permits, the leading facts in the history of Jerusalem, showing the number of its sieges and the different dynasties and races that have held the city. We have stated the principal passages in the historical evidence which bear upon the sites, showing what Josephus says, what Eusebius, what the pilgrims have said, and what the Mohammedan historians say. And, lastly, we have given the principal points of difference on the rival theories. Now, let Captain

Warren's work be read and considered, and let the reader, if he pleases, take theory after theory, and try how far the new facts fit into each. He need not take Captain Warren's conclusions, but he *must* take his facts, because they are of a nature which cannot be disputed. And even if he be one who is content to wait till others have reconstructed the city for him, he will surely feel an interest in the tale which the stones have been made to tell, of incredible labour for ages, of former magnificence, of destruction, ruin, and disaster. "Who is left among you that saw this house in his first glory? And how do ye see it now?"

CHAPTER IX.

CAPTAIN WARREN'S EXCAVATIONS.

THE preceding chapters will have prepared the reader for a clear understanding of the main objects of Captain Warren's work in Jerusalem. It was not to consist of mere purposeless digging, though even that alone would have been interesting in such ground. It had for object the determination of those difficult points, without the settlement of which the ancient city can never be understood, and the history of the Bible never completely appreciated.

LAMP, WITH CHRISTIAN INSCRIPTION.

He landed at Jaffa, on February 15, 1867, armed with a vizierial letter from Constantinople to the Pasha of Jerusalem, authorizing him to excavate anywhere, *except in the Haram Area, and sites sacred to Christians and Moslems*—an exception of the greatest importance, as it prevented

H

him from digging where results would have been
certain, and gave the Pasha opportunity to inter-
fere, whenever he thought it prudent, on some
vexatious plea of possible damage to the walls
of the Haram Area. His party, from first to last,
consisted of Sergeant Birtles, and Corporals Phil-
lips, Hancock, Turner, Mackenzie, Cock, Ellis,
Hanson, and Duncan. The last of these died in
Jerusalem. It is fair to record Captain Warren's
often expressed opinion as to the worth and
ability of his staff. The work was begun immediately after his arrival, and continued till April,
1870, for a space of three years; when Captain
Warren judged that, with the means at his command and the limitation imposed on his powers
of excavation, he had done all that could be done
in his special work, and returned home. In the
autumn of that year appeared the full account of
his labours, in the volume entitled the "Recovery
of Jerusalem," from which we make our abridgment of his work. We had been prepared, by
Captain Wilson's report of the Ordnance Survey,
for a vast accumulation of rubbish. At the same
time, its actual details proved far greater than
any one had anticipated. This *débris* is described
as consisting of "stone chippings"—that is, not
long chips, but small hemispherical or cubical
pieces lying in layers. Between these layers are
broken stones, of 2 to 6 in. cube, or great lumps
of broken cut stone, and sometimes a layer of
earth from 1 to 3 ft. thick. Before reaching the
rock itself, there is a layer of mould from 2 to 4 ft.,

and sometimes more, in thickness, which abounds
in potsherds, and in those old lamps, the oldest
known, made for burning fat. Remember all
the sieges of the city. The lowest layer represents
the earliest period of all, the time when no great
building had taken place, and no destruction.
The successive layers represent the work of destruction, and the occasional layers of earth a
long period of repose.

The "shingle," as it is called by Captain Warren, runs like water. It has no cohesion, except
where, as in the city along the Tyropœon Valley,
water has percolated through it, and given a certain amount of mud to keep it together; consequently, when it is "tapped," it will run for days
together. Another annoyance was the fact that
when the shingle was at all moist it was in a
certain degree poisonous, and a wound in the
hand, however slight, would fester instead of
healing at once.

The shafts which were sunk through this
dangerous stuff were long pipes 4 ft. clear outside the city, 3 ft. inside, so as to take up the less
space. They were sheeted round with mining
cases—that is, boxes of wood, without top or
bottom, put in as the work of excavation went on.
The great difficulty here was, that the rubbish
behind one of the sides of the case would begin
to run, and leave a great void outside the shaft;
most dangerous, because it led sometimes to the
fall of the rubbish beyond, with a violence enough
to smash in the shaft itself. By a series of

"lucky escapes," by the constant exercise of the
most careful personal supervision, and by the
ntelligent care of his staff, Captain Warren was
enabled to carry on the work with no fatal acci-
dents, and only one or two at all serious.   Yet
the danger was very great.   The lives of the explorers were exposed to risks such as were certainly not contemplated by the promoters of the
expedition. Any shaft might at any moment col-
lapse through a rush of the shingle; great blocks
of masonry hung tottering over their heads; in
the foul air below, their lights would not burn;
the careless workmen dropped their tools down
the shafts in which they were; and any serious
accident, attended with loss of life, might have led
to the suspension of the works altogether.

At first it was supposed that the shafts would
lead not only to topographical but also to archæological discoveries. This expectation was not real-
ized.   No weapons at all were found, except a solitary spear-head or two; and no hoards of treasure,
which some people in Jerusalem looked for.
Considering the great portions of the city which
have been already turned up in the many recent
public and private buildings with such small
results, we may fairly expect that we shall find
little to reward us from an archæological point of
view in any future research.   Probably, in some
old aqueducts and sewers, or in some secret
caves, there may exist treasures hidden away
in troublous times; but we have not yet found
any.

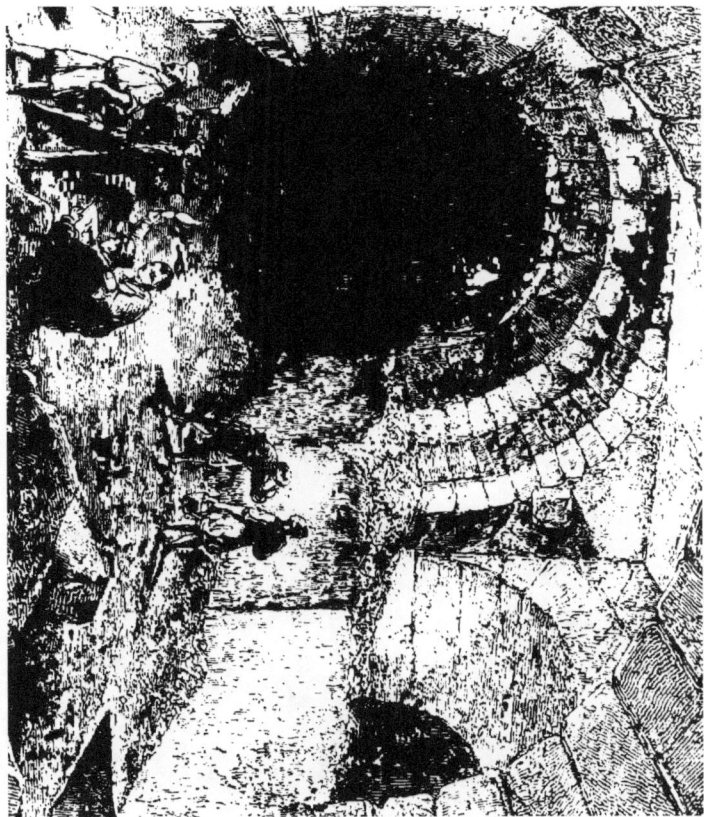

The first shaft sunk was at the western wall, at Wilson's Arch.

The western wall of the Haram Area has been already described. Here there were formerly four gates to the Temple—three of which have been identified with Wilson's Arch, Barclay's Gateway, and Robinson's Arch (see p. 107). Captain Warren examined each in turn. We give only those of his results which appear the most important, referring in this, as in all other cases, to our larger work, the "Recovery of Jerusalem," for fuller explanation.

Under Wilson's Arch is an old disused cistern, the pavement of which was broken through, and a shaft sunk along the wall. The stones here were about 3 ft. 8 in. to 4 ft. in height. They were all in their original positions, and appeared to Captain Warren to be probably one of the *oldest portions of the Sanctuary now existing*. If so, they formed, without doubt, part of the original enclosure wall of the Temple. At a depth of 24 ft. they came upon a mass of masonry and voussoirs, apparently those of a fallen arch. Hence we may conclude that the present arch, which may be late Roman, stands upon the site of an older one. Lower down, they came to the foundations of the wall in the rock, and here running water was found; and observations, extended over a long period, proved that a fountain of water exists in the city, and is running to this day far below the surface. It ran along the wall; but no trace of the stream was found lower down at the excavations near Robinson's Arch. There is.

a tradition among the Jews that when flowing
water has been found three times under the
Temple walls, the Messiah is at hand. Now,
according to their accounts, it had been found
twice before, so that this made the third time;
and the Rabbis came down to look at the discovery, with cries of joy and thanksgiving.

There came next the point whether, if this
was one of the suburban gates of the Temple, the
second could be found. A gallery was run along
to the south, along the valley, to look for it, but no
signs were found; and Captain Warren thinks
that if a second gateway existed south of Wil-

CAPITAL OF PILASTER FOUND AT WILSON'S ARCH.

son's Arch, and similar to Barclay's Gate, it would have been visible in the shafts or gallery, or in some part of the wall exposed in the vaults which lie under the Hall of Justice.

Another shaft uncovered the pier of Wilson's Arch; and galleries running out from this first revealed the existence of a very singular viaduct of arches supporting the roadway above. There are two rows side by side, of different span and different width, one being 21 ft. wide, and the other 23 ft. wide. In some cases, a second arch is found below the first. These arches form chambers, which may have been used for storehouses, perhaps for merchandize, like a modern railway arch.

Mejr-ed-Deen, an Arabic writer of the thirteenth century, mentions a subterranean gallery, "which David caused to be made from the Gate of the Chain to the citadel, called the Mihrab of David. It still exists, and parts of it are occasionally discovered." This subterranean passage was actually found in the course of their explorations at Wilson's Arch. It lies westward of the vaults' entrance just described. It was followed up by Captain Warren to a distance of 250 ft. from the wall of the Haram. It there ended in a tank, the owner of which refused permission to examine it further. It is a well-built arched passage, 10 ft. high and 14 ft. wide, and was evidently intended as a secret way of communication between the citadel and the Temple, by which troops could be brought, in case of an *émeute*, without exciting suspicion. Unfortunately, it is impossible to say where this passage began and ended.

The lower part of the pier was found to be, for 19 ft., built of very rough boulders, as if, for that height, it was covered up and hidden with earth or rubbish when built. Above that it was built with large squared stones, like those *above* the drafted stones at the Wailing Place.

There are thus several historical points brought out by these shafts. The arch, as it now stands, is not the first. It is probably either Herodian, or built by Hadrian. This seems to point very clearly to its having been one of the four gates mentioned by Josephus. A viaduct connected the gate with the upper part of the city, having vaults and chambers beneath it; and a secret passage ran nearly parallel with the viaduct, probably connecting the Temple Area with the citadel, just as Herod made a secret passage connecting the Temple with the fortress of Antonia.

The next series of excavations were those at Robinson's Arch, which yielded discoveries perhaps the most important and interesting of any. First, the pier of the arch was found 51 ft. 6 in. long, and 12 ft. 2. in. thick, built of the same stone, with the same draft and chisel marks as in the wall at the south-west angle. There is a hollow of 5 ft. wide inside, a method of building adopted to save stone. Between the pier and the wall there was a pavement, on which lay the fallen voussoirs of the arch. At

the north end of the pier a tank was found, and
at the east of this a passage leading to the wall,
where it branched off north and south. It was
traced as far as the Gate of the Prophet, a distance

of about 180 ft., where a breach occurred. This
proved that the wall runs in an unbroken line
from Robinson's Arch to the Prophet's Gate.

The pavement was broken through, and found

to be placed over a mass of rubbish 23 ft. deep.
At the bottom of this there was found a canal
cut in the rock, and running north and south.
Across the canal lay voussoirs, which must of
course have belonged to an arch *older* than that
whose ruins lay upon the pavement above. This
very curious canal was traced north and south
(see plan of Haram Area) for a long distance. It
may possibly have been the same down which
ran the stream of water which Captain Warren
discovered at Wilson's Arch. Several lamps,
weights, jars, &c., were found in it. It runs occasionally into circular pools, one of which is cut
across by the Haram wall, showing that the pool
is older than this portion of the wall. The canal
is arched over, and at intervals holes have been
cut for buckets to be dropped through. The
conclusions that Captain Warren came to are so
important that we give them in his own words :—

"1. The winding aqueduct was cut in the rock.

"2. The Temple and Solomon's palace were
constructed, and a bridge leading over the Tyro-
poeon valley connected the palace with the Lower
city in the plateau below and east of the upper
city.

"3. The arch of the bridge fell (two voussoirs
still remain), breaking in part of the arch of the
aqueduct.

"4. The Temple was reconstructed by Herod,
who took in the Palace of Solomon, and built
the present south-west angle of the Sanctuary ;
and the new wall, cutting across portions of the

rock-cut canal, connections were made by means of masonry passages. At this time, the rubbish had begun to choke up the valley at this point to 22 ft., and the wall to that height was built with rough-faced stones, the portion above being made to resemble the older parts of the wall. A pavement was laid on the rubbish, and the pier and arch of Robinson's Arch and viaduct were built. In order to obtain water readily, shafts, which still exist, were constructed at intervals from the pavement to the canal and pools.

"5. The arch fell, and now rests upon the pavement.

"6. *Débris* began to fill the valley, and the pier of the arch, sticking out, was removed for building purposes, all except the three lower courses.

"7. When Wilson's Arch and pier were built, a second pavement was made along the west wall of the Sanctuary, level with the site of the Prophet's Gate, and a few feet above the pavement at Robinson's Arch, reaching out to the Dung Gate. Mention of this road is made in the 'Norman Chronicle,' and parts of the pavement still exist, and also a drain running underneath it. Houses were built near this pavement.

"8. The houses and walls becoming ruins and *débris*, filled the valley to its present height, which at this point is 45 ft. above the *lower* pavement."

About 270 ft. north of the south-west angle is the great lintel of an old gate, discovered by Dr. Barclay (author of "The City of the Great King"), and called the Gate of the Prophet, or Barclay's

Gateway.   Excavations have shown that the sill
of the gate was 50 ft. below the level of the
Haram Area, while the gate itself was about
30 ft. high, and 19 ft. wide.   There was found an
embankment in front of the gate, which was
kept up by retaining walls, 46 ft. above the
bottom of the valley.   Here, then, is another old
gate of the Temple; so that three out of the four
mentioned by Josephus appear to have been
found.   Where was the fourth?   Captain Warren
thinks he has ascertained that it certainly does
not lie south of Wilson's Arch.   Now, according
to the theory of Mr. Fergusson, the Temple was
never north of Wilson's Arch at all.   According
to Captain Warren, it was; and he thinks he has
found the gate in a spot twenty feet south of the
Bab el Mathara, where is a large cutting, running
east and west, and piercing the Haram wall.   It
is very much like the vaulted passage leading
from Barclay's Gate; it is of the same width,
and runs the same distance into the Haram
Area; but it does not appear to turn round at
the eastern extremity, as the other passage does.
If this is the fourth gateway, which cannot yet
be clearly proved, of course the Temple had an
extension north of Wilson's Arch.   The question
of the gates is a very curious and difficult one.
It depends on a passage in Josephus, which is,
like all Josephus's descriptions, apparently clear
and precise, really vague and uncertain.   He
says that there were four gates on this side.   The
first (which is the first?—the most northerly, the

most southerly, or the first in importance?) led
to the palace by a passage across the intervening
ravine. Unfortunately, we do not know where
the palace was, or if Herod's palace is meant.
It has been placed on the eastern side of the
citadel; so that, provided Josephus means Herod's
palace, and the palace was really there, the first
gate would be Wilson's Arch. Then there were
two gates leading to the suburbs—Barclay's Gateway for one; but where can the other be? The
fourth gate, leading to the other city, "being carried down into the ravine by a great number of
steps, and then up again by the ascent." Well,
that may be Robinson's Arch, or it may be
Wilson's Arch. Certainly, one thing is very remarkable: no signs of a continuation of Robinson's Arch by means of other arches could be
found. There is only the one pier. Could the
"steps" have begun at this arch?

Clearly, the excavations at the western wall
alone will not be sufficient to decide our difficulties for us. It is not sufficient—although it is certainly a great point—not to find the fourth gate
south of Wilson's Arch, because the wall may have
been so much demolished as to destroy all traces
of it. It appears, however, to Captain Warren
clear that Herod built the south-west angle:—
"Herod breasted up with the wall the area around
the Temple, so as to enlarge it to twice its former
extent." What, then, are the remains of the
older arch? They might be the remains of that
bridge which was destroyed by the followers of

I

Aristobulus (B.C. 63), during Pompey's siege. There would in that case have been a wall further eastward, of which no trace now remains above ground.

Surely, we have here a great contribution to our knowledge of the old city. Three gateways found out of four; traces of evidence, conjectural at present, of the fourth; the stones of an older arch under Wilson's Arch, and those of two arches where the spring called Robinson's Arch now stands; vaults, secret passages, subterranean chambers, aqueducts, and drains. And besides all this, the clear proof that a stream of water actually ran through the city, *because it is running still.* Where it comes from, where it goes to, we have not yet ascertained. The great fact remains that it is there.

Let us turn the corner at the south-west angle, and follow Captain Warren in his work along the south wall. It must be always borne in mind that, while Dr. Porter makes the Royal Cloister of Herod extend along the whole length of the wall, Mr. Fergusson supposes the Temple to have extended 600 ft. east of the south-west angle, and then to have terminated in a wall, which was the eastern wall of the city until [the building of the great wall by Agrippa. In the first place, Captain Warren has noticed—what had previously escaped observation—that a course of great stones runs continuously from the eastern angle as far as the Double Gate, where it suddenly comes to an end. He, therefore, concludes that the wall to this point was built *before the continuation to the west*—a very important conclusion, if it is correct, as, if so, Mr. Fergusson's theory (where Mr. Lewin and Mr. Thrupp follow him) at once collapses. All the stones below the surface of the ground in the south wall appear to be *in situ*, and to have the marginal draft. The rock, which is 60 ft. below the surface at the south-west angle, slopes down till it reaches a depth of 90 ft. below the surface. It then rises rapidly; is 30 ft. below the surface at the Double Gate, level with the surface at the Temple Gate. This is an important point; because if the old east wall of the Temple lay over here, it would not have looked down upon a deep valley at all, but upon a rock sloping about one in three. The Double and Triple Gates nearly bisect the south wall, being respectively 300 ft. distant from the east and west angles. The Double Gate has been generally identified with the "Huldah" Gate of the Temple. Captain Warren thinks that the whole portion of the wall from the east of the Double Gate formed Solomon's Palace; and, in the absence of the course of great stones west of this gate, finds confirmation of his theory that Herod built the south-west angle. It may be remembered that the heaviest stone in the whole wall, weighing over 100 tons, is in the south-east angle; while the longest (38 ft. 9 in.) is at the south-west angle. Another point has been noticed, confirming this theory. A pavement of "mezzeh" stone has been found running along part of the south wall, at a depth of 40 ft. Now, up to this pavement the stones were drafted with rough faces. Probably, therefore, they were never exposed to view at all; and therefore were purposely left rough. At the other end of the south wall, the stones are all smooth-faced down to the rock. But above this pavement, about 23 ft. below the present surface, is another pavement, under which were found "Haggai's seal," and several Greek lamps, one of which has a Christian inscription. What is the date of this pavement? Most likely we are brought to the time of Justinian or Constantine.

Before we go on, let us state clearly the reasons why Captain Warren believes the south-west angle to be of later date than the rest of the south wall, and to be the work of Herod. The importance of this conclusion, in a reconstruction of the city, cannot be overrated:—

(1.) The wall is built over one of the circular aqueducts at the bottom, and is therefore later than the aqueduct.

(2.) From Barclay's Gateway to Wilson's Arch the drafted stones have their faces finely worked. South of Barclay's Gateway there are stones at a higher level with their faces rough.

(3.) A course of great stones runs from the south-east angle along the southern wall to the Double Gate, where it suddenly stops.

(4.) The stones of the south wall near the western angle are rough up to a certain pavement, whose date is probably about that of Herod.

(5.) The west wall here is not built on the *eastern* but on the *western* slope of the Tyropœon Valley, and probably at a time when rubbish had choked up the valley, so that it was here partially covered in.

The course of great stones is on a level with that of the vaults of the eastern angle, known as the " Stables of Solomon," and one storey of these Captain Warren considers to be modern; and one circumstance seems to strengthen his opinion —namely, that the wall was evidently all destroyed above the great course. It is therefore extremely unlikely that the vaults should have been left standing. It is interesting to note that he found under the single gateway a passage 9 ft. wide and more than 60 ft. long, running between the piers on which the upper vaults rest. What the object of this passage was, it is impossible to say; but it seems to point to the fact that the uncovered space between the level of the Haram and the rock was not all filled up with earth, but is in part built up in vaults and chambers.

Captain Warren has given an account of his deepest shaft at this south wall, which, as it shows vividly the kind of work and the risks run by the explorers, we give in full:—

" On Friday, October 11th, 1867, having arrived at a depth of 79 ft., the men were breaking up a stone at the bottom of the shafts. Suddenly the ground gave way, down went the stone and hammer—the men barely saving themselves.

They at once rushed up and told the sergeant that they had found the bottomless pit. I went down to the spot and examined it; and in order that you may have some idea of the extent of our work, I will give you a description of our descent.

"The shaft mouth is on the south side of the Haram wall, near the south-west angle, among the prickly pears; beside it to the east, lying against the Haram wall, is a large mass of rubbish which has been brought up; over the mouth itself is a triangular gyn with an iron wheel attached, with guy for running up the excavated soil. Looking down the shaft, one sees that it is lined with frames 4 ft. 6 in. in the clear; farther down, the Haram wall and soil cut through is seen, and a man standing at what appears to be the bottom. An order is given to this man, who repeats it; and then, faintly, is heard a sepulchral voice, answering as it were from another world. Reaching down to the man who is visible is a 34 ft. rope ladder, and on descending by it one finds oneself standing on a ledge which the ladder does not touch by 4 ft. This ledge is the top of a wall running north and south, and abutting on the Haram wall; its east face just cuts the centre of the shaft, which has to be canted off about 2 ft. towards the east, just where some large loose stones jut out in the most disagreeable manner. Here five more frames have been fixed to keep these stones steady. On peering down from this ledge, one sees the Haram wall with its project-

ing courses until they are lost in the darkness
below, observing also at the same time that two
sides of the shaft are cut through the soil and
are self-supporting. Now, to descend this second
drop, the ladder is again required. Accordingly,
having told the man at bottom to get under
cover, it is lowered to the ledge, from whence it
is found that it does not reach the bottom by
several feet. It is therefore lowered the required
distance, and one has to reach it by climbing
down hand over hand for about 12 ft. In passing along, one notes the marvellous joints of the
Haram wall stones, and also, probably, gets a
few blows on the skull and knuckles from falling
pebbles. Just on reaching the bottom, one recol-
lects that there is still a pit of unknown depth to
be explored, and cautiously straddles across it.
Then can be seen that one course in the Haram
wall, near the bottom, is quite smooth all over,
the stones being finely dressed, all other courses
being only well dressed around the marginal
drafts; one may also see two stout boards lying
against the Haram wall, under which the men
retire whenever an accidental shower of stones
renders their position dangerous. We are now
at a depth of 79 ft. from the surface, and from
here we commence the exploration of 'the bottomless pit.' After dropping a rope down, we
find that it is only 6 ft. deep, though it looks
black enough for anything. Climbing down, we
find ourselves in a passage running south from
the Haram wall, 4 ft. high by 2 ft. wide, and we

explore this passage. It is of rough rubble masonry, with flat stones at top. The floor and sides are very muddy, as if water gathers there in the rainy weather.

" It struck me that this might be one of the overflow aqueducts from the Temple of Solomon, and that there might be a water conduit underneath. We scrambled along for a long way on our feet, our skulls and spines coming in unhappy contact with the passage roof; after advancing thus for about 200 feet, we found that the mud reached higher up, and we had to crawl by means of elbows and toes. Gradually the passage got more and more filled up, and our bodies could barely squeeze through, and there did not appear to be sufficient air to support us for any length of time; so that having advanced 400 feet, we commenced a retrograde movement, having to get back half way before we could turn our heads round. On arriving at the mouth of the passage underneath the shaft, we spent some time in examining the sides, but there is no appearance of its having come under the Haram wall. It seems to start suddenly, and I can only suppose it to have been the examining passage over an aqueduct coming from the Temple, and I am having the floor taken up to settle the question. This passage is on a level with the foundations of the Haram wall, which are rough-hewn stones, perhaps rock, I cannot yet tell. The bottom of the shaft is $87\frac{1}{2}$ feet below the surface of the ground."

It is impossible to avoid the reproach of being

dry in dealing with work like this of Captain
Warren's. Not only—though we do not profess
to give here a complete account—is it necessary
to state his own conclusions, and the reasons
which have led him to adopt them, but also, in
most cases, to state other facts which may possibly
lead us to other conclusions. But it is hoped that
the apparently uninteresting nature of many of
these details will have had light thrown upon
them by what has gone before—the account of
the city, its history, and the results of the Ordnance Survey.

We have followed our explorer along the west
and south walls. Let us now see what he found
at the east wall. We omit henceforth many details
of work, because the difficulties have been already
sufficiently indicated.

The results at the south-eastern angle were of the
greatest importance. It was there found that at
the bottom of the shaft there was an accumulation
of 8 to 10 ft. of fat mould, filled with potsherds.
This was the layer of earth on the rock, and is,
perhaps, the actual layer found by Solomon when
he began his work of building. Close to the wall
it was cut away, gradually closing in to it. This,
of course, was to allow the stones to be lowered
into their position. The rock in which the lowest
stones stand is very soft. It is cut through for
2 ft., for the purpose of placing the stone in
position. Close to the angle was found a hole
cut in it 1 ft. across and 1 ft. deep. In this hole
was a little earthenware jar standing upright, as

though it had been purposely put there. Was it

left there by a work-
man, or was it some
quaint fancy of one of
Solomon's Phœnician
masons, to be found
again after 2,000 years?

On the stones them-
selves were found—the
most important thing of
all—characters in red
paint, and others in-
cised. These have been
most carefully traced,
and photographs taken
of the tracings. They
have been examined by Mr. Emanuel Deutsch,
who saw them in Jerusalem, and pronounced
them to be probably Phœnician, and representing numerals.* Then, concludes the world at
once, we have here the stones of Solomon's
Temple, with the works of his Phœnician
workmen. Hiram, the great master mason,
doubtless stood on this spot and superintended
the lowering of these stones. Chippings, but no
signs of extensive stone dressing were found
about, so that these were those stones wrought
in the quarries, and brought here to be set in
their places—see 1 Kings, vi. 7: "And the house,
when it was in building, was built of stone made
ready before it was brought thither: so that there

* See Appendix, p. 342.

was neither hammer nor axe nor any tool of iron
heard in the house, while it was in building." And
upon that layer of "fat mould," where lie the
potsherds of the Jebusites, the great King has

often stood watching his work rise slowly. It is
a dream that every one has had who visited the
shafts, or who has read the accounts of the discoveries. But it must, for the present at least,
remain a speculation—until we are quite certain

that Captain Warren's conclusions are correct;
that the characters are really of Solomon's time;
until further research has added, bit by bit, to the

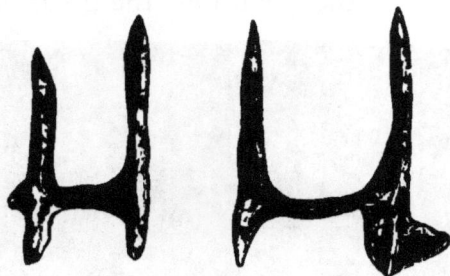

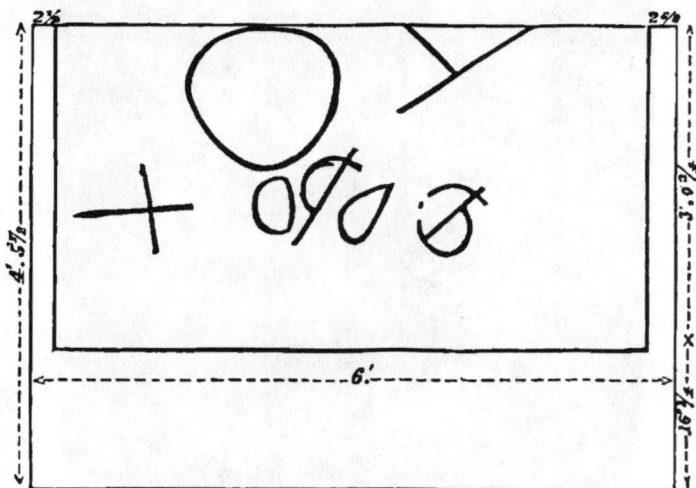

facts we have accumulated, ready stored up, till
they are enough to fill up every hiatus and clear up
every difficulty.   Meanwhile, let those of us who
please—only with this uncomfortable reservation
of doubt—go on believing that we have before

us the veritable works of King Hiram's workmen. One little thing more, to strengthen us in our belief. On the original layer of "fat mould," belonging, that is, to a later time, were found handles of jars, two of which had on them legible

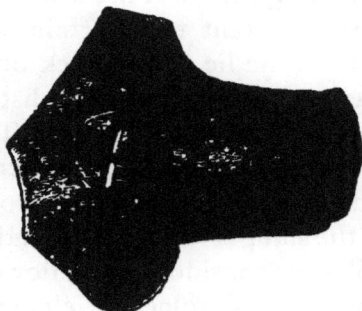

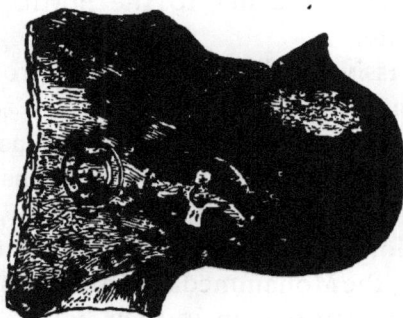

inscriptions in the Phœnician character, with the royal crest of an eagle. The words on one appear to be [Le] McLeK zePHa (of or belonging to King Zepha).

Leaving the south-east angle, we go northwards till we come to the Golden Gateway; all excavation here being difficult, if not impossible, on account of the tombs all along this wall, and the strong feeling of the people against any desecration of the resting-places of the dead. As, however, it was very important to ascertain something, if possible, about the lie of the rock on this side, a gallery was sunk at a spot 143 ft. distant from the south end of the Golden Gateway. The results of this were important, though the gallery had to be abandoned before work there was completed, on account of the shingle which ran in and filled it up. Captain Warren considers the following points to be ascertained with tolerable clearness, though not certainty:—

1. At the Golden Gate, the Haram wall extends 30 ft. below the present level of the ground.

2. The rock inclines to the north, near the Golden Gate.

3. A massive wall runs along in front of the Golden Gate.

These are facts which may be put aside until their full importance is seized by means of other discoveries. It is very difficult to do anything with the Golden Gateway, on account of a tradition among the Mohammedans, that Jerusalem will not permanently remain in their hands, and that the conquering Christians will pass through this gateway in order to take possession of the city. As if to hinder, as much as possible, the fulfilment of this prediction, they have blocked up the entrance, and would resist to the utmost all attempts at excavation near it.

In deference to these prejudices, then, a gallery was opened lower down in the Kedron Valley, and by making a double entrance the suspicions of the Moslems were diverted. The tunnel was driven in a direction perpendicular to the wall, in hopes of arriving at its foundations, and perhaps some further masons' marks, which might help in fixing the date of the building of the wall. It has been already mentioned that different opinions are held as to the Golden Gateway itself, and its original building. The tunnel yielded some very curious information, but not of the kind sought for. It was stopped by a massive wall, running north and, after a little, north-west. In the gallery they came upon an inverted pillar—suspended, so to speak, in the rubbish—on which were engraved characters, as if it had been the face of a dial. It was concluded, though not with perfect certainty, from the nature of the ground and other reasons, that the Golden Gateway stands from 30 to 40 ft. above the rock. The very dangerous nature of the rubbish obliged Captain Warren to close up the shaft.

Higher up, at the north-east angle, we were much more fortunate, and our discoveries here were of far greater importance. So many shafts were sunk that it is impossible to give more than the general results.

1. On reference to the map of the Haram Area,

it will be observed that the city wall seems to be a
continuation of the east wall of the Haram, while
there is a projection of the stones, marked in the
plan. This projection has the modern name of the

INVERTED COLUMN IN GOLDEN GATE SHAFT.

Tower of Antonia; though it is needless to observe
that it was not, and never could have been, the
famous tower. Another instance, this, of the eager-
ness with which sites are identified: the remains

of a strong place near the Temple—therefore, the Tower of Antonia. The "tower" is, however, ancient, and as old as the wall. The stones at this part of the wall are described as carefully dressed, with irregularly projecting faces. There is a "batter" (*i.e.*, a slope back, caused by setting back each stone a little behind the one below) running regularly up the wall for a height of 48 ft. Thus, the builders began to form their tower by the simple process of continuing the original batter for the wall—viz., of $4\frac{1}{2}$ in. in each course—and giving a much less batter—viz., of $1\frac{1}{2}$ in.—to the tower; so that in 22 ft. the projection is 2 ft., and at the surface of the ground it is 7 ft. It is remarked, too, that the level of the point where the tower begins is only a short distance below the surface at the *south-east* angle, where there is a check in the wall, as if just such another tower were commencing. This method of construction is very curious. A similar instance may be observed in the wall of the Haram at Hebron, where a sort of pilaster springs from the wall of bevilled masonry much in the same manner.

2. Continuing the gallery southwards, it was found that the rock dipped so considerably that at the lowest point reached the surface course of the wall is actually 120 ft. above the rock. The valley, therefore, which begins in the Bab-az-Zahiré, and was supposed to run into the Kedron through the Birket Israil, really runs out to the south of the north-east angle altogether. Remembering that the south-

K.

west angle of the Haram also runs across a
valley, we have thus two valleys, one at either
angle, filled up; one more than 90 ft., the other
more than 100 ft., before the present level is
reached. A similar process would have to be
carried on at the south-east angle; and, in a less
degree, along the west wall. It has been calcu-
lated that not less than 70,000,000 cubic feet of
earth or rubbish would be required to fill up this
enormous great space; that is to say, a solid
cube of earth as high as St. Paul's, and 400 ft.
square. Of course, it may very well be that at all
these corners, as at the south-east corner, vaults
have been built one course above another.

3. Characters in red paint were found on the
broken stones of this Haram wall near the southern end of the tower, at the north-east angle.
These have been pronounced of the same character as those found at the south-east angle and
already described.

4. One of the most curious, if not a very important discovery, was that of an old chamber
or aqueduct leading from the Birket Israil. We
extract the account which Captain Warren himself gives of this singular and ancient construction. It was at a point 26 ft. north of the north-
east angle and 32 ft. below the surface that a
sort of slit was observed, 18 in. wide and 4 in.
high, in the Haram wall itself.

"At first," says Captain Warren, "it was impossible to squeeze through, but after a few hours
it became easier, though it is now only 7 in. high.

The passage from this slit is difficult to describe; the roof falls by steps, but the floor is a very steep, smooth incline, falling 12 ft. in 11½ ft., like the slit and shoot for letters at a post office.

This shoot ends abruptly, passing through the roof of a passage. The passage runs east and west: it is 3 ft. 9 in. high, and about 2 ft. wide; it runs nearly horizontally, and at its eastern end opens out through the Haram wall. At the

K 2

western end it goes (by measurement) to the east
end of the Birket Israil, but is closed up by a
perforated stone.   This passage is 46 ft. in length.
On the south side is a staircase cut in the masonry, and running apparently to the surface,
but it is jammed up with stones.   The roof of
this passage is about 48 ft. below the surface.
The stones forming it are of great size, but do
not show large in comparison with those at the
sides, which are from 14 to 18 ft. in length, and
vary from 3 ft. 10 in. to 4 ft. 6 in. in height.   To
the west of the staircase the bottom of the passage slopes down rapidly, so that in one place it
is 12 ft. high.   The roof is also stepped down 4 ft.
about 11 ft. from the western end.   Altogether,
this passage bears a great resemblance to that
which we found under the Single Gate.

"At the eastern end, where the passage opens
out through the Haram wall, a rough masonry
shaft has been built round, so that we can see a
few feet up the wall and about 7 ft. down it below the sole of the gallery.   It is evident that
there has been some tinkering here at a comparatively modern date.

"In the course forming the sole of the passage
there is a waterduct leading through the Haram
wall, about 5 in. square, very nicely cut; but in
the next course lower, a great irregular hole has
been knocked out of the wall, so as to allow the
water to pass through at a slightly lower level,
and so run into an aqueduct 9 in. wide and 2 ft.
high, which commences at this point, and runs

nearly due east from the Haram wall. All this botching and tinkering looks as if it had been done quite recently, and the workmen have left their mark on the wall in the shape of a Christian cross, of the type used by the early Christians, or during the Byzantine period.

"At the farther end of the passage to the west the same large massive stones are seen until the eye rests upon a large perforated stone closing it up. This is the first approach which we have yet found to any architectural remains about these old walls (which I believe are now admitted to be of the times of the Kings of Judah); and though it merely shows us the kind of labour bestowed upon a concealed overflow aqueduct, still it has a bold and pleasing effect, and until something else is found will hold its own as some indication of the kind of building at an early period. It consists simply of a stone closing up the end of the passage, with a recess or alcove cut in it 4 in. deep. Within this recess are three cylindrical holes $5\frac{1}{4}$ in. in diameter, the lines joining their centres forming an equilateral triangle. Below this there appears once to have been a basin to collect the water; but whatever has been there, it has been violently removed. It appears to me probable that the troops defending this portion of the wall came down the staircase into this passage to obtain water. At first sight this passage appears to be cut in the rock, as stalactites have formed all over it, and hang gracefully from every joint, giving the place a very picturesque appearance. It seems probable that we are here 20 ft. above the rock.

"There can be little doubt that this is an ancient overflow from the Birket Israil, which could not at that time have risen above this height—about 25 ft. above the present bottom of the pool, and about 60 ft. below the present top of the pool.

"It is also apparent that the Birket Israil has been half full and overflowing during the Christian period, and that for some purpose or other the water was carried away by an aqueduct into the Kedron Valley. At the present day, when there is such a dearth of running water in Jerusalem, it is rather mystifying to find that within our era the Birket Israil has probably been constantly full up to a certain point, and flowing over."

We must leave the north-east angle, in spite of the many other points of interest in the history of the shafts sunk there, and turn the corner which brings us to the Birket Israil. This great pool, now dry, nearly 400 ft. long, is, as has been stated, the traditional Pool of Bethesda. Another opinion, perhaps based on better grounds, will be found given on the Pool of Bethesda, below. Captain Warren's object was to find out as much of its construction as possible. At the western end of the pool are two passages, which had been already partially examined by M. De Saulcy and others. Captain Warren began by examining them to their termination. One ends in a masonry wall, and the other in a modern passage, built, apparently, "to enable the rubbish to be thrown down." Next, for the bottom of the pool. It was found to be in complete preservation, 80 ft. deep, with an accumulation of 35 ft. of sewage and rubbish.

If this was not the Pool of Bethesda, where was it? Two sites are advanced, one by Captain Warren, in which he agrees with many writers before him; and the other, which had been already advanced and ably defended by Mr. George Williams and by M. Clermont Ganneau. The second is given in the Appendix. The former is that the Pool of Bethesda was the twin pool under the convent of the Sisters of Sion. It is marked in our plan of the Haram Area, just outside the north-west corner of the Haram—two parallel pools. The first of these was already known, and had been described by Captain Wilson ("Ordnance Survey Notes"). The second was discovered while Captain Warren was in Jerusalem, in extending the buildings of the convent. The first pool is a deep fosse cut in the rock, about 53 ft. wide and 165 ft. long; the second is 127 ft. long, and from 20 ft. to 26 ft. across. The south-eastern end in both is cut off by the same line of scarped rock. At the south-west corner of the first, a passage runs in a southerly direction. This passage was doubtless formerly connected with the ancient water supply. It is a splendid rock-cut passage,

30 ft. high. It was full of sewage, 5 ft. deep, and
was 4 ft. wide. By means of three old doors,
Captain Warren and Sergeant Birtles managed
to investigate the passage. It was a perilous
passage. The doors kept sinking, and they had
the greatest difficulty in keeping their balance.
Presently, however, a dram was reached, crossing
the passage, beyond which the sewage grew
harder and firmer, until they were able to walk
upon it. The passage ended, after 200 ft. and
more, by the roof sloping down till it was only
8 ft. high, and a block-up of masonry. Soon
after Captain Warren left the city it was cleansed
of its filth, and thoroughly examined. The bottom is plastered. The masonry at the end was
taken down, and it was found that the passage
turned round to the east, just where it stops in
one place, and ended by running against a massive wall lying along the western boundary of
the Haram enclosure. What was this passage?
It is a question which cannot yet be answered.
Like most of the discoveries we have been de-
scribing, it is one more contribution to the mass
of facts which have been accumulated about the
city, and are waiting for the final discovery which
will give a key to the whole, and enable us to
sort our facts, and explain how, bit by bit, they
all fit in with the story of the Bible.

Let us next get inside the Haram, and see
what has been done there. It will be understood
that very little is to be expected here, except by
way of windfall and accident, until permission

can be got to dig in it—a permission which we seem further from obtaining every day. First, with regard to the water supply. No obstacle was put in the way of Captain Warren's examining the cisterns with which the Area is honeycombed in every direction; the Moslems only considering the occasional disappearance of Captain Warren into one of the tanks as a piece of eccentric curiosity. Most of the tanks were examined and fully described by Captain Wilson. In Pierotti's account of the cistern, he pretends to have found from tank No. 1 (see the plan of the Haram Area) a passage running straight to the Bir Arwah, and to have recognized the marble slab. To this Captain Warren very pertinently replies by asking, first, how he knew the bottom of the slab, having only previously seen the top; secondly, how he knew he was under Bir Arwah, when he had no one to communicate with him above; and thirdly, how he got there at all, seeing that *no passage exists* from cistern No. 1.

No fewer than three and thirty tanks are numbered in our plan, and described by Captain Warren in the "Recovery of Jerusalem," and Captain Wilson in the "Ordnance Notes." One of these, a discovery of Captain Warren's, is very curious and unlike any of the rest. We give his account in his own words. It is that cistern numbered 16, 17, in the north of the Haram, near the Birket Israil. On sounding the opening which he found there, Captain Warren measured 42 ft. down to the water.

"I tried to descend, but to no purpose, until I had nearly stripped to the skin; and even then, in my contortions, I managed to slip the rope over one arm. The narrow passage was only for 3 ft., and 10 ft. from the surface I came upon the floor of a little chamber about 6 ft. square, apparently on a level with the Haram Area. The shaft down to the cistern continues through the floor of this chamber, and is a moderate-sized opening. On getting down to the water I found it only 3 ft. deep, and concluding from the size of the cistern that help would be required in measuring, I signalled for Sergeant Birtles to come down.

"On lighting up the magnesium wire and looking about me I was astonished, my first impression being that I had got into a church similar to that of the cathedral (formerly a mosque) at Cordova. I could see arch upon arch to north and east, apparently rows of them.

"After floundering about for some little distance, however, I could see that there was a limit to these substructures at no great distance north and east. In the meantime Sergeant Birtles was making great efforts above with very little result; do what he would, he could not get past the narrow opening to the cistern, and at last he had to give up the trial, and go and get leave from the owner to pull down the upper part of the shaft, and then he very soon appeared at the bottom, his shoulders considerably injured by his exertions. In the meantime the excitement of our 'find' had begun to wear off, and the water felt cold. I was just giving the sergeant some sage advice as to how he should direct his steps to the best advantage, when I stumbled over a large stone, and fell into the water flat on my face. As just at present the weather is frosty, and the rain generally accompanied by sleet or hail, a bath in one's clothes is anything but agreeable."

The cistern, of which a plan was afterwards published, is 63 ft. long by 57 broad, and has a roof supported on piers and pointed arches. Now, it will be remembered that a deep valley runs down here, so that the cistern is not rock-cut, but built in the *débris*, at what date is uncertain. The rock-cut cisterns are probably the oldest, the *montes cavati sub terrâ*, as Tacitus calls them. They served a double purpose. They held so much water that, even supposing there was no stream running into them, which is exceedingly improbable and contrary to history and tradition, there would have been enough at all times to last through a good long siege, protected as they were from the sun, and therefore not exposed to evaporation. And, moreover, they supplied the water for the sacrifice. Captain Warren protests very sensibly against the idea that these tanks were connected with the blood, &c., of the victims, and points out that what was wanted was a series of culverts, so connected with the tanks that they might be easily flooded, and passing from the place of sacrifice to one of the valleys. When this series of culverts is found, of course we shall not be far off the site of the Altar.

A discovery was made on the north side of the platform on which the Dome of the Rock stands, which may possibly turn out to be of the very greatest importance.

Referring back to our previous pages, unless you remember what was said there, you will find several important facts. Tradition and many eminent scholars and architects fix the Temple of Herod on this platform. On the site of Herod's Temple, Hadrian set up a Temple of Jupiter, which was the cause of the revolt of Bar Cochebas. During this wild insurrection the Temple was, naturally, destroyed. Constantine built his great Basilica (180 years later) opposite the Holy Sepulchre. Mr. Fergusson puts the Basilica in such a position that its apse would fall just where the discovery was made.

Read it first in Captain Warren's own words. The original plan and sketch of the arches is given also. The italics are our own, and intended to call attention to the more important points:—

" Passing by the northern edge of the platform of the Kubbet es Sakhra, I saw that the earth had been lately disturbed at the foot of the eastern steps; and on asking the sheikh of the mosque about it, he said that after the heavy rains, three days before, the ground had given way, and that they had found an entrance to substructions as large as those at the south-east angle. I suggested to him that the hole had been badly filled

tine Exploration Fund
lan Nº 27 referred to in Mʳ Warren's letter
of Decʳ 8ᵗʰ 1868.

Rubbish

A ⸱⸱⸱ B

Scale 40 or 20 to 1 inch

Rock

16.3

Door

Rubbish

Magnetic Bearing of Vault 250°

Lavir Arch

section of South end
of Bay

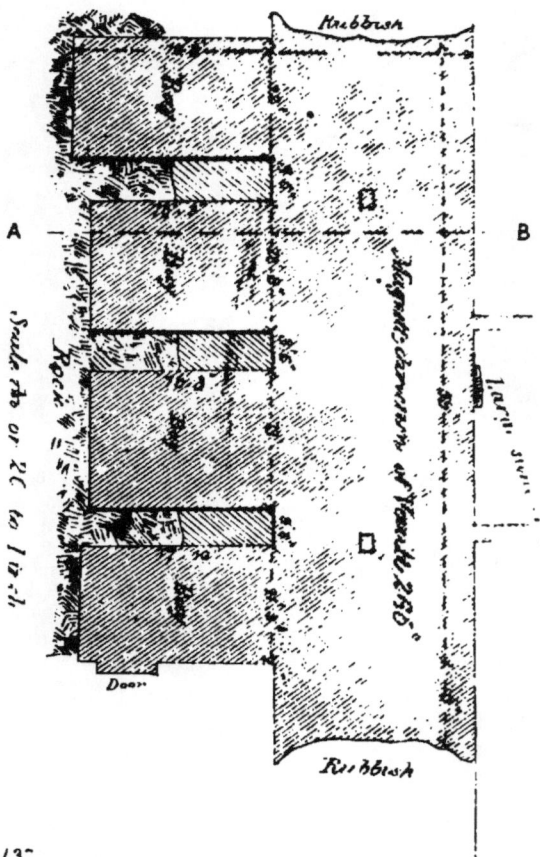

Rubbish

el or Mosque Platform 3437

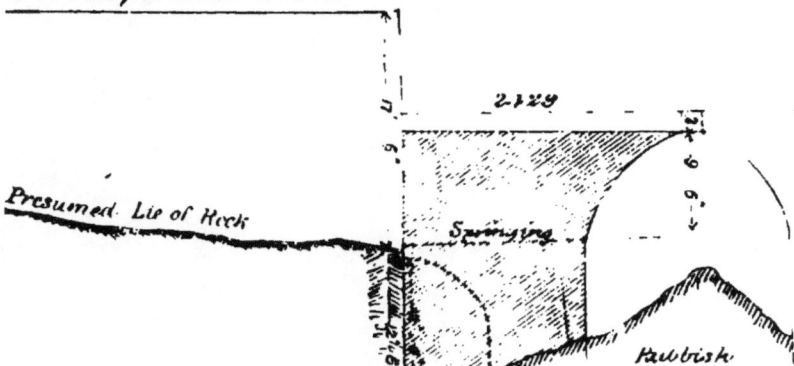

2429

Presumed Lie of Rock

Springing

Rubbish

in, and that it would probably give way again. This morning we went early to the Haram Area, and happened to come upon this place just a few minutes after the hole had opened a second time. We went down into it and made an examination.

"It is a subterranean passage running east and west in the line of the northern edge of the platform. It consists of an arched passage 18 ft. span, with bays to the south of 12 ft. by 17 ft. arched over, the piers being 3 ft. 6 in. thick. The *southern side of these bays is scarped rock, and on it the wall supporting the northern edge of the platform is built.* Portions of the piers are also scarped from the rock, which appears to shelve down rapidly to the north; so that if the earth and vaults were removed, the *northern edge of the platform would present the edge of a perpendicularly scarped rock, with excrescences on its face 3 ft. 6 in. wide, 12 ft. apart, and projecting about 6 ft.*

"The vault was examined for about 70 ft. east and west, and four bays were surveyed. The crown of the arch of the vault, and also of the bays, is about 2 ft. below the surface of the ground, which is here about 8 ft. below the surface of the platform; the distance from the crown to the springing of the arches is 9 ft. 6 in.; the arches of the bays being perpendicular to, and forming groins with, that of the vault. The arch over the vault has a span of 18 ft.; it is not semi-circular. *It appears to have a parabolic curve, while the arches over the*

bays are decidedly pointed. On the northern side
of the vault I could see no appearance of rock,
except in one place, for about 5 ft., where there
is either rock or a large stone, the top of which
is about 10 ft. below the springing; the northern portions of the piers are also of masonry, but
from their centres to their southern ends they
are cleanly scarped from the rock, just as are the
southern ends of the bays.

"The masonry of the walls is of a very miscel-
laneous character, in some cases large and small
squared stones, in some places coarse rubble.
On the northern side of the vault are two passages about 2 ft. wide and 8 ft. high, which are
blocked up about 8 feet: *they have the appearance
of being in connection with other vaults to the
north;* they are roofed over with stone slabs.

"To east and west the passage is choked up
with rubbish, fallen in from above; but it appears to extend in both directions, though towards the west there is an indication of a portion of the arch having given way. . . . . The
passage has no appearance of having been constructed for a tank; there is not a sign of plaster
about, and the rock appears to have been scarped
for view; it differs in most respects from the
tanks in the Haram Area, and was apparently
built for the purpose of raising the Haram Area
to a general level. The arches appear to be
Saracenic. For several months I have been
seeking an opportunity to examine the ground
on the northern side of the platform, near the

western steps, as I am convinced that there are
vaults there (from the hollow sound of the
ground), and my impression now is that the passage just discovered extends all along the northern edge of the platform."

What is this "subterranean passage?" Notice
particularly that the platform is rock, and not
built; that the passages to the north seemed to
lead· to other vaults, and that more remained,
east and west, than Captain Warren was able to
examine. Foundations perhaps, certainly remains,
of ancient buildings; and perhaps the entrance
to that vast system of vaults which, as many
believe, is built up in those immense spaces which ·
it would require such an immense quantity of
earth to fill in.

The substructures at the south-east angle,
called "Solomon's Stables," were thoroughly
examined. They have been described in every
book on Jerusalem, and the position of the
arches is made a strong point in Mr. Fergusson's
argument on the position of the Temple. Captain Warren thinks that they are a modern reconstruction, chiefly out of old materials.

A few more details of his work in the Haram
will be found in the full account. Thus, there is
at the Triple Gateway a passage running up to
the platform by an inclined plane. Two of the
rival theories—that of Mr. Fergusson and Mr.
Lewin—place the east wall of Herod's Temple
here. This, then, should be the *west* wall of the
passage. Captain Warren has given a very ac-

curate examination of this wall, and has pronounced his decided opinion that there is nothing
whatever in it that can give it the slightest pretensions to be considered as the exterior wall of
the Temple, while the remains of ancient engaged columns, *in situ*, tend to show that it was
a gateway of about the same style as the Double
Gate. Also, he finds no traces of the colossal
monoliths stated to be there in Murray's Handbook.

And now we must leave the Haram—the Noble
Sanctuary, as Captain Warren calls it—for a
little, and describe other work in its neighbourhood. South of the Haram Area is the
Hill of Ophel. On this hill Mr. Lewin places
the Palace of Solomon. As we shall see afterwards, Captain Warren has found reasons for not
agreeing with him. King Manasseh, we are
told (2 Chron., xxxiii. 14), "compassed about
Ophel, and raised it up a very great height."
Here, also, Jotham (chap. xxvii. 3), "built
much." The wall in Ophel was, doubtless, part
of the wall of the city in the time of Herod.
Mr. Fergusson puts it as beginning at the Triple
Gate. Now we learn from Josephus that the
old wall of Jerusalem, on reaching the place
called Ophla (or Ophel), joined the eastern porch
of the Temple. Captain Warren, after sinking
a great number of shafts, has arrived at the following facts:—

A great wall (marked in the plan of the
Haram) still exists, though buried in rubbish,

joining the Haram wall at the south-east angle.
It was evidently built for purposes of fortification, for it is 14 ft. thick. As the stones below
a depth of 30 ft. are not squared, and as this is
the case all along, it is apparent that the wall
was not built till long after the building of the
Sanctuary wall at the south-east angle. No sign
of any gate was discovered. It is not built in
the rock like the Haram wall, but on the hard
layer of clay resting on the rock. The wall was
traced (see plan) for 700 ft. from the first tower.
It there terminated, within a few feet of the surface, in a rocky knoll, having been probably
taken away in detail by the fellahin. There are
several towers projecting from the wall, one of
which is very remarkable, as it projects more
than any of the rest, standing upon scarped rock,
and having another wall leading from it going
down towards the Kedron. It may possibly be
"the tower that lieth out." It is also remarkable that many of the stones in this wall are
polished, reminding us of the "polished corners
of the Temple." Observe, too, that if all the
rubbish were taken away there would be this
great wall of Ophel standing out above the
valley, even now 40 ft. to 60 ft. high. Yet the
upper stones of the wall do not appear to be *in
situ.* The wall, then, is, in its present form, a reconstruction. Whose? It is more modern than
the Haram wall. If Solomon built the latter, did
Manasseh build this wall? If Agrippa, who
built the Ophel wall? Some remains of a great

L

wall were also found, leading, apparently, to the eastern jamb of the Triple Gate, which Captain Warren thinks may have been a recess running from the Ophel wall.

On the slope of the Ophel Hill a great many curious things were come across. Among these were lamps, a good deal of pottery, stone weights, dishes, &c., notice of which will be found further on. It was there, too, that the very curious little seal with the Hebrew inscription, " Haggai the son of Shebaniah," was found. The accompanying engraving represents its actual size. Its date

may be *possibly* 500 B.C., but it is very difficult to say within any accurate limits. A cavern was found in this hill, in which was a copper lamp

stand, perhaps of the Byzantine period. The
cavern is cut out of the rock, and consists of two
chambers. Round one of them are cut vats,
mangers, or troughs. It was last used for a
stable; but as the earth was 11 ft. deep, it is obvious that this was not its original purpose; and
it is more likely to have been, as Captain Warren
suggests, a fuller's shop. Tradition tells us that
St. James was thrown over the outer wall at the
Temple enclosure, and that a "fuller took the
club with which he pressed the clothes, and
brought it down on the head of the Just one." In
the earth above the cave is a drain, which is of
course more modern than the cave. Here were
found glass and pottery, supposed to be early
Christian. This takes us to the antiquity of the
"fuller's shop," a very long time back.

Come with us next to the other side of the
city. According to the theories of Mr. George
Williams, Dr. Porter, and other writers, the
second wall ran over a part of the ground close to
and perhaps forming part of the place now called
Muristan. It is a large open space, partly belonging to the Greek Patriarch and partly to the
Grand Master of the modern representatives of
the Order of St. John, whose church and buildings formerly stood there. The excavations conducted here were entirely with a view of finding
the foundation of the second wall. The result
was not satisfactory for those who expected to
find it, for no trace of the foundation was discovered. Captain Warren thinks that the second

wall may possibly be found along the northern wall of the Muristan.*

Other excavations were made at the Damascus Gate, at the southern slope of Zion, at the "Gate Gennath," which was proved to be of modern construction, and in the valley of the Kedron. At the last place it was ascertained that the enormous mass of rubbish now lying in the valley has displaced the old bed of the stream, shifting it 90 ft. to the east, and lifting it 40 ft. higher than its former position.

Very few objects of high antiquity were found in the shafts. None were such as to be pronounced of distinctively Jewish workmanship. The whole pottery found may be divided into Phœnician, Græco-Phœnician—*i.e.*, made in Cyprus and elsewhere, where these Phœnician colonists were influenced by Greek culture—Roman, Christian, and Arabic.

Of the first kind are the two jar handles already mentioned (p. 125), with five others bearing the same figures, but more or less defaced. They were found 63 ft. deep, lying in the well, at the south-east angle of the Haram enclosure. On each handle is impressed a more or less well-defined figure resembling a bird, but believed to be a winged sun or disc, probably the emblem of

---

* South of the Muristan, was found in a shaft, while digging for the foundation of Dr. Chaplin's house, an old and massive wall, with towers at intervals. This discovery has not yet been followed up. An account of it is given in Lewin's "Siege of Jerusalem."

the Sun God, and possibly of royal power. The
Phœnician letters close to the figure have been
read by Dr. Birch, of the British Museum, thus:—
On the first handle (see the figure, p. 125), "To or
of King Zepha;" on the second, "King Shat;" on
the third, a part of the word "Melek," *king;* on
the rest the letters are obliterated. Now we
know from 1 Chronicles, iv. 23, that there was an

establishment of potters at Jerusalem—"These
were the potters. . . . . there they dwelt with
the king for his work."

Of Græco-Phœnician, our attention is especially
called to the ancient jar found in a cavity scooped
out of the rock at the south-east angle; to the
"fat" lamps—*i.e.,* lamps adapted for people too
poor to burn oil (these are considered by Mr.
A. W. Franks to be of the second century before

Christ); to a dish of brown ware, with feet perforated like handles, as if for the purpose of
suspension when not in use; to some very
curious fragments, ornamented with designs like

those on the pottery of the aboriginal Kabyle
mountaineers of Algeria, and on that of the
almost unknown Riff people of the Empire of

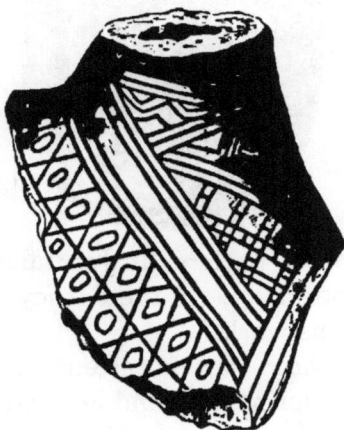

Morocco.   Large quantities of similar pottery
have been found at Cyprus.   The largest is a
portion of a single-handed jar (see figure), and,

from the perforated stoppage in the interior of the neck, was probably used for water.

The excavations in the Birket Israil brought to light certain vases, of an extremely hard, massive black ware, coated in three instances with a dark crimson glaze, perhaps produced by cornelian. They are shaped like the pine cone, or Thyrsus, the emblem of Dionysius on gems.

Very few specimens were found of Roman pottery. A fragment of the so-called "Samian"

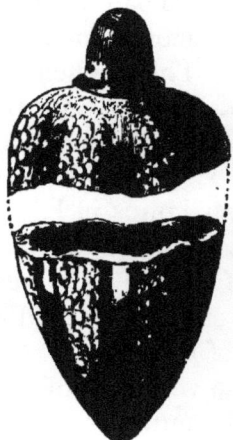

ware was found near Wilson's Arch, in a passage leading south; another came from Ophel; and a third was found. This last piece has a potter's mark in the shape of a foot and the letters CANRI. Three or four lamps, a jar with circular horizontal flutings, earthenware water-pipes, fragments of a large amphora of pale red ware, and one or two other things, exhaust the list. On one (see figure) is the word BARNÆ, implying that it was from the shop of one Barna or Barnas.

We have a much larger number of objects of the Christian period.

"Many lamp types of more Western Christendom, from the catacombs of Rome, Syracuse, and Carthage, such as the Good Shepherd, the Sacred Monogram, the Dove, the Cock of St. Peter, and the Chalice, are entirely absent; and the same may be said of the disgusting and probably Gnostic device of the Toad with the Cross, so often found on the catacombs of Alexandria and elsewhere in Egypt. The earthenware bottles with the effigy of St. Menas, an Egyptian saint who flourished in the fourth century, and whose name recalls the first Egyptian king, so commonly found with Christian lamps in Egypt, are also absent. The usual symbols of the Jerusalem lamps, which are all of a rude and cheap description, and which give an affecting indication of the poverty of the 'saints' of the early Church of Jerusalem, are the Cross, the very sign of their salvation; the seven-branched candlestick, which reminded them not only of the dimmed glories of Zion, but of Him who is the Light of the World; and the palm branch, which was dear to them not merely from its own exquisite grace and beauty, but by its association with Psalm xcii., with the gospel narrative (John, xii. 13), and with the Apocalyptic vision, wherein the glorified saints are described as 'clothed with white robes and palm branches in their hands' (Revelation, vii. 9).

These emblems, which the Christians of the
'Mother of Churches' used and rejoiced in, in
common with their brethren in more western
lands, are all more or less conventionalized in
their treatment, and are represented in a distinctive and different manner, occurring in every
instance, not as is usual in the west and even in
Egypt, in the *centre*, but along the edge and near
the outer lips of the lamps, which are pear-shaped,
and in no instance round. *Un*inscribed round

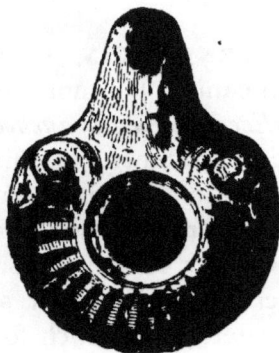

lamps of a different description have, nevertheless,
been discovered, and probably belong to this
period. (See Figure.)

"The following inscriptions occur. They are
written in barbarous Greek, the words being often
misspelt, and the letters frequently braced together or turned upside down. It is noticeable that
one form of the A which is used is that which is
constantly found upon contemporary work in
Egypt, and, indeed, is frequently employed as a

potter's mark for ware made at Alexandria, which seems to have been to Egypt what Stoke and Worcester are to England, and Dresden to Germany.

"1. LYXNAPIA KALA. *A Seven-branched Candlestick, conventionalized.* The first word is not classical Greek, but the inscription seems to signify 'good' or 'beautiful lamps.'

"2. ΦΩΣ ΧΥ ΦΕΝΙ ΠΑΣΙΝ. *A Cross.* This misspelt inscription may be translated, 'The Light of Christ shines forth to all,' or 'gives light to all.'*

"3. ΦΩΣ ΧΥ ΦΕΝΙ ΠΑΣΙΝ, followed by two letters whose meaning has not been explained. *A conventionalized Seven-branched Candlestick.* There are several specimens of this type.

"4. The inscription on this lamp appears to begin with the letters IΧΘ, which may stand for Ιησους Χριστος Θεος, or it may possibly allude to our Lord under the well-known symbol of the fish, IΧΘΥS, the letters of which form the initials of the Greek equivalent of 'Jesus Christ, the Son of God, the Saviour.'

"Some other lamps have a running pattern of the conventionalized tendrils, leaves, and fruit of the vine, executed with considerable freedom and elegance; but although they exhibit something of Greek freedom of treatment, they may probably be assigned to the Christian period, and the design may have reference to the

* Compare a lamp in the Museum at Leyden, which bears the inscription ✝ΩΣ ΕΚ ✝ΩΤΟΣ, *Light of Light.*

mystery of the Holy Eucharist. One of the Jerusalem lamps bears the letters I + I, probably for Jesus; and another of somewhat different fabric, besides two palm branches, exhibits a tree within a circular fence. It may be conjectured that this is intended to represent the Tree of Life. The writer has seen a somewhat similar tree in a mediæval Hebrew map of the Holy Land. The Christian lamps have been found not only in tombs, but in numerous other excavations in and about Jerusalem. It is remarkable that none of them bear potters' marks on the under-side."

Very little Arabic pottery has been found.

As for other objects, we have found objects in glass, mostly in fragments, some of which are very curious. Thus, there is a two-headed vase, found in a sepulchral cave on Olivet.

"It is double, with two handles, and a third, now unfortunately broken, originally arched over the top. The colour is a pale green, with circular and zigzag lines running over it in relief, of a much darker tint, approaching to blue. To the Roman period belong also several fragments of glass mosaic of the ordinary type, which have been found in various parts of the excavations. Of Arabic glass, three lamps are worthy of especial notice. Two of these are of a pale green colour, with three dark blue rings or handles, by which they were formerly suspended by means of chains, and contain perforated stems designed apparently to hold a wick."

In stone there were selected by Mr. Greville

Chester for notice, a shallow trough, used probably for grinding grain; certain balls of flint, a great number of some weight; the "seal of Haggai" (see p. 146); three sepulchral chests of the Christian period. These are among the most interesting objects found. They are all formed of white or pale-red limestone, and the style of their execution is of considerable

SEPULCHRAL CHEST FROM JERUSALEM.

elegance. When discovered they contained human bones and skulls, and it is much to be regretted that the latter were not preserved. Captain Warren states that the skulls and other bones found in these chests are "generally adult." They must, therefore, have been disinterred for some particular reason, and placed in the chests after the decomposition of the bodies. Is it possible that the individuals thus interred were martyrs ignominiously buried at first, and afterwards exhumed and honoured with more careful interment?*

Of metal objects, we may mention a bronze dagger, the bronze boss of a shield, a copper lamp-stand (p. 146), and a few other objects.

As we have given the different theories which Captain Warren's excavations will help to prove or disprove, it will not be considered as departing from our strict impartiality if we proceed to state what conclusions he himself has arrived at. And it is the more unnecessary to apologize for doing so, inasmuch as Captain Warren himself, with the admirable modesty which distinguishes all his utterances, advances his conclusions simply as those which have been forced upon him as one shaft after another yielded up its secrets; but which he is prepared to abandon to-morrow should fresh light convince him he is wrong. For even yet, after all his work, our light is but gloom, or, worse still, cross lights, such as those which his candles might have thrown from one gallery to another, illuminating the stones on which they were turned, but leading to confusion and danger along the side passages, along which their rays throw a fitful and uncertain light.

* In some places at the present time, as in certain Italian convents, it is customary to dig up the bones or skulls of the dead after a certain time, and then to arrange them fantastically, or with the names attached, in churches or crypts. A similar custom used to be followed at Ripon and Hythe.

And, first, let us enumerate some of the points which Captain Warren considers proved:—

THE WESTERN SIDE.—Here Robinson's Arch has been found, the voussoirs lying are those of a former arch; an aqueduct in the rock older than the wall; the wall *crossing* the Tyropœon Valley; a stream of running water at the foundations; Wilson's Arch, like Robinson's, at least the *second* on the same site; a secret causeway, apparently connecting the Temple Area and the citadel, large enough to march an army through; vaults, chambers, viaducts, everywhere underground. Barclay's Gateway examined. No traces found of the fourth gate between Wilson's and Robinson's Arch ; the masonry at the south-west angle apparently of more recent date than that at Barclay's Gateway.

THE SOUTH WALL.—The Triple Gate is on the rock, which, after rising to the surface in 600 ft. from the west, for 300 ft. more shelves rapidly down to the east, where the wall is 90 ft. below the platform. In other words, which is important, while the rock to the north of the platform (perhaps artificially) is made level with the platform, it slopes from thence with a dip down to the Triple Gate of 60 ft. in four hundred—*i.e.*, say, one in six and a-half. At the Single Gate an entrance was found to vaults lower than those called Solomon's Stables. Abutting on to the east corner was found an old wall of fortifications, with towers—itself a reconstruction of older material.

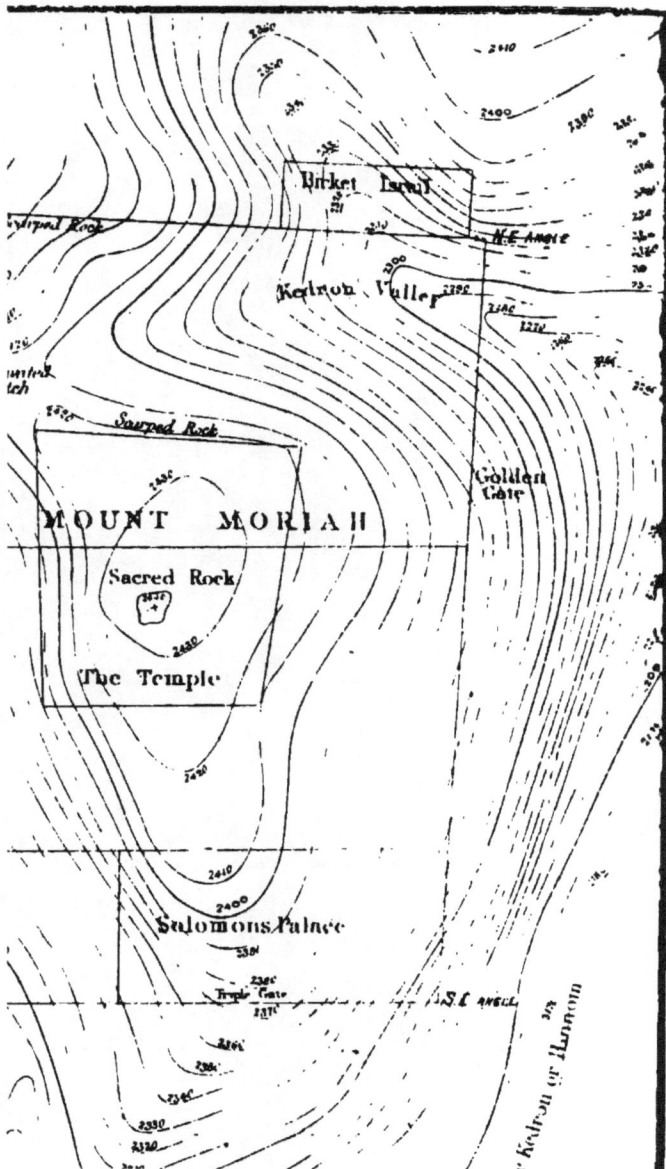

THE EAST WALL.—The stones let into the rock, apparently dressed before laid in their places; the rock hollowed to receive them ; Phœnician marks upon them. The Golden Gateway, 30 ft. at least above the rock; a massive wall in front of it. At the north-east angle, more Phœnician marks on the turret courses. Masonry very curious in character ; a valley running right across the north corner; proof that the Birket Israil was built for a pool.

INSIDE THE HARAM.—The platform not built, but of rock scarped in the north. The tanks examined and described ; new tanks discovered, a *contour map of the whole Haram Area obtained* from rock observations in the cisterns and elsewhere. From this it appears that from the platform (not the rock) of the Sakhra to the south-west angle there is a dip of 140 ft., to the south-east angle of 160 ft., and to the north-east angle one of 110 ft.; and if the place assigned by Messrs. Fergusson and Lewin for the Altar of the Temple be correct, a depth of nearly 50 ft. would first have had to be filled up to get the level of the Altar; while Araunah's Threshing Floor was on a slope of one in six. This is not advanced as an objection, but as a fact.

And now, with these facts before our eyes—all quite new ones—let us hear Captain Warren's own conclusions.

The accompanying plan shows what these are. It will be seen his reconstruction of the city differs very considerably from any previously attempted.

His reasons for these conclusions are given in full
in the " Recovery of Jerusalem," chap. xii.

He first argues, from the contour plan of the
Haram which he has been able to form, that it
is incredible that the Temple of Solomon should
have been built upon the slope of a hill as steep
as the Rock of Gibraltar to the west, down in a
hole, or anywhere except on the ridge. Now,
this ridge is somewhat flattened near the top.
Further, the Altar stood on the threshing floor of
Araunah, and threshing floors to this day are on
the highest points or ridges, exposed to every
breeze. If the Temple, then, was on the ridge,
it could not have been at the south-west of the
Haram, or the north-east, or even the north-west;
because there, too, is a small valley, or depression, of 30 ft., overlooked by the north side of the
platform. Nor could it have been in the south-
east. We may, therefore, place it somewhere
near the platform. Where, then, was the Altar?
Not, thinks Captain Warren, over the raised rock,
but where is now the Dome of the Rock—the
same rock having formed part of the Chel, through
which the gate Nitsob led underground to the
gate Tadi. Solomon's Temple, then, was a rec-
tangle, about 900 ft. from east to west, by 600
from north to south. Wilson's Arch would, therefore, be Solomonic, and all the portion of the
Sanctuary on the eastern side.

Then comes a difficulty. There is every reason
to believe that the wall at the south-east and north-
east parts is as old as any other portion of the

JERUSALEM AT THE TIME OF KING HEROD.

SKETCH SHEWING APPROXIMATELY THE LIE OF ROCK.

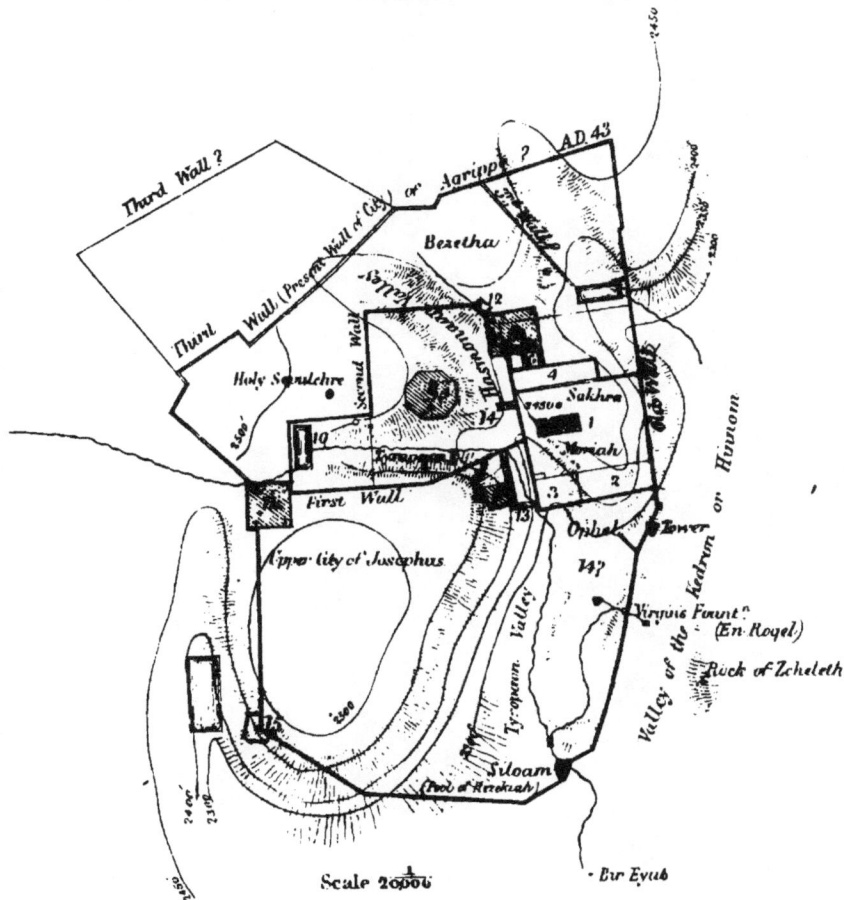

Scale 20000

REFERENCE.

1. Temple of Solomon
2. Palace of   do.   } Herod's Temple
3. Added on by Herod
4. Exhedra (The Tower, Baris or Antonia)
5. Antonia (The Castle)
6. Cloisters joining Antonia to Temple
7. Xystus
8. Agrippa's Palace

9. Iron & Acra
10. Lower Pool of Gihon or Amygdalon
11. Herod's Palace
12. Bethesda or Struthion
13. Bridge built by Herod
14. The lower City called sometimes Akra
15. British Cemetery. A.D. 1870.

wall. This is met by placing the Palace of Solomon in that space, 300 ft. from north to south, and 600 ft. from east to west. In the south-east corner of the Haram, the Porch of Solomon, "which overlooked the Kedron," would be built on the wall between Solomon's Palace and that continued part which, turning to the west at the north-east angle, formed the north part of the second wall.

Mr. Lewin has proved that the Palace of Solomon was near to the Temple, and must have been south of it. As for the south-west angle, that is Herodian. Antonia, Captain Warren thinks, must have been double—*i.e.*, there was a *Castle* of Antonia (see the plan) connected by cloisters with a *Tower* of Antonia; the name Antonia being given to the whole fortress, with all its buildings. The second wall he places nearly where Mr. Williams puts it. The third wall he is not certain about.

In giving this plan we are not advancing it as one more likely to be correct than any that have preceded it. It does not belong to the functions of the Committee to embrace any theory. But the opinions of Captain Warren are thus roughly set forth as an act of justice, and to show what bearing his discoveries had upon the questions at issue in the mind of the discoverer.

Rough and bald as is this sketch of Captain Warren's work, it is hoped that it will be found a sufficient introduction to a further study of this great subject. To reproduce the ancient city,

M

to make it clear where each incident in that Life which is our example and pattern took place, with what surroundings it was accompanied, is truly no mean ambition, no unworthy task.   It is attempted in every Sunday school, where the children learn to associate their Saviour's history with illustrations which are only unfaithful because we have not yet fully accomplished our object.   They can follow the history of the chosen people in maps which mislead or are imperfect because our work is not yet finished.   They can illustrate the ancient customs by reference to the modern, with a fullness which every intelligent traveller increases.   And here we would fain offer a word of warning and advice.   The facts yet found and stored up—the historical evidence, the architectural evidence, the witness of the stones—altogether, are not yet enough.   We want more, before we can describe with certainty.   Let our readers learn that many theories have been advanced, that the chain of evidence in each is weak at some points, that nothing can be considered fixed till more has been discovered.   And to discover more, we must fain look to Jerusalem herself, and examine further among the stones of the City of David.

Let us finally bear witness to the untiring perseverance, courage, and ability of Captain Warren.   Those of us who know best under what difficulties he had to work, can tell with what courage and patience they were met and overcome.   Physical suffering and long endurance of heat, cold, and danger, were nothing. There were, besides, anxieties of digging in the dark, anxieties as to local prejudice, anxieties for the lives of those brave men, Sergeant Birtles, and the rest of his staff—anxieties which we may not speak of here.   He has his reward, it is true. So long as interest in the modern history of Jerusalem remains, so long as people are concerned to know how sacred sites have been found out, so long will the name of Captain Warren survive.

CHAPTER X.

THE FIRST EXPEDITION.

WE have taken our work in Jerusalem first, although in point of chronological order it should have been second; for the expedition of which Captain Warren was in command had been preceded by a preliminary expedition under Captains Wilson and Anderson. It is their work that we propose to detail next, following it with the topographical work of Captain Warren and the journey of Professor Palmer in due order.

Captain Wilson's previous acquaintance with the country, acquired during the progress of the Ordnance Survey of Jerusalem, was a very great assistance to the Committee in this first expedition. His instructions were general rather than particular. He was asked to make such a general survey as would enable the promoters of

the Fund to fix on particular spots for future investigation, and also to collect such special information as would throw light on the points mentioned in the original prospectus issued by the Committee.

Following their reports, we will endeavour to give in detail an account of all the work which these two officers accomplished in six months. It began at Beyrout itself, where they landed on November 22nd, 1865, with a series of astronomical observations for fixing the position first of Beyrout itself, and afterwards in succession of Mejdel Anjar, Baalbek, Surghaya, Suk Wady Barada, Damascus, Tel Salhiyeh, and Harran el Awamid. These places belong, it may be urged, to Syria rather than Palestine; but they are all indirectly, if not directly, connected with that volume whose elucidation is the sole object of our Society. Thus, Beyrout, never mentioned at all in the Bible, is historically interesting as being the scene of the mock trial of Herod the Great's two sons, Alexander and Aristobulus (Josephus, Antiq., xvi. 11). It was a favourite place with Agrippa, who adorned it with baths and theatres, which latter were afterwards used by Titus for the gladiatorial exhibitions held after the destruction of Jerusalem. In these the miserable Jews had to take part. Mejdel Anjar is near the old city of Chalcis. Baalbek, the Greek Heliopolis, has been supposed by some to be on "the plain of Aven" (Amos, i. 5), and by others to be the Baalath built

by Solomon (1 Kings, ix. 6). Its importance
architecturally need not be mentioned. Then
Suk Wady Barada is the old Abila, which belonged to Philip the Tetrarch (Luke, iii. 1). Its
present name, "the Fair of Wady Barada," is
derived from the fact of the place having been
taken by the Mohammedans during a fair which
was being held in the place at the time. The
Barada is the Abana of Scripture. Tel Salhiyeh is a mound near Damascus, where excavations appeared likely to lead to valuable results;
while Harran el Awamid is, according to Dr.
Beke's theory, the Haran where dwelt Laban.

Besides the astronomical observations, plans
were made, with occasional detail drawings, of
the old temple at Deir el Kalah near Beyrout,
the temple at Mejdel Anjar, the old city of
Chalcis, the Basilica of Theodosius at Baalbek.
At Tel Salhiyeh an Assyrian slab, previously
known and now in England, was examined and
photographed.

Leaving Damascus, on the road to Banias,
Kaukab, Jeba, and Banias itself were astronomically fixed. Kaukab, "near Damascus," is the
traditional site of St. Paul's conversion. It was
certainly near here. "A mile or two backwards
or forwards," says Dr. Porter, "makes no difference in the leading features of the landscape.
We see them to-day just as Paul saw them: the
snow-capped peak of Hermon on the left; the
long, bare ridge of Anti-Lebanus running eastward, with the rounded top of Jebel Siniyeh

rising in the midst of it; the broad plain, with its various tinted foliage, and deep green corn fields, here spreading out to the horizon, and there bounded by groups of graceful hills; the village embowered in orchards to the right and left, and the bright buildings of the city itself just appearing above the foliage; the same cloudless sky, and the same fierce sun pouring down a flood of light from the midst of Heaven upon city, plain, and mountain."

It was on the first day of the new year that work commenced in Palestine proper, near Banias. Banias, called Panium by Josephus, is perhaps the site of "Baal Gad, in the valley of Lebanon, under Mount Hermon" (Joshua, xi. 17), the northernmost point of Joshua's conquests. Herod built here a temple in honour of Augustus Cæsar. The city round this temple was afterwards, by Philip the Tetrarch, called Cæsarea Philippi. It was near here that our Lord asked Simon Peter (Matthew, xiv. 3) the memorable question, "Whom do men say that I the Son of man am?" It was near here, on "a high mountain apart," that the Transfiguration took place. The ruins lie on a triangular terrace 500 ft. above the level of the plain beneath. At its innermost angle there issues from the rock a spring, which rises a full-grown stream. It is one of those springs which constitute a peculiar charm in Palestine scenery, welling up from the rock, and forming at once a full-grown river. Such are those of Ain Jalûd, of Ras el Mukatta, of Fijeh. They

can only be found in a rocky country. "The Lord
thy God bringeth thee into . . . a land of brooks
of water, of fountains and depths that spring out
of valleys and hills" (Deuteronomy, viii. 7). The
statement by Josephus that this fountain was
connected with Lake Phiala was proved to be
impossible, from the physical features of the
country. The ruins of the once-famed city, Cæsarea Philippi, lie about this terrace; and about
1,000 ft. above this place, at an hour's ride, is the
great Castle of Banias, "Kalaat es Subeibeh,"
one of the most magnificent ruins in Syria. What
the age of the earlier portions of the castle may
be it is difficult to say with any precision. Captain
Wilson thinks not earlier than the eighth or ninth
century, A.D.; but Dr. Porter would give them
a much higher antiquity. The castle became
afterwards one of the strongholds of the Christian
kingdom, during its brief and stormy existence.
It finally succumbed, in 1165, to Noor-ed-deen, or
"Light of Religion," the great predecessor of
Saladin.

Near Banias, that is to say at three-quarters of
an hour's ride distant, lies a curious grassy mound
now known as Tell el Kady, "the Mound of the
Judge." Here was Laish, the site of Dan. There
can be no question as to its being the place.
Neglected as it is now, and abandoned to shep-
herds and nomads, the Mound of the Judge is the
place where stood Laish, the Phœnician colony.
The children of Dan sent five men from their coasts
to spy out the land. "The five men saw the

people . . . here they dwelt careless, after the
manner of the Zidonians, quiet and secure; and
there was no magistrate in the land that might
put them to shame in anything; and they were
far from the Zidonians, and had no business with
any man." A quiet, peaceful colony, forgotten
by the mother city, happy in their land, "where
there was no want of anything that is in the
earth." Then the six hundred Danites went up
"and smote them with the edge of the sword,
and burned the city with fire. And there was
no deliverer, because it was far from Zidon, and
they had no business with any man."

Standing on the west side of the hill, says
Captain Anderson, "we hear the sound of a great
body of rushing water, and on penetrating through
the thick oleander bushes, and traversing a most
rocky slope, we discover a large pool, 50 or 60
yards wide, and the water, bubbling out of the
ground, rushes away another full-grown stream.
The pool is partially filled up and entirely surrounded by shapeless basaltic stones, and it is
evident that all with any architectural detail, or
with well-dressed faces, have been removed long
ago for building in other parts of the plain.
The two streams join and form a large pool, 150
yards wide, delta shaped, and covered with
bushes. From the apex of the delta, the stream
flows away in a south-west course across the
plain. This tributary of the Jordan, called by
Josephus the lesser Jordan, is twice as large as
the fountain at Banias, and three times as large

as the main stream of the Jordan running from
the north. The southern ridge has still traces of
the wall which was built there to command the
plain towards the south, and a position so well-
chosen, when fortified, might well be considered
secure." Extending the reconnaissance down the
valley, the exact spot was found where the principal tributaries unite—the streams passing through
a succession of terraces before reaching the plain.
On the right bank of the stream were observed
three caverns, the largest tenanted by cattle.
The Banias and Tel el Kady streams unite down
the valley, the lake having parted with most of
its waters to irrigate the upper part of the plain.
A quarter of an hour farther on is the junction
with the main stream, a point whose latitude
was astronomically observed. The Jordan here
is 45 ft. wide, of a dirty yellow colour, and flowing between banks 25 ft. below the general level
of the plain; whilst the united streams flow in a
channel 90 ft. wide. Lake Hûleh lies seven miles
south of this point, the whole of the intermediate
plain being marshy and the lower part overgrown
by babeer canes, which are used by the villagers
of Monsourah for building their huts. Between
Tel el Kady and Hunin we pass the site of the old
town of Iron, which was taken and plundered when
Dan was also taken by Benhadad (1 Kings, xv.
20), and again by Tiglath Pileser (2 Kings, xv.
29). The site is a rich and beautiful little plain,
now called Merj Ayûn, at the northern end of
which is a mound called Tel Dilbin. Farther on

is Abil, the probable site of Abel Beth Maacha, where the curious siege by Joab took place (2 Samuel, xx. 14—22). The town was saved then by the "wise woman's" speech and the sacrifice of the fugitive Sheba; but it fell afterwards into the hands of the Syrians (see 1 Kings, xv. 20). On the rising ground beyond Abil, the watershed of the country was reached, and the explorers—whose object it was to lay down this watershed accurately from this point to Jerusalem—began to follow it up, as they proceeded southward, step by step. It proved to be at first an extremely narrow and well-defined ridge, widening as they went on. It may be stated at once that this object was successfully carried out, and that one of the chief results of the expedition was the establishment for the first time of the backbone of the country from Banias southward to Jerusalem.

The first day's journey brought them to Hunin, a place about which absolutely nothing is known. Yet it possesses the ruins of a very old and important fortress, so old that it bears the stamp of every successive conquering race—Jewish (in the Phœnician "bevel" or marginal draft), Roman (in the arch), Saracenic, Christian (the period of the Christian kingdom), Turk, and Arab. The site is by nature designed for a fortress: it commands the mountain pass by which is the high road from Acre to Damascus. The advantages of position have also been thoroughly understood, if the extent and strength of the castle be any proof.

The whole northern portion is surrounded by a
ditch cut in the solid rock, to a depth of, in some
places, 20 ft.—a work, says Captain Wilson, apparently of great antiquity. From this place the
plain of the Jordan may be looked down upon on
the one side, and the hill ground sloping to the
Mediterranean on the other; the whole valley of
the Jordan appearing like a vast fissure with an
elevated plateau on each side of it. Just below
Hunin the river overflows the entire valley, and
converts it into a vast swamp; and again, a few
miles below it, converts itself into a triangular
lake, known as Lake Huleh, where Mr. Macgregor,
in his canoe voyage, made his discovery of the
floating papyrus. It is strange, in a country
where every village has its mound and every hill-
top its ruin, about which cluster the traditions of
the people or the sacred associations of the Bible,
to find remains of so vast a fortified place, with
no tradition—or none recorded—and no history.
Dr. Robinson, however, would identify the place
with Beth Rehob (Judges, xviii. 28; mentioned
also in Numbers, xiii. 21; and 2 Samuel, x. 6).

The position would seem to warrant this theory,
but there is nothing in the name which corrobo-
rates it.

The reconnaissance survey along the watershed
from Hunin led across a succession of mountain
peaks, forming the great western vale of the
Jordan. The highlands—we are in the tribe of
Naphtali, "the hind let loose"—form a series of
valleys with which the country is intersected, the

ridges between them being described as somewhat
of the character of open glades, gently sloping
towards the sea. The hills are well wooded,
though the oaks are being thinned out to supply
the Damascus market with charcoal. At the last
peak the hill slopes to the southward, overlooking
a little plain, one mile wide and two long, lying
sheltered among the surrounding hills. This is
the plain of Zaanaim, where Heber the Kenite
had pitched his tent when Sisera, defeated down
below in the plain by Barak, was flying up from
the lowlands to meet his death. In the middle
of its western side is the undoubted site of
Kedesh Naphtali (now Kedes). It is built upon
a tongue of land, once regularly fortified, as the
ruins of its walls and towers show. Below this,
however, is another tongue of land, stretching out
into the plain a quarter of a mile, lower than the
first and rocky, where are some remains of undoubted antiquity. Among these are two or
three magnificent sarcophagi, one of them a
double one, made to hold two persons under one
lid, the stone pillows being at alternate ends.
Some excavations were made among the ruins,
and photographs taken. "The western building,"
says Captain Wilson, "is a tomb containing
eleven loculi; the eastern one, called by some
travellers a Jewish synagogue, is a Temple of the
Sun, of about the same date as Baalbek. The
lintel over the main entrance was dug up : on its
under-side is a large figure of the sun (I think),
and over the architrave is a small cornice, beauti-

fully worked. It consists of a scroll of vine leaves, with bunches of grapes; in the centre is a bust, and facing it on either side is the figure of a stag. On either side of the main entrance is a small niche, with a hole communicating to larger niches within the building, like a sort of confessional; in one of the niches is part of a figure, clothed in a robe, with a spear in the left hand; over one of the side doorways is the figure of an eagle. Close to the temple, and evidently belonging to it, an altar with a Greek inscription was found, which I have copied and taken a squeeze of. It is apparently dedicated to Baal Comos, Lord of Sports, as was the temple Deir el Kalah, near Beyrout. In the group of sarcophagi, one buried in the ground was dug up, and the decorations found in better repair than those exposed to the air. It consisted of a wreath, held up at the sides in two folds by nude male figures, and at the corners by four female figures, with wings and flowing drapery. The figures have been purposely defaced, but the arms and feet still remain, and the whole is finely sculptured. After seeing this better preserved one, similar designs can be traced in the others, one of which has a sword and shield cut on it."

The ancient city was originally a city of refuge for the northern tribes. It was here that Barak was born; and it is with a knowledge of this place and its surroundings that the fourth chapter of the book of Judges may be studied.

A short distance to the south-east of Kedesh

stands a hill called Tel Hara. It was visited for
the first time by Captains Wilson and Anderson.
Here were found the remains of an ancient fortress; a city with its walls and towers are still
to be traced; and on the eastern slope, the usual
concomitants of old ruins, broken glass and
pottery. Here, they both agree in thinking, was
the long-lost Hazor, which "lay over" the Lake
Huleh, according to Josephus; which was the
city of that Jabin who attempted to face Joshua,
and that other Jabin who sent Sisera to oppress
Israel. "The position," says Captain Wilson,
"is one of great strength, and overhangs the lake.
Every argument which Robinson adduces in
favour of Tel Kureibeh applies with much greater
force to these ruins." Now, at Tel Kureibeh,
selected by Dr. Robinson as a probable place,
there is, it is true, a position overlooking the lake,
and of great possible strength; but there are no
old ruins, no traces of former occupation, and *no
cisterns*. Clearly, Tel Kureibeh must yield its
claim to Tel Hara; but Dr. Porter refuses to
accept either theory, arguing that as the strength
of Joshua's Jabin, as well as Barak's, lay in
chariots, we must look for Hazor on the lower
slopes of the mountains, so as to be easily acces-
sible for chariots.

Leaving Kedesh, it was found that the watershed was pushed westward by the plain of Zaanaim, and after struggling for several hours with
steep and difficult ravines, the watershed was
again reached at Kefr Birim. On the way they

N

passed the villages called Maroon and Yaroon.
The second of these, on a solitary hill-top, has
the ruins of an early Christian church, and
may perhaps be identified with Iron, one of
the cities of Naphtali (Joshua, xix. 38). Half a
mile to the eastward of Yaroon was found a nameless heap of ruins; among them a temple, built of
hard, white limestone, almost like marble. Before
arriving at Maroon again is the village of Ainath,
which may be the Beth Anath of Joshua, xx. 38,
also one of the fenced cities of Naphtali. We
are now in the centre of the wooded hills of
Naphtali; and from the summit of a prominent
hill, near the village of Khunin, could be seen,
to the west, the Mediterranean Sea, the ridge of
Cape Carmel, and the town of Acre. To the
north is visible the old crusading castle of Tibnin,
built on the ruins of an old fortress, by Hugh de
St. Omer, and called Toron; it was taken, after a
lapse of eighty years, by Saladin. The second
husband of Isabella, Queen of Jerusalem, Hum-
phrey de Toron, was the Seigneur of this castle.
Farther north, too, can be seen the far more important place now called Kaláat esh Shukif—the
Crusaders' Belfort—a castle which held out after
the Battle of Hattin for a whole year, and then
only surrendered to Saladin on honourable terms.
The ruins, however, show that there was a fortress here in much older times than the Crusades.

At a little village called Shalaboon was found
an immense sarcophagus, large enough to contain one of the giants of old. Here were also

two stone coffins, with extremely curious designs, in a good state of preservation.

Kefr Birim, where the watershed was reached, is a place which no one has yet identified with any scriptural town. It is, however, an exceedingly interesting place as a place of pilgrimage, in the early Christian centuries, of the Jews of Safed and other places. Here were the traditional tombs of Barak and of the prophet Obadiah. The ruins still stand of one of the most remarkable synagogues in the country. They were photographed by Captain Wilson. There was a second synagogue at Kefr Birim, of which the doorway alone remains; but on this there is an inscription in Hebrew, which Mr. Deutsch was enabled to read from the photograph.* Close to Kefr Birim is the village of Sasa, where an old Jewish tomb was explored. It is cut in the rock, having a small entrance leading to a chamber 12 ft. square; and around this space coffin-shaped tombs or recesses, in which the bodies were placed, some very small, as if for an infant. The mouth of each tomb had at one time been sealed with a stone. The entrance was so low that it was *necessary to stoop in order to get in*, reminding one of St. John (xi. 38).

Captain Wilson† divides the tombs of Palestine into three classes: "Rock-hewn tombs," "Masonry tombs," and "Sarcophagi." The rock-hewn

---

* See Photographs of the Fund, Nos. 67—70.

† See " Quarterly Statement," First Series, No. II.: "Captain Wilson on the Remains of Tombs in Palestine."

tombs are the earliest in date—the softer strata
of limestone, especially the white chalk in some
districts, being well adapted for sepulchral. excavations.   There are many different kinds of these
tombs.   The simplest is when a grave-shaped
loculus has been sunk in the rock, and a reveal
cut round its mouth to receive a covering slab,
which in some cases is flush with the surface of
the rock, and in others raised above it, and ornamented in the same way as the lid of a sarcophagus.   Examples of this kind were found,
among other places, at Kedesh and Yaroon.
Another form (found at Meiron) was an arched
recess cut in the face of the rock, and a loculus
"sunk" under it.   And a third simple form is
that in which a single deep loculus is cut in the
face of the rock, and its mouth closed by a rough
stone slab.

The commonest kind, he says, is that in which
a number of deep loculi are grouped together in
one or more chambers of the same excavation; and
he divides them into three classes—1. Where a
natural cavern has been used, loculi being cut in
its sides.   2. Where a square or oblong chamber
is cut in the rock, loculi being ranged along its
sides.   3. Where one entrance leads into several
sepulchral chambers, each having several loculi.
This class, of course, is the most important and
the most costly.   Examples were found at Tibneh
and at Jerusalem.

As the number of rock-hewn tombs seems
hardly sufficient for a large population, Captain

Wilson suggests that it was the custom to use the same loculus for several burials, a second taking place when the body of the first had decomposed. He also observes that while many of the highly finished and ornamented tombs were for noble and princely families, some of the larger ones may have been public tombs for the poorer classes of society, and perhaps provided by the Government.

Of the second great class of masonry tombs there are but few, and these are confined to the northern portion of the country. They were found at Kedesh, Tel Hum, Malul, and Teyasir.

The sarcophagi were found all over the country, the most elaborate being that already described at Kedesh ; but near this a large number were found in good preservation, made of black basalt. Two brought home by Captain Warren are in the collection of the Fund at the South Kensington Museum.

To return to the reconnaissance survey. A few miles brings us from Kefr Birim to Jebel Jermûk, the highest mountain in Galilee, whose summit is 4,000 ft. above the sea. No identification has been made of this mountain with any scriptural place. On the top of it, never before visited, they found an inhabited village, the people of which refused to give them any information whatever. Following the narrow ridge of the mountain, the land falls on either side, and the water parting is here defined exactly. The southern peak descends precipitously 2,000 ft.

into the plains of Rameh, which was identified
by Dr. Robinson with the Ramah of Naphtali
(Joshua, xix. 36). If this is so, we are near to
the southern limit of the tribe of Naphtali.

A good deal of the country in this district was
carefully explored, and many plans and photographs taken, besides astronomical observations.
Among the places visited was Safed, important
chiefly from its position, which commands one of
the most magnificent views in Palestine. Its
castle was built by the Crusaders, and garrisoned
by the Knights Templars. Saladin took it, and
buried it in ruins; but it was rebuilt some years
later, only to fall into the hands of Bibars, who
flayed the commandant alive. An earthquake
destroyed the whole place in the year 1837,
killing some 5,000 of the inhabitants. Tradition
has made Safed the site of Bethulia, the scene of
the events recorded in the Book of Judith. But
this is very uncertain; and Sanur, some few miles
north of Samaria, has been proposed as a more
probable site. At Meiron plans were made of
the synagogues, drawings of some of the tombs,
and photographs of the shrines. This interesting
place, though it has no Biblical history, is one of
the most venerated spots in all Palestine for the
Jews, who go on pilgrimage there every May;
for here are the tombs of those great Rabbis,
Hillel and Shammai, and of Simeon Ben Jochai,
the reputed author of the Kabbalistic book
"Zohar." At a little place called Nebartein
were discovered the ruins of an old synagogue,

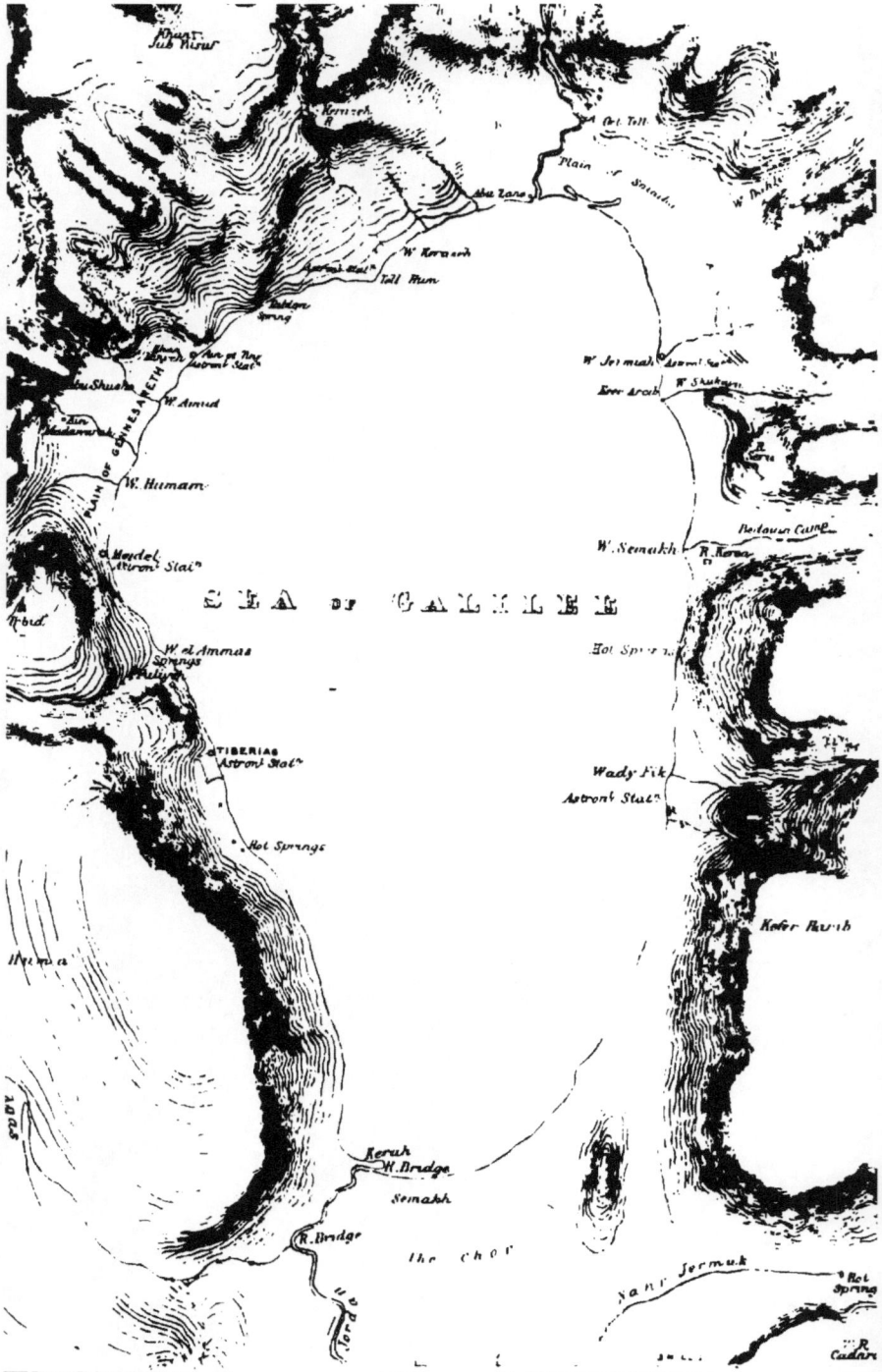

on the lintel of which was a Hebrew inscription, and over it a representation of the candlestick with seven branches, similar to the well-known one on Titus's tomb at Rome; and at Kasyur the ruins of a small temple with a mutilated Greek inscription.

Come with us now from the mountains of Naphtali to the shores of the Sea of Galilee, while Captain Wilson takes us round this, the most interesting place in all Palestine, save only the Holy City.

The accompanying map will be necessary to help us. It is as well to state that this is the only accurate map of the lake ever published.

Without any pretensions to boldness of scenery, with no lofty precipices to cast their shadows in the waters, the Lake of Galilee, says Captain Wilson,* has yet a beauty of its own which would always make it remarkable. The hills, except at Khan Minyeh, where there is a small cliff, are recessed from the shore of the lake, or rise gradually from it; they are of no great elevation, and their outline, especially on the eastern side, is not broken by any prominent peak; but everywhere from the southern end the snow-capped peak of Hermon is visible, standing out so sharp and clear in the bright sky that it appears almost within reach, and, towards the north, the western ridge is cut through by a wild gorge, "the Valley of Doves," over which rise the twin peaks or horns of

* See "Recovery of Jerusalem," article "Sea of Galilee."

Hattin. The shore line, for the most part regular, is broken on the north into a series of little bays of exquisite beauty; nowhere more beautiful than at Gennesareth, where the beaches, pearly white with myriads of minute shells, are on one side washed by the limpid waters of the lake, and on the other shut in by a fringe of oleanders, rich in May with their "blossoms red and bright."

The surrounding hills are of a uniform brown colour, and would be monotonous if it were not for the ever-changing lights, and the brilliant tints at sunrise and sunset. It is, however, under the pale light of a full moon that the lake is seen to the greatest advantage; for there is then a softness in the outlines, a calm on the water in which the stars are so brightly mirrored, and a perfect quiet in all around, which harmonize well with the feelings that cannot fail to arise on its shores. It is perhaps difficult to realize that the borders of this lake, now so silent and desolate, were once enlivened by the busy hum of towns and villages; and that on its waters hostile navies contended for supremacy. But there is one feature which must strike every visitor, and that is the harmony of the Gospel narrative with the places which it describes, giving us, as M. Renan happily expresses it, "un cinquième évangile, lacéré, mais lisible encore."

The lake, shaped like a pear, is twelve and a quarter miles long by six and three-quarters broad. The plain of Gennesareth, now called El Ghuweir, is on the north-western shore. It is two miles and a half long and one mile broad. On the north-east is another plain, now a swampy marsh, called El Batîhah. On the west there is a recess in the hills containing the town of Tiberias; and in the east, at the mouths of Wadys Semakh and Fik, are small tracts of uninhabited ground. On the south, the valley of the Jordan stretches away southward.

The lake is between 600 and 700 ft. below the level of the Mediterranean. The water is bright, clear and sweet to the taste, and it abounds with fish. Sudden storms are frequent. Captain Wilson saw one. "The morning was delightful; a gentle, easterly breeze, and not a cloud in the sky to give warning of what was coming. Suddenly, about midday, there was a sound of distant thunder, and a small cloud, 'no bigger than a man's hand,' was seen rising over the heights of Lubieh to the west. In a few moments the cloud appeared to spread, and heavy black masses came rolling down the hills towards the lake, completely obscuring Tabor and Hattin. At this moment the breeze died away, there were a few minutes of perfect calm, during which the sun shone out with intense power, and the surface of the lake was smooth and even as a mirror; Tiberias, Mejdel, and other buildings, stood out in sharp relief from the gloom behind; but they were soon lost sight of as the thunder gust swept past them, and, rapidly advancing across the lake, lifted the placid water into a bright sheet of foam: in another moment it reached the ruins, driving myself and companion to take refuge in a cistern, where for nearly an hour we were confined, listening to the rattling peals of thunder and torrents of rain.   The effect of half the lake in perfect rest, whilst the other half was in wild confusion, was extremely grand.   It would have fared badly with any light craft caught in mid-lake by the storm; and we could not help thinking of that memorable occasion on which the storm is so graphically described as 'coming down' upon the lake."

The lake does not appear to have anything volcanic in its origin, the hill on either side being limestone, capped in places with basalt.

So much for the general appearance of the lake.   Come now, with Captain Wilson, round its shores, beginning at the mouth of the Jordan, at the northern end.   On the western bank, we observe a few small mounds and heaps of stones, called Abu Zany, which Dr. Thompson considers the site of the Galilean Bethsaida—the birthplace of Peter, Andrew, and Philip.   On the other bank are ruins, which the same author identifies with Bethsaida Julias—the birthplace of Philip the Tetrarch.   Two miles along the shore, with no ruins, bring us to Tel Hum, which Captain Wilson believes to be Capernaum.   The ruins, which lie close upon the shore, cover a space of half a mile long and a quarter of a mile broad.   Dr. Robinson seems to have been the first to draw attention to these remarkable ruins, and especially to those of a large and important building called the

"White Synagogue." Captain Wilson discovered
that it lay within a later building, which may be
the ruins of the church said by Epiphanius to
have been built at Capernaum, and described by
Antoninus as a basilica, including the house of
Peter. The original building is 74 ft. 9 in. long
and 56 ft. 9 in. broad, built north and south, with
three entrances at the southern end. That it was
a synagogue, and built for no other purpose, is
proved by Captain Wilson's own researches into
the peculiarities of synagogue building.* The
interesting point about these ruins is, that if the
town be Capernaum, here we have, without any
possibility of doubt, the site of the identical
synagogue built by the Roman centurion (Luke,
vii. 4, 5), where our Lord pronounced the discourse
of John, vi. These very stones before our eyes
have echoed to His words. We can trace the outlines of the building in which He stood. Surely,
if there be any sacred place upon the earth, it is
this!

Here, alas! as elsewhere, the cold breath of
doubt chills the rising enthusiasm. Is it, after
all, the site of Capernaum? To us, reading
Captain Wilson's arguments in its favour, it
would almost seem as if there could be no doubt.
But, supported as Captain Wilson is, not only
by his own reasoning, but by the weight of
many travellers, he is opposed by Dr. Robinson,
Dr. Porter, Mr. Macgregor, and others, who be-

* See " Quarterly Statement," First Series, p. 37.

lieve Khan Minyeh to be the real Capernaum.
Let us, however, agree with our guide, and
follow him to Kerazeh, which is two and a half
miles away from the shore of the lake. In
Kerazeh we may recognize Chorazin, though
this depends mainly on Tel Hum being Capernaum. The ruins, which consist chiefly of dwell-
ing-houses, with one synagogue, are built of
black basalt, and not of limestone, like those of
Tel Hum. In such a house as any one of those
before us, our Saviour must have passed his childhood. They are generally square, of different
sizes—the largest measured was nearly 30 ft.—
and have one or two columns down the centre to
support the roof, which appears to have been
flat, as in the modern Arab houses. The walls
are about 2 ft. thick, built of masonry or of
loose blocks of basalt; there is a low doorway in
the centre of one of the walls, and each house
has windows 12 in. high and 6½ in. wide. In one
or two cases the houses were divided into four
chambers.

Returning to the lake, we find, a mile and a
half from Tel Hum, the little bay of Et Tabigah,
where is the great spring, the fountain of Caphar-
naum, mentioned by Josephus as watering the
plain of Gennesareth. Here there are no ruins
except those of works which were once erected
for the purpose of raising the water to a higher
level, and conveying it to the plain of Gennesareth.
Passing round the cliff of Khan Minyeh, at the
southern end of the bay, we are at the "Fountain

of the Fig-tree" (Ain et Tin), standing at the head of the plain; and close to it the ruins of Khan Minyeh, the site (according to Dr. Robinson, Dr. Porter, and others) of Capernaum. The ruins are not so large as those of Tel Hum or Kerazeh, nor are there any remains of large buildings yet discovered among them. South of Khan Minyeh is the plain of Gennesareth, now covered over with brushwood, and here and there a few isolated patches of corn. For a description of the plain as it was, read the account of Josephus, who loved it well. "One may call this place," he says, "the ambition of nature, when it forces those plants that are naturally enemies to one another to agree together. It is a happy contention of the seasons, as if every one of them laid claim to this country; for it not only nourishes different sorts of autumnal fruits beyond man's expectation, but preserves them a great while; it supplies man with its principal fruits, with grapes and figs continually during ten months of the year, and the rest of the fruits, as they become ripe together, through the whole year; for besides the good temperature of the air, it is watered from a most fertile fountain." This fountain, we have seen, is that of Et Tabigah. Some travellers find it in the "Round Fountain," Ain Mudawarah, where, however, there are no ruins of waterworks or traces of aqueducts. In it exists the fish which Josephus mentions as common to the fountains of Capernaum and the Nile, the Coracinus.

At the south of the plain is Mejdel (Magdala),

the home of Mary Magdalene. In the Wady
Hamám are the caves of Arbela, the scene of
that most extraordinary battle in which the
assailants were lowered in boxes by means of
chains, and the defendants fought from the caves.
It ended in the complete destruction of the
robbers (Antiq., xiv. 15, 4). The caves were
afterwards used, in the time when Palestine was a
greatnest of hermitages, for monks and cœnobites.

Near the caves are the ruins of Arbela, now
called Irbid. Southward we have the "Horns
of Hattin," the traditional site of the Sermon on
the Mount; and the plain of Hattin, where the
great battle was fought which crushed the Christian kingdom, on the fifth of July, 1187. The
battle ended with the capture of the King, the
murder of the Templars and Hospitallers who
were taken prisoners, and, as a natural consequence, the loss of Jerusalem. But the efforts of
the Crusaders were by no means ended here, as
many a bloody fray fought in the next hundred
and fifty years can testify. Nor must it be forgotten that there was another Christian King of
Jerusalem, when Frederick the Second, abandoned
by the Church, excommunicated by the Pope,
and attended only by his Teutonic knights,
marched up to the Church of the Holy Sepulchre,
and crowned himself where King Baldwin and
King Amaury had been crowned.

Between Mejdel and Tiberias is a little triangular plain covered with nebek trees, which was
pointed out to Arculf as the place where the five

thousand were fed. Later tradition places the spot on the brow of the hill between the Horns of Hattin and Tiberias (see John, vi. 3). Modern writers put the spot on the eastern side of the lake.

The ancient city of Tiberias occupied a much larger area than that occupied by Tabariyeh, as is proved by the ruins stretching southwards towards the hot springs, the temperature of which was observed to be 137·7 deg. at the time when Captain Wilson visited the place.

Kerak (Tarichaea) lies at the southern extremity of the lake; and commanding not only the end of the road along the western shore of the lake, but also the three bridges over Jordan, in its immediate vicinity, was once a place of considerable importance. Nothing now remains of the town except a heap of rubbish covered with broken pottery and fragments of sculpture. For the connection of the place with history, see Josephus (Wars, iii. 10, 1—6, and 9). The exploration of the eastern side of the lake was attended with difficulty, on account of the Bedawin being at the time at open war with the Turkish Government. After vainly endeavouring to get any assistance short of a guard of 100 soldiers from the Governor, the travellers determined to manage for themselves; and hiring one of the three boats which represent the modern fleet of Galilee, they made arrangements for walking along the shore, the boat coming daily to meet them with a tent and blankets at fixed points.

But the eastern side is by no means so full of interest as the western. The plain of Butiha was crossed, ruins being found at the Wady Daly, and again at a place called Kefr Argib (see the map). Just south of this is a curious oval mound, partly artificial, and built in two terraces, supported by loose stone walls.

On the left bank of the Wady Semakh are the ruins of Khersa, the ancient Gergesa (Matthew, viii. 28). The remains of the town are enclosed by a wall three feet thick. Among them is a large rectangular building, lying east and west.

"About a mile south of this, the hills, which everywhere else on the eastern side are recessed from a half to three-quarters of a mile from the water's edge, approach within forty feet of it; they do not terminate abruptly, but there is a steep, even slope, which we would identify with the 'steep place' down which the herd of swine ran violently into the sea, and so were choked. A few yards off is a small intermittent hot spring.

"That the meeting of our Lord with the two demoniacs took place on the eastern shore of the lake is plain from Matthew, ix. 1; and it is equally evident, on an examination of the ground, that there is only one place on that side where the herd of swine could have run down a steep place into the lake, the place mentioned above." The eastern coast has since been carefully examined by Mr. Macgregor in his canoe, and he

has come to exactly the same conclusion. A
difficulty has arisen with regard to this locality,
in consequence of the different readings in the
three Gospels. In Matthew, our Saviour is said
to have come into the country of the Gergesenes;
in Luke and John, into that of the Gadarenes.
The old MSS. do not give any assistance here;
but the similarity of the name Khersa to that of
Gergesa is, as Dr. Thompson points out in the
'Land and the Book,' a strong reason for believing that the reading of Matthew is correct;
and we have also the testimony of Eusebius and
Origen that a village called Gergesa once existed
on the borders of the lake. Perhaps the dis-
crepancy may be explained by supposing that
Gergesa was under the jurisdiction of Gadara.
There do not appear to be any rock-hewn tombs
near Khersa; but the demoniacs may possibly
have lived in one of those tombs built above-
ground, which have been noticed under the head
of Tel Hum, a form of tomb much more common
in Galilee than has been supposed."

The remains of Gamala are on a hill just up
the Wady Fik. Many portions of the wall still
stand, though the town is only a mass of ruins.
It was entirely destroyed by the Romans in that
cruel and sanguinary campaign by which the
conquerors endeavoured to strike such a terror,
once for all, into the country, as to prevent the
people from ever rising again. But the ruins of
a church prove that the place was occupied again,
doubtless in those quiet times after the revolt of

O

Bar Cochebas. The exploration of the lake and its neighbourhood terminated in a visit to Um Keis, the ancient Gadara, which had been formerly visited and described by Burckhardt and Dr. Porter. We subjoin Captain Wilson's own account:—

"On reaching the summit we found ourselves in front of the eastern theatre, the form of which is perfect, though the upper part has fallen down and covered the seats with stones. A few yards to the east of this is the large cemetery, which forms one of the most peculiar features of the place. There are both rock-hewn tombs and sarcophagi: the former are cut in the limestone, without any attempt at concealment. A flight of steps leads down to a small court, from which two or three doors give access to the tomb chambers; the doors are of stone, and many of them are still almost perfect. These tombs are now occupied by Fellahin, who bear rather a bad character, but we seemed to attract little attention. There are a large number of sarcophagi, ranged in two rows, one on either side of the great military road, which after passing through the city went eastwards. The sarcophagi are all of basalt; and the universal use of this material, which, though more enduring, does not take such a fine polish as the limestone on which they rest, can only be accounted for by a caprice of fashion. The best general view of the ruins is from the eastern theatre, from which the western and larger theatre is about three hundred yards distant. This building is in an almost perfect state of preservation, and were it not for a little rubbish on the floor we might imagine that the earthquake, which appears to have ruined the city, was an affair of yesterday. The seats, which are very comfortable, appear to have left the mason's hands but a few hours, so fresh and sharp are the mouldings. In the vaults of the passages and vomitories hardly a stone is out of place, and they are so wide and lofty that we rode through them with ease. The approach to the theatre must have been extremely grand, passing from the main street over a grand plat-form, on each side of which were columns with Corinthian capitals. The main street running east and west through the city can be easily followed. The basalt pavement is in places quite perfect, and retains traces of the marks of chariot wheels; along each side of the road lie a row of columns just as they fell."

And now, turning our backs upon the Sea of Galilee, for space presses, we must hasten on the southward journey. Zebulon, lying south of Naphtali and north of Issachar, stretched from the Mediterranean to the Lake of Gennesareth. We are still in a hilly country, though the hills are lower and the strips of plain more fertile than in its northern neighbour. As we go on, the ridges becoming less elevated and the plains still more raised, "we find at last," says Captain Anderson, "plain and ridge blending together in a plateau ending abruptly near Nazareth, where the range of hills forms the great natural step

O 2

leading to the great plain.   There is something
very striking in the position of Nazareth.   It is
completely shut in by hills which cluster round
it on all sides, and shelter it from the bleak winds.
The town is built principally on the slope of the
western hills; the houses, constructed of the white
limestone of the neighbourhood, are of dazzling
brightness in the sunlight. . . . . The Nazareth
hills have for the most part become rocky and
barren, and the effect is to make the little town
and basin of Nazareth appear more beautiful—a
lovely little spot shut in on all sides by dreary
and unprofitable hills.   And yet, in spite of the
beauty of the place, it had a very mean reputation
nineteen hundred years ago.   We hear the question put, 'Can any good thing come out of Nazareth?' and the very villagers spoke with a rude
and uncouth provincialism that marked them
at once as Nazarenes.   The hills of Nazareth,
although at one time under cultivation, are for
the most part neglected now."   As the scene of
our Saviour's childhood, Nazareth must ever
possess an overwhelming interest to all Christians.
And yet, as Dr. Porter points out, there was not
a single Christian in the place in the time of
Constantine, and no pilgrimages were paid to it
before the sixth century.

Mount Tabor is two hours' journey east of
Nazareth.   On it are the remains of a fortress
and modern Greek Church.   In the middle ages,
a tradition was set up that this was the scene of
the Transfiguration.

Descending from the Nazareth hills by a deep gorge, we find ourselves in the great plain of Esdraelon, twelve miles from north to south, and twenty-five miles from east to west. This large tract—the battle-field of Palestine—is an undulating expanse, mostly planted with corn, bounded on the west by the range of Carmel, on the south by the hills of Samaria, and on the east by Mounts Gilboa and Tabor. This is the "plain of Megiddo," where Barak conquered, and which was, perhaps, in the mind of the Apostle John when he spoke of "Armageddon." (See Judges, iv. 3—7; v. vi. 34; vii. 1; 1 Samuel, xxix. xxxi.; 1 Kings, xx. 26; 2 Kings, xiv. 17, &c., &c.) The modern inhabitants have forgotten both the old name and the Greek name of Esdraelon. They call it " Merj Ibn Amer."

On the way across the plain, after leaving Nazareth, the village of Fûleh is passed, where the French, under Napoleon, defeated the Turks, in April, 1799. The battle is known as the battle of Mount Tabor. This village is also the site of an old Crusader's castle, called Faba. Farther south, and at the western end of Gilboa, we come to a miserable little village of some twenty tottering houses, standing in a noble position overlooking the plain. Open the Bible, and read here how Ahab had a palace in Jezreel; for this is the spot on which we stand. But there is a yet more interesting history connected with this place; for here it was that Gideon's three hundred struck such a panic in the mighty hosts of the Midianites and Amalekites that they fell upon each other and routed themselves; and at our feet is the very spring where they drank the water, lapping it from their hands. And another scene we may recall. The army of the Philistines is upon the plain, and it is the last day but one of King Saul's life. He is at Jezreel. He puts · on other raiment to disguise himself, and taking two men only as companions, he goes by night to · Endor, where dwelt a woman who had a familiar spirit. Now, Endor lies at the back of the hill called Little Hermon—a little village where there are caves still inhabited by the people. It is six miles and a half from Jezreel; and the way by which the unhappy King crept round in the darkness, in his long and miserable expedition, may be traced step by step. And near here was Naboth's vineyard. But this old city, where so much might be looked for, is nothing but an immense heap of rubbish, covered with modern hovels. The search for Ahab's palace was quite hopeless, for not a vestige of any old building remains to be seen. Perhaps we may yet find traces by excavation. From Jezreel to El Lejjun, on the western side of the plain, camp was pitched by the waters of the ancient Megiddo, where Sisera lay encamped the night before his defeat by Barak.

After visiting Beisan, the ancient Bethshean or Scythopolis (1 Chronicles, vii. 29), where the dead bodies of Saul and his sons were hung up to the wall by the Philistines, the work on the plain of Esdraelon was completed. The water-shed which had been followed across it was lost unfortunately, after passing the summit of Gilboa, a district which has never yet been examined by any traveller.

In the continuation of the plain, a little to the westward, is the hill called Dotan, recognised as the site of Dothan, where Joseph's brethren were feeding their flocks when he went down there from Hebron. It is noticeable that there are to this day numerous cisterns still existing, hewn in the rock, into which he might have been dropped. These are shaped like a bottle with a narrow mouth, so that it would be impossible for any one ever placed in them to get out without assistance. Another story connected with Dothan is found in the victory of Elisha (2 Kings, vi. 8—23), when the Syrians were miraculously smitten with the "confusion of sight."

The way now led through a succession of narrow valleys, occasionally relieved by strips of plain, which are the chief characteristics of this the central portion of Manasseh's territory.

Nâblûs, the ancient Shechem, has been described by every traveller in Palestine. Situated in the most beautiful position possible, the modern town is also on the site of an overwhelming crowd of scriptural events. Mount Gerizim, "the Mountain of Blessing," is on its south; Mount Ebal, "the Mountain of Cursing," on the north. Its history begins 4,000 years ago, when as yet Jerusalem had no existence. To run through it seems like

running through the history of the Bible, from
Abraham to our Lord. Here is Jacob's Well, a
site accepted universally; here is the traditional
tomb of Joseph; here was the ancient temple of
the Samaritans; here where they annually kept
the Feast of the Passover; here where the Law
was read, Israel standing half over against Mount
Gerizim, and half over against Mount Ebel.

Captain Anderson conducted the excavations
at Gerizim, while Captain Wilson simultaneously
worked at Sebastiyeh (Samaria). The whole of
the mount was systematically explored, and the
octagonal building which stands in the centre of
the old temple enclosure was proved to be a
church, Captain Wilson thinks, of the date of
Justinian.

" Anderson," he says, " opened out the foundations of Justinian's church within the castle; in
many places but one or two courses of stone
are left. The church is octagonal, on the eastern
side an apse, on five sides small chapels, on one
a door; the eighth side too much destroyed to
make out, probably a sixth chapel. There was
an inner octagon, and the building without the
chapels must have been a miniature Dome of
the Rock. A few Roman coins were found.
The southern portion of the crest has been excavated in several places, but no trace of any large
foundations found. In an enclosure about four
feet from the Holy Rock of the Samaritans, a
great number of human remains were dug up,
but nothing to tell their age or nationality. We

have since filled in the place and covered them up again. The Amran says they are the bodies of those priests who were anointed with consecrated oil, but may more probably have been bodies purposely buried there to defile the temple, or rudely thrown in and covered up in time of war. An excavation was made at the 'twelve stones,' which appear to form portion of a massive foundation of unhewn stone."

Captain Anderson also effected a descent into Jacob's Well. He says:—" A chamber has been excavated to the depth of ten feet, and in the floor of the chamber was the mouth of a well, like the mouth of a bottle, and just wide enough to admit a man's body. We lowered a candle down the well, and found the air perfectly good; and after the usual amount of noise and talking, I was lashed with a good rope round my waist and a loop for my feet, and lowered through the mouth of the well by some trustworthy Arabs, directed by my friend Mr. Falscher, the Protestant missionary. The situation was novel and disagreeable. The numerous knots in the rope continued to tighten and creak; and after having passed through the narrow mouth, I found myself suspended in a cylindrical chamber, in shape and proportion not unlike the barrel of a gun. The twisting of the rope caused me to revolve as I was being lowered, which produced giddiness; and there was the additional unpleasantness of vibrating from side to side and touching the sides of the well. I suddenly heard the people from

the top shouting to tell me that I had reached
the bottom; so, when I began to recover, I found
myself lying on my back at the bottom of the well,
looking up at the mouth. The opening seemed
like a star. It was fortunate that I had been
securely lashed to the rope, as I had fainted
during the operation of lowering. The well is
75 ft. deep, 7 ft. 6 in. in diameter, and is lined
throughout with rough masonry, as it is dug
in alluvial soil. The bottom of the well was perfectly dry at that time of the year—the month of
May—and covered with loose stones. There was
a little pitcher lying at the bottom unbroken; and
this was an evidence of there being water in the
well at some seasons, as the pitcher would have
been broken had it fallen upon the stones. It is
probable that the well was very much deeper in
ancient times, for in ten years it had decreased
ten feet in depth. Every one visiting the well
throws stones down, for the satisfaction of hearing
them strike the bottom; and in this way, as well
as from the *débris* of the ruined church built on
the well in the fourth century, it has become filled
up to probably more than half of its original
depth."

After leaving Nâblûs, the reconnaissance survey
was extended to the valley of the Jordan, in
order to determine the confluence of the Zerka.
This done, the work of tracing the watershed was
proceeded with. Among other interesting places
visited were the sites of Shiloh and Ai. There
is very little to mark the site of the former, now

called Seilûn. A ruined mosque stands beside
an immense oak, and there is a curious.excavation
in the rock which may possibly have been the
"actual spot where the Ark rested, for its custo-
dians would naturally select a place sheltered
from the bleak winds that prevail in these highlands." About half a mile from the ruins are the
spring and well of Shiloh, which must have been
the spot where the daughters of Shiloh came out
to .dance when they were carried away by the
survivors of the tribe of Benjamin. In the neighbourhood of this spring are many rock-hewn
tombs, in which, according to Jewish tradition,
were laid the bodies of Eli and his sons. Nine
miles south of Shiloh lie the ruins of Bethel
(Beitin). This is but a heap of ruins. However,
on the hill adjoining and east of Bethel are the
remains of a fortified Christian church, and on a
hill-top east of the church, called by the Arabs
Et-Tel (the heap), is without any reasonable
doubt the site of Ai. "It corresponds exactly to
the description, when we know the site of Bethel
and the site of Abraham's encampment, where he
built an altar; for we read that he pitched his
camp having Bethel in the north and Hai in the
east. There is a valley behind the ruined heap
where Joshua placed his ambush. There is the
spot opposite, across the intervening valley, where
Joshua stood to give the preconcerted signal;
and there is the plain or ridge down which the
men of Ai hurried in pursuit of the retreating
Israelites, so that the men in ambush rose and

captured the city, and made it 'a heap' (or 'a Tel') for ever.   Mr. George Williams has pointed out that the word which is translated heap in our version exactly corresponds to the Arab rendering 'Tel.'"   (For an able paper on the site of Ai, see Captain Wilson in the "Quarterly Statement," First Series, p. 123.)

After passing Bethel, the land of Benjamin is traversed, where nothing is found but rocks, stones, ruined heaps, with low ranges of hills having nothing prominent to vary the scene. The great high road from Bethel to Jerusalem follows the line of the watershed; and on both sides valleys take their rise, and /become at once rocky ravines, descending precipitously on the left hand to the Jordan, and on the right hand more gradually to the Mediterranean.   And after three hours and a half from Bethel the last ridge was crossed, and the city of Jerusalem, half a mile distant, burst into view.

Such was the first expedition under Captains Wilson and Anderson.   We have passed by a large portion of their work, for fear of crowding these pages with detail.   Thus, we have said nothing of the work at Tibneh (Timnath), where the tombs were opened and examined; at Cæsarea, at Tantura, at Athlit, and Sebastiyeh.   Nor has anything been said about the valuable photographs brought home, with which many of our readers are acquainted.

Let us conclude this chapter by quoting the words of Captain Anderson.

"Our reconnaissance survey has embraced the western highlands down to this point; and the amount of work accomplished, compared with what remains to be done, is *as the seam of a coat to the whole garment.* The vast system of valleys east and west of the line we have followed, has still to be examined. There is not a hill-top on the ridges between them that does not contain the ruins of some ancient city; and the work that has been commenced should not cease till the topography of the whole of Palestine has been carefully worked out. The length of the Holy Land, from Dan to Beersheba, is only 140 miles, and its breadth 60 miles; and yet this small area, the theatre of the most engrossing portion of the world's history from the earliest time, still remains only partially explored. A knowledge of its topography is indispensable for an accurate comprehension of the varied scenes which are described, and without which the significance of the records must remain more or less obscure. . . . . . . The land is undergoing changes, the people are dying out or migrating, the old habits and customs are disappearing, and no time should be lost in completing this work before the levelling hand of civilization shall have effaced the relics of the past."

[NOTE.—It may be interesting to give a portion of the report drawn up by the President of the Society (the Archbishop of York), the Dean of Westminster, and Professor Owen. Short and concise as it is, it has been made still shorter to fit our scanty space.]

" The expedition was constantly employed in the country from December, 1865, to May, 1866, and its results may be briefly stated as follows :—

" 1. *Topography.*—By accurate observations for time and latitude, made at forty-nine separate points between Beyrout and Hebron, and by a line of azimuths carried through the country from Banias to Jerusalem, a series of detailed maps has been formed, on the scale of one mile to an inch (the scale of the English Ordnance Survey), of the whole backbone of the country, from north to south, including the Lake of Gennesareth and all the watercourses descending to its western shores.

" Two debated questions have been definitely settled : the confluence of the Jabbok (Wady Zerka) with the Jordan, and the course of the Wady Surar.

" 2. *Archæology.*—Materials have been collected for making about fifty plans, with detailed drawings, of churches, synagogues, mosques, temples, tombs, &c., amongst which are the plans of the cities of Beisan, Sebastiyeh, and Cæsarea ; of the Holy Place of the Samaritans, and the ruined Church of Justinian, on the summit of Mount Gerizim ; of ancient churches at Baalbek, Yarun, Sebastiyeh, Beitin, Birch, Cæsarea, Lydda, Beit Jibrin, Kuryet el Enab, and Jerusalem ; of seven Jewish synagogues ; of the Grand Mosque at Damascus, of a mosque at Nâblûs ; of temples at Deir el Kalah, Mejdel-Anjar, and Kedes, and of numerous tombs in various parts of the country.

" Inscriptions were found and copied at the Nahr el Kelb, Der el Kalah, Masi, Damascus, Tel Salhiyeh, Harran el Awamid, Banias, Kedes, Yarun, Nebartein, Kefr Birim, Kasyun, and Nâblûs ; several of these are new, two of them in the Hebrew character, and others in the Samaritan. Squeezes were taken of the most important, including the tablets of Sennacherib at Nahr el Kelb.

"The position of Chorazin at Kerazeh, a couple of miles north of Tel Hum—which had been indicated by the Rev. G. Williams in 1842—now seems to be fixed with tolerable certainty, by the presence of extensive remains, including those of a synagogue.

"The ancient system of irrigating the plain of Gennesareth can still be traced, and may help to throw light on the site of Capernaum. From the streams which descend the three wadys of Hammam, Rubadiyeh, and Amud, water was carried to the right and left by small aqueducts, and beyond these towards the north-east the plain was watered by the spring of Tabighah. The Round Fountain seems to have irrigated a comparatively small extent of ground between W. Rubadiyeh and W. Hammam, the aqueducts from both of which can be traced nearly up to their sources, the latter one being still in use. By carefully using the water derived from these sources the entire plain was perfectly irrigated, and from the richness of its soil must have been of great fertility. Neither Ain-et-Tin nor the Round Fountain answer to the account given by Josephus of the Fountain of Kepharnome; they are too small, and hardly come into the scheme of irrigation—the former not at all; but, supposing it to be Ain Tabighah, his allusion is at once explained by the copiousness of the supply, and the excavated channel through the rock above Khan Minyeh, by which the water was carried into the plain; the fertilizing powers of the fountain are still attested by the rank vegetation around the mills, more noticeable there than at any other point on the lake.

"Near the mouth of Wady Semakh, on the eastern shore of the lake, some ruins called Khersa were visited, possibly those of the ancient Gergasa, and between this and Wady Fik (opposite Tiberias) appears to have been the scene of the destruction of the herd of swine; indeed, no other point on that side of the lake is so suitable. From the eastern plateau the ground slopes steeply, in a few places almost precipitously, down to the level of the lake, leaving a margin of fertile land from half a mile to a mile broad between the base of the hills and the water; but at this particular point, and only at this, a spur runs out to the shore; there is no 'cliff,' but a slope sufficiently steep to fulfil the requirements of the Bible narrative.

" Excavations were made in three places in the mound of Tel Salhiyeh, apparently an Assyrian monument, near Damascus, during which the sculptured slab mentioned in Porter's ' Five Years in Damascus' was rediscovered. Owing to the badness of the weather it was not advisable to persevere with the exploration at that time; but it has been since resumed by Mr. Rogers, her Majesty's Consul at Damascus, to whom a sum of £50 has been voted by the Committee for that special object.

" Besides determining the general form of the authentic synagogues, the excavations made at Kedes confirm the conjecture that the supposed synagogue there was a Greek temple, of about the same age as those at Baalbek. At Jerusalem, the gate Gennath, so-called, was found to be of comparatively modern construction; and the continuation of the passage from the Bab el Burak of the Haram was discovered. The vault is of massive, well-built masonry, and there seems no reason to doubt that it is one of the original entrances to the Herodian Temple.

" On Mount Gerizim numerous excavations were made, under the direction of Lieut. Anderson. Within the ruin known as the ' Castle,' the foundations of an octagonal church were laid bare, probably the one known to have been built there by Justinian. On the eastern side of the church is an apse, on the northern side the main entrance, and on each of the others doors leading to small side chapels. In the interior are the piers of a smaller octagon, apparently intended to carry a dome. The church and castle were found to be built on a rough platform of large stones laid together without mortar, and of this—which may possibly be that on which the Samaritan Temple stood—the so-called 'twelve stones' form a portion. No trace of large foundations could be found on the southern portion of the small plateau on which the castle stands. Close to the Holy Rock of the Samaritans a number of human remains were dug up, but no clue could be obtained to their age or nationality.

"3. *Photographs.*—A series of photographs (9 by 6), 166 in number, have been taken, the majority for the first time. They comprise views of sites, details of architecture, inscriptions, &c., the Samaritan Pentateuch, and a few natural objects."

CHAPTER XI.

CAPTAIN WARREN'S COUNTRY WORK.—
I. PHILISTIA.

DURING the three years spent by Captain Warren in Palestine, his work was by no means confined to excavation in Jerusalem. By way of rest he was accustomed to take long and laborious journeys, accounts of which have appeared in different

MONUMENTAL SLAB.

numbers of the "Quarterly Statement," surveying, exploring, and sketching. In this volume it is impossible to give the results of the survey work, which belong to our future map. But in accordance with our design of narrating, as nearly as may be, all that we have done since our work first began, let us take up Captain Warren's work in the country. It will be seen that, although its importance has been eclipsed by his splendid work in Jerusalem, the contributions which he has made to geographical knowledge are neither few nor unimportant.

We begin with the first expedition in chronological order—that to the plain of Philistia in 1867. As much as possible, we follow Captain Warren's own words. The land of Philistia consists of an undulating plain 32 miles long and 9 to 16 broad, lying from 30 to 300 ft. above the level of the sea. To the east is found a series of, low spurs and undulating ground, culminating in hogs' backs, running nearly north and south, and rising in places 1,200 ft. above the ocean; to the east of these is a steep descent, of 500 ft. or so, to valleys which break through the barriers much in the same way as we find the rivers forming passes through the chalk hills between Aldershot and Chatham. To the east of these again, the hill country begins.

In the hill country the spurs, not more than one mile or so apart, are often separated by narrow ravines 1,500 to 2,000 ft. deep, at the bottom of which, in the rainy season, rapid torrents roll. Follow them into the plain, and see what becomes of them; but first look at the existing maps. In one they appear to traverse the plains in a different direction to what they do in the next. The fact is, the bulk of the water reaches the ocean underground; on coming into the plain

it forms marshes and pools, and quietly sinks
away, while the bed of the stream itself in the
plain is merely a narrow ditch some 6 ft. wide
and 4 ft. deep. You may leave the water at the
commencement of the wady mouth, ride over the
plain without seeing anything of it, and meet it
again welling out of the ground close to the sea-
shore, forming wide lagoons there. Now, if
proper precautions were taken, were the people
industrious, and the country cultivated and clothed
again with trees, the water flowing in the ravines
might be conducted over the plains in the early
summer months, and induce the rich soil to yield
a second crop.

Meantime, not only is this fertile soil neglected,
but its very existence is threatened by the slow
approach of that persistent enemy, the sand—
which is advancing step by step, and against
which no action whatever is being taken. The
method of progression is plainly visible. The
sand lies in a long ridge, with a windward slope
of 10 deg., and a slope on the north-east side of
30 deg.—that is to say, the natural slope of the
sand is 30 deg. When the wind blows the sand
over the ridge, little by little it slides down,
making a silent but steady advancement, inch by
inch, over the land it means to engulf.

It is curious in traversing these sandhills to
come upon the site of some orchard which has
been covered perhaps for hundreds of years.
You suddenly meet with a sort of crater in the
sand, 40 ft. deep, at the bottom of which flourishes

an apple tree; then you come upon a fig tree
growing in the same manner; and lastly upon a
little patch of ground, quite below the level of
the sand, with a house attached; but even this
patch of ground has several feet of sand over it.
The husbandman's chief duty appears to consist
in dragging up the sand in baskets from the
bottom of the craters to the surface. The trees
growing in these little hollows are very fruitful,
and no wonder, for they have no wind, plenty of
sun, and good moist earth to grow in; the super-
incumbent sand, being a non-conductor, prevents
evaporation from the soil below, and keeps it
moist through the summer.

One of the places which it was desirable to fix
was the site of the ancient Gerar, the city where
Isaac lived (Genesis, xxvi.). It had been identified
by Mr. Rowlands (see Williams, "Holy City," vol.
i., p. 464) with a place called Joorf el Gerar, the
Rapids of Gerar, where there are ancient ruins,
lying south-south-east of Gaza. Van de Velde
found Gerar in "Um el Jerar, at the foot of Tel
Jema in Wady el Adar, recognized by a few
scattered stones in the vicinity of some fine
springs."

Obviously, the thing to do was to go first to
Tel Jema. This was found to lie about eight
miles south of Gaza, in a position quite different
to that marked in Van de Velde. But where were
the "fine springs?" There were none. The Tel
itself is a mound like those at Jericho, artificial,
and covered with pottery and broken glass; no

doubt the site of some ancient stronghold. Water there was none, and the natives knew of no other ruins near except those of Tel Sheriah, a name which suggested Gerar to Robinson. So that Van de Velde is apparently mistaken, and Dr. Rowlands's site not yet rediscovered.

Gaza, a large and flourishing town of 15,000 inhabitants, is not, it is believed, on the exact site of the ancient Gaza, which stood nearer the sea, now three miles distant. They still, however, point out the traditional position of that gate which Samson carried off. Between the present city and the shore, wherever the ground has been turned over, hewn stones, fragments of wall, and innumerable pieces of pottery—the surest signs of an ancient city—have been found. Gaza, indeed, is one of the most ancient cities in the world. It was a city in the time of Abraham, and was a stronghold from that time until its final occupation by the Arabs.

The city of Ascalon is known to us chiefly in connection with Samson's exploit, told in Judges, xiv. 19. The city stands on the very shores of the Mediterranean, its walls having been built along the ridge of a rock, which follows a semi-circular course, sweeping round inland, in a sort of continuation of the cliffs along the shore—a very singular position. Like Gaza, it is an extremely ancient city, though its history has been of more importance since the Biblical periods than during them. It was here that that great battle was fought—the first of a long series, and the most brilliant—between the Crusaders and the Egyptians. It should have been followed up by the taking of the city, but jealousy on the part of Count Raymond prevented it; and for a long time Ascalon was a thorn in the side of the Christian kingdom. It was taken at last by Baldwin the Third. It was taken again at the fall of the kingdom, and retaken by Richard Cœur de Lion. Finally, its fortifications were destroyed by the Sultan Bibars, in the year 1270.

The city is four and twenty miles, as the crow flies, from the present ruin of Timnath, whence Samson came to plunder the thirty change of garments for the payment of those who had expounded his riddle. Though this is the only incident with regard to the whole city recorded in the Bible, yet it is impossible to visit these ruins at the present day without realizing—perhaps more than in any other ancient city west of Jordan—the utter overthrow of power that has taken place, the desolation which reigns supreme. The walls of indurated sandstone, though now of small-sized stones, were once formed of massive blocks, as is seen by the remains here and there that have not been cut down for other purposes, or carried away to Acca or Saida; great columns of granite 17 to 18 ft. in length, and 2 to 2½ ft. in diameter, project from the faces of the existing walls, used as thorough bonds, though hardly necessary it seems, for the intensely hard mortar has united the stones into one solid mass, which has only again been broken by some great force,

probably gunpowder. Examine these walls, great
discs of masonry overlapping each other in confusion, and it is apparent that they have been
overturned at no very remote period. Some of
these walls may have been built by the ladies of
England as an offering to their country and the
lion-hearted King during the Crusades.

"Gaza shall be forsaken," says the prophet
Zephaniah, "and Ashkelon a desolation: they
shall drive out Ashdod at the noonday, and
Ekron shall be rooted up." Ashdod, often
mentioned in the Old Testament, and once
a place of such power and importance that
it held out against Psammetichus, King of
Egypt (B.C. 630), for twenty-nine years, is now
a mean Mohammedan village, with no signs
of its former greatness. The villages round it
are all alike, and all void of interest. At El
Tasar a marble column and effaced capitol were
seen, and at Summeil a few bevelled stones. All
this time, of course, the survey work was going on.
Remains of a castle were found at Kerdua, five
miles south of Tel es Safiyeh, the Blanche Garde
of the Crusaders. And at Deir Dubân were
found great caves, in one of which were several
inscriptions in Syriac, said by the Syrian Bishop
of Jerusalem to be the work of Christians who
went there from the Holy City at the time of the
Persian invasion. Captain Warren here makes a
suggestion as to the position of the Cave of
Makkedah, where the five kings took refuge
when pursued by Joshua (x. 5).

"We have (Joshua, xv. 41) the towns 'Gederoth, Bethdagon, and Naameh, and Makkedah' placed together; and we have at the present day, Kutrah and Mughâr close together, Naameh six miles north-east, and Beit Dejan about twelve miles to north. I have to suggest that the village of El Mughâr (the cave) is the modern name of the ancient Makkedah, and the desirability of making further researches at this place. It is true that several authorities place Makkedah farther to the south of this point by several miles, but the writer of the article 'Makkedah,' Smith's 'Dictionary of the Bible,' appears to establish the fact that it must have been situate at no great distance from Ramleh, and El Mughâr is less than eight miles from that city."

From Tel es Safîyeh to Yebneh; thence to Jaffa; thence back to Ekron (now called Akir), where there is not a single trace left of its former greatness. It is, however, interesting in connection with the history of the Ark (see 1 Samuel, v. 10, 12; vi.)

"The village of Sùrah, the ancient Zoreb," says Captain Warren, "stands about 1,150 ft. above the sea, and is situated on the southern end of the hill crest overlooking the valley of the same name. On the opposite side of the valley, low down, is the ruin of Ain Shems (the ancient Bethshemesh), and from our stand-point it is easy to see the line which the milch kine would have taken in coming up from Ekron, and also the valley which the men would have ascended in carrying the ark up to Kirjath-jearim. Looking across the valley to the opposite crest, we can see the ruin of the Tibneh (the ancient Timnath), where dwelt Samson's betrothed.   It is 740 ft. above the sea, and therefore not in the plains, as some writers have stated.   Samson, in going down to it, would descend 700 ft. into the valley, and then ascend again 350 ft. to Timnath.   It is apparent from the sacred narrative, Judges, xv., that the corn was growing in the valley, as it does at present, with the vineyards and olives lining the sides of the hills; for we are told that the Philistines *came up* to Timnath, and burnt Samson's wife and her father with fire."

The rest of the journey among the villages and ruins of the plain may be followed in Captain Warren's own account, published in the "Quarterly Statement" of April, 1871.   The latitudes and longitudes are given in that of October, 1871.

EAST OF JORDAN.

East of the Jordan no survey work of any importance had ever been attempted before Captain Warren visited it.   Other travellers had ridden across the country (Dr. Porter, Dr. Tristram, Burckhardt, &c.), and have described some of the ruins which remain; but a systematic survey of any portion had not been thought of.   In the eyes of the Palestine Exploration Fund, this whole country now belongs to America; for the survey of east of Jordan, including Moab, will be

undertaken by them. It is well here to reiterate
· our previous caution. *Nothing is useful, for Biblical purposes, but a scientific exploration.* Let not
the reader imagine that a private expedition can
accomplish anything of lasting importance. Some
additions it may make to our geographical knowledge, some illustrations of ruins; but what is
gained in this way is lost in another, for the
cupidity of the natives is aroused, prices are
raised, jealousy excited. It is very greatly to be
hoped that, just as the English reader is asked to
help our own work, not by exploring himself,
but by giving us money to explore by means of
scientific agents on a well-defined plan, so he may
help the Americans by not encouraging small
expeditions into that tempting country east of
the Jordan, where so many treasures lie hidden.
These little forays into a dangerous district are
like dashes into an enemy's country. They result
in a small amount of plunder, and each one
makes the next more difficult and costly;—unless,
indeed, like Professor Palmer and Mr. Tyrwhitt
Drake, travellers are prepared to travel without
escort, or servants, or baggage, to "mess" with
the people, to do everything for themselves, and
to talk their language as the Bedawin talk it.

Captain Warren's journey was made in July,
1867. The work he accomplished was a reconnaissance survey of all the country passed over;
the taking of a great many photographs of the
old cities of Rabbath Ammon, Jerash, Ramoth
Gilead, and others; observations of latitude and

longitude in fourteen places; and a long list of
350 names, of which 84 agree nearly with 84 out
of the 135 taken by Dr. Robinson. He observed
the proofs, in the pointed arches lying in older
work, that a domesticated people lived here long
after the fall of the Roman Empire, and that it
is but a short time since the Bedawin held sway.

As for the ruins, they are everywhere. At a
hill known as Tamak, for instance, Captain
Warren says:—

"Here are columns, pedestals, and capitals
lumbering the ground, and no idea of the ground
plan of the temples or public buildings of which
they formed part could be obtained during the
short time we were able to examine them.

"Some of the capitals are Corinthian; there are
a great many pilasters about, and the pedestals
appear to be peculiar to this country.

"We had now arrived in a very remarkable
piece of country. Over a tract four miles square
there is a never-ending succession of ruins. On
each spur there appears to have been a village,
on each hill-top a temple or public building. In
one square mile I have shown six of these on the
plan; but I could not put a fifth of them in, they
seemed to turn up in every direction. This tract
appears to have been more like one large town
than anything else, and yet there is at present
very little water here. It is, however, a portion
which most decidedly merits a more lengthened
visit than I was able to afford it, for in names
alone it is most rich."

It is no use attempting to describe the route taken, because no map exists which gives the names mentioned in Captain Warren's journals, and the wadies, even in Van de Velde, appear to be all incorrectly laid down; so that the course as described in the journals is impossible, if read with an eye to the map. This is another proof of the necessity of making a survey of the whole country. The ruins, again, want the most careful examination, with excavations in likely spots. The country is rich in materials for illustration of the Bible, and cries aloud for examination. May it be but a very short time before the reproach of indifference is entirely removed from us, and the perfect map of the Holy Land be given to the world!

UP THE JORDAN.

This journey was undertaken in February, 1868, in company with Dr. Chaplin, of Jerusalem, and a small party. It consisted of a ride up the left and down the right bank of the river, a journey never before accomplished. Geographical observations were taken during the expedition. On returning, the party visited Callirhoë, the hot springs of the Dead Sea, and proposed to go on to Kerak in Moab, but were prevented from doing so by the illness and subsequent death of one of the party.

The account sent home by Captain Warren was printed before the publication of the first

"Quarterly," and had but a very small circulation. We therefore reproduce it, so far as our limits will allow, verbatim. The reader should accompany the account with the best map at his command:—

"The weather at Jerusalem and throughout the country had been very severe, and we heard that the communication (by boat) across the Jordan had been broken, but Goblan assured us that such was not the case, and insisted that he 'had crossed by the boat on the previous day. We accordingly made our preparations, and moved down to Ain-es-Sultan on 24th February, 1868. This place is supposed to be the site of the ancient Jericho and Elisha's Fountain (2 Kings, ii. 19); it is about 600 ft. below the Mediterranean, and 700 ft. above the Dead Sea. Here we remained two days starting the excavations. The weather was very cold at this time, the wind from the north seemed fresh from the snows of Lebanon, and at night the thermometer fell to the freezing point; at mid-day, however, when the wind dropped, the heat was felt.

"On 26th February, we started for the ford at Damieh, twenty-three miles distant, on the direct road from Nâblûs to es-Salt. The weather was chilly, and we wore our overcoats; but the country was green everywhere, and flowers of every hue lay in our path. Passing Kurn Surtabeh and over Wady Ferrah, we arrived at dusk at the ford of Damieh, and camped half-way up the bank separating the upper and lower plains of the Jordan, where we found a small space which was not quite covered with shrubs. We had a fine view of the Jordan from this spot: the country one mass of green, and down below us the lower Jordan plain—a great flat, covered with an early crop of corn, with here and there branches of the overflowing Jordan meandering through it. We thought little of these floods, and discussed our crossing in the morning.

"At daybreak, 27th, we hurried down to the water, and to our dismay found that the rope had been broken by the wood brought down by the floods, and the ferry-boat itself lay stuck in the mud some yards from its proper place. This ferry had been established about six months. The boat is in shape like a decked launch; it is about twenty feet long, and eight feet wide, and is eminently unfitted for the work required of it. A thick rope is fastened across the river, and to this are attached the bows of the boat, and it is hauled across by lugging in the rope. This boat was made on the Jordan, but it has a keel instead of a flat bottom, and drawing nearly as many feet of water as it has beam, it is most unsafe for passing over animals; also there is a bulwark of about two feet in height round the deck, and no means of letting it down, and as there are no steps up or down to the boat, horses have generally to be hauled in by the legs if they will not jump; when the Jordan is at its full, the bulwarks of the boat are four feet above the bank, and when the Jordan is low there is a drop of six feet or more into the boat.

"This boat, however, bad as it was, was our only means of crossing the Jordan; for during the floods it was quite unsafe to attempt to swim. The water was running like a mill race, quite sixty yards in width. Goblan commenced his blarney with us, and we spent the whole day in making plans for getting the rope stretched across. Each hour they said the flood would go down, and each hour it appeared to rise. We were told that men were coming down from Nâblûs to put things to rights, but we

Q

could hear nothing for certain; and as it was impossible
to cross without the boat, we had the alternative either to
go back or to try and go along the western bank of the
Jordan to the north. This latter was an unknown route:
we could not hear that it had ever been traversed by Euro-
peans. We sent for the Sheikh of the Mesa'ad Arabs, who
camp on Wady Ferrah, and entered into an agreement
with him to escort us round by Jisr Mejamia for five
pounds sterling. He arranged to meet us next morning
and take us on. Unfortunately, Goblan got leave to go
and sup with the sheikh that evening, and a little plot
against us was the result. During the night we had a
storm of wind and rain, so violent that for a portion of the
night we were outside the tents keeping them up; in the
middle of it all our horses were driven past us, but we
thought it was only to get shelter under the hill-side.

"In the morning (28th) we got all ready to start at sunrise; but something was evidently wrong, and soon the
muleteer came up to say that four horses and a mule were
absent. After searching for them for an hour, we came
to the conclusion that Goblan had stolen them in order
to prevent our leaving the ford. We told him so; upon
which he struck his breast, and talked about his honour
being wounded. Goblan is not a pleasant-looking gentleman. He has a great sabre wound down one cheek and
on one wrist, but these he keeps concealed: he never
shows more than his nose and two eyes—one of the latter
is a revolving light; he is very dark, and his eyes are
bloodshot. He is quiet and gentle so long as he is not
roused.

"On the east banks of the Jordan were the tents of Mustafa Aga, the Government nominee over the lower Ghor;
but we had no means of telling him of our mishap. We

therefore wrote a letter to the Governor of Nâblûs, telling him that Goblan had stolen our horses, and asking for assistance. We had great difficulty in sending this letter, as the people insisted that the ford was not under the Governor of Nâblûs, and would not see that Mustafa Aga, being cut off from us, was as far as if he had been sixty miles away. Eventually we got the letter off, and then insisted that all our luggage should be mounted on the remaining animals. The head muleteer was in a frenzy about it, but nothing could induce us to believe that he was not aware of his beasts having been driven away; and our only consolation was that he had to give up his mule for the baggage and walk himself. We were so overloaded that the muleteers could not find room to stow everything away, and one of them had an iron fireplace mounted on his back for the first hour. We started off to meet our escort, the Sheikh of the Mesa'ad. He looked rather sheepish on coming up to us, and said he supposed we understood that he wanted five pounds a-day. Of course we did not understand anything of the sort, and told him we would go without him. Dr. Chaplin told Goblan he had acted infamously towards us, but he only struck his breast in reply, and affected to be more aggrieved than any of us. We then started off north by ourselves, trusting to fortune. Goblan rode after us, and tried to dissuade us from it, but to no purpose; and for a long time after, we saw him, motionless, gazing after us and meditating over his next move, for we told him we should hold him responsible for any mishap that might befall us.

"We left Makrûd at 11 a.m., all our baggage being packed on six mules and three donkeys, which before had required nine mules; but the animals were very much overweighted, and delayed us a good deal. We had to keep round them, in skirmishing order, for fear of an attack from the Mesa'ad Arabs. At noon the Jordan valley gradually began to close in, the west upper plain being about a mile and a quarter wide; the plain began to be much cut up with wadies, and we were very anxious to keep our baggage together. We soon came upon a Bedawin encampment, and the dragoman was sent in with the soldier to say that the sheikh must come and escort us during the day, as we were in haste. He came out in a flurry, and travelled with us the whole day. Great was his astonishment, on leaving, to receive a present. The idea of travellers coming by such a road never entered his head, and he thought we were a Government party travelling by a short cut to Tiberias.

"On our right we saw Jebel Ajlûn, covered with snow. After passing several wadies, of which the names are shown on the sketch, we found at 3 p.m. that the whole Jordan valley just here was less than two miles wide. Our path now led over the hills, but we could see that farther north the hills come close down to the Jordan banks, the river passing through a gorge. We were ascending for some hours, and quite losing sight of the Jordan, the country being much broken up with ravines.

"At 5 p.m. we found ourselves overlooking the Jordan again, and about a mile and a half from it ; to our north, a great plain extending for several miles—the plain of Beisan ; we could see Beisan in the distance, and, scattered over the plain (the upper Jordan plain) were innumerable mounds and ruins. We descended, crossing Wady Malih after its junction with W. Shûk, the water flowing in a copious stream.

"After traversing the plain to the N.W., we arrived at Tel Humah at 6.30 p.m., where was a Bedawin camp clustered round a spring of delicious water. Just before we arrived at the Tel we heard firing behind us, and, on going back to see what was the matter, we found our missing beasts coming up. Goblan, having failed to keep us, evidently thought it better to send them on, and the muleteers were firing away for joy at not having another day's walking before them.

"The Bedawin at this camp received us kindly, and wanted us to feed with them. We declined, although it was some hours before our dinner could be got ready; in the meantime we made what examination of Tel Humah we were able to do in the dark, and concluded that it was an artificial ruin. Late in the evening the sheikh of the camp came to pay us a visit; he seemed to fear that, if rains continued, the corn crop would be damaged by a worm eating at the roots.

"At sunrise, on 29th February, we were off to east to visit Ain Sukût; a beautiful morning, the clouds hanging over the Jordan, thermometer at 5 a.m., 36° Fah. We visited the hot spring at Ain Sukût—air 52°, water 79° 9'; left at 8.30 a.m., passed Ain Helweh to west of Sukût; and at 9.25 another hot spring, a mile and a half from Tel Humah, water 78°.

" 9.35 a.m.—Passed the site of an old city, near Tel Sheikh Saleh. Here we bade farewell to our yesterday's escort, giving him four dollars for his aid; he left us delighted. We kept on towards Beisan, now and then going out of the way to examine Tels and springs. This plain is wonderfully well supplied with water; the Tels we passed are shown on the sketch. Arrived at Beisan at noon; much disappointed in the ruins, but the abundance of water made the country delightful; we examined the bevelled stones in the khan on the northern side of the

stream, and declined visiting some tombs on account of
our being separated from our baggage.   Leaving Beisan
at 1.45 p.m., we passed over the hills into the plain, which
again is narrow.   At 3.5 p.m. passed Wady Shûhabeh, a
rivulet with water; and, cantering on, arrived at our camp
to west of Jisr Mejamia at 4 p.m.   Here was another
Bedawin encampment, the people of which appeared very
curious about us.   We started off at once to visit Kaukab,
but our guide would not follow us, and at sunset we found
ourselves alone close to the ruined castle; the view is
magnificent, reaching for miles in every direction.   Kaukab
will be an important point when the trigonometrical survey
of Palestine is commenced.   No observations were taken
on this journey, except with the prismatic compass; my
object being to select points for a survey at some future
period.

"We paid the sheikh for Saturday's work four dollars.
On Monday, 3rd March, we started off for the bridge
Mejamia.   Something was wrong again, and our mules
were delayed; but at 8 a.m. we were all assembled at the
bridge.   Our new sheikh, however, refused to cross, saying
he had a quarrel with the tribe on the other side, and left
us under the protection of a man with a stick.   The bridge
Mejamia has one large pointed arch and three small ones;
it is in good preservation.   After passing the bridge our
guide seemed to lose all confidence in his stick, and eventually disappeared, and we were again alone.

"After passing some ruins we came upon a very large
Bedawin camp.   We sent in the dragoman and the soldier
to ask for a guide, and soon there issued out five strapping
big Bedawin, armed with spears, commanded by a noble-
looking sheikh, armed with a handsome sabre, silver
mounted.   The sheikh said he was an emir, and called

himself a very great man. The Bedawin of these parts
are all mounted. The sheikh is the finest specimen of a
Bedawin I have yet seen. The poor fellow had a gunshot
wound in his leg, which had been open for years, and he
was very anxious to obtain advice about it, but quite
refused to come up to Jerusalem to have it looked at. We
explained to him that we did not wish him to attend us,
that we only wanted one man with a spear, but he insisted
on coming. The country we passed through was delightful, but the wind had changed to the south, and we felt it
very hot. We lunched at Fahil, perhaps the ancient Pella,
where there is much water and cultivated lands.

"About 4 p.m. our party began to get uneasy, and soon
we saw rushing down upon us a troop of Bedawin, armed
all with spears. We had nothing to do but try and look
as if we thought it great fun. They came dashing up,
with their spears lifted on high, until a few yards from us,
and then one rode out and gave us a salaam. It proved to
be Sheikh Arabeh, the government nominee of Jerash, who
had come down with fifteen men to look after us, sent by
Mustafa Aga. After looking askance at each other for
some minutes, our two parties coalesced and became
friendly. This Sheikh Arabeh is uncle or cousin to Shiekh
Dieb, the former independent head of the Adwans.
Arabeh turned against his family and tribe, and led the
Turkish army during the summer of 1867 into all their
strongholds, and pointed out the granaries. For his
treachery he was rewarded with the government command
of the hill country about es-Salt; but the Bedawin would
have nothing to say to him, and still call Dieb's son and
Goblan their heads.

"At sunset we had got as far down as Tel Salahat, where
we camped; here are trees and cultivation, and it would

have been very pleasant but for the quantities of scorpions under every stone. We gave our parties a couple of sheep for their food, and they seemed well satisfied. In the morning I gave the great sheikh five dollars, all in silver. He said nothing, but complained to Dr. Chaplin that he was a very great man, and had been insulted—that he expected several pieces of gold; that he had only been half a day with De Saulcy, who had given him two rifles and thirty napoleons, and so on. We believed a little of what he said; but it was suggested that such a great man could not think of taking anything, and that the silver was for his followers. We found now that we were in the narrowest part of the Jordan valley, the hills reaching down to the river, and the plains together not being more than half a mile in width. Down towards Tel es-Sa'idiyeh we saw the ground cultivated to the water's edge. At 10 a.m. we passed over the bridge and ruin of Ferjaris. The bridge was apparently an aqueduct. There are four pointed arches. At 10.15 a.m. the Jordan valley opened out into the Zerka plain, and we saw before us the wely of Abu Obeideh and the many Tels surrounding it.

"We now saw the great sheikh and his men dodging about in the underwood, and we expected an attempt to secure some of our baggage. We left the soldier always in the rear to look after it. Sheikh Arabeh now tried to persuade us to go up to Jerash with him; failing in that, he said we must go and stop with Mustafa Aga, who was making ready for us; finding us unwilling to do that, he insisted that we could not reach Damieh that night. And soon our mules began to wander about wildly, evidently getting sly kicks from the Bedawin. We pushed on through the cultivated and irrigated land between the Rajib and Zerka; at noon we reached the point where the

Zerka emerges from the hills. We had to pass through a hole in the rock, and then crossed the Zerka, which was here a foaming torrent. As we pushed on, Arabeh still insisted we could not get to Damieh that night, and then we saw he had some object in getting us to wait. About 1 p.m. we arrived at the open plain, south of the Zerka, and were now told that Mustafa Aga was coming to meet us. Looking out, we saw in the distance two troops of Bedawin coming towards us from different quarters full speed; they seemed to consist of about twenty men each. Full gallop they came; one had a little the advantage of the other and reached us first. Suddenly reining in their horses, as they reached us, the chief rode out—a dark-looking, cunning little man, with a beautiful blue abba embroidered with silver lace, his horse's appointments being covered with small silver coins. It was Mustafa Aga. We had hardly time to salute him when the other party came charging up; our old friend Goblan and company. It was a curious sight to see the two meet—the government head and the outlaw chief. Goblan for once looked quite dignified and haughty when he distantly returned Aga's salutation. The parties were equal, and it would not have been etiquette to have quarrelled before us; so the respective suites kept together, while the chiefs came out and tried each in his way to get our ear.

"Then arose a difficulty: each of these chiefs wanted to take us down the Ghor. We soon disposed of Arabeh, and it remained between the Aga and Goblan. No doubt it was the Aga's duty to take us, and yet he did not know the road and dared not venture beyond his post; in fact, we suspected that he would have been glad to escort us as an excuse for visiting the country. On the other hand,

Goblan was only a nominal sheikh, and his only hold on his tribe was their ancient fear. After weighing the matter over, we concluded that the Aga would be more expensive than Goblan, that we should be sure to lose our road and our baggage with him, and that Goblan would be preferable. Accordingly, we thanked Mustafa Aga for his courtesy, and told him that we had our own government soldiers, and did not require more, and that Goblan would probably go with us; and then we parted. We thought that the lesson Goblan had learnt about stealing the beasts would keep him from such deeds next time he was tempted. And after all, Goblan, in spite of his stealing our mules, and other faults, is as good a specimen of an old rascal as can be met with in these degenerate days of Bedawin.

"We arrived at Damieh at dusk, and camped close to the ferry boat, which was now plying across whenever wanted, the rope having been repaired. We now raised the question whether we should return to Jerusalem or not, and it was decided that we should go on.

"The ford at Damieh is just below the junction of the Zerka and Jordan. The Zerka, soon after it emerges from the hills, flows through the lower plain of the Jordan, which is sometimes on either side of it half a mile wide.

"Next day (4th March) up early and rode along the east bank of the Jordan until we reached Nimrin. Stopped here three hours, and then, crossing the old Roman road from Amman to Jerusalem, arrived at Ain Suwaimeh (a distance of thirty miles) at sunset; here we encamped. On our way we had met with several impediments; Goblan wishing us to stop at his camp near Nimrin. We, however, paid his camp a visit, and made the acquaintance of his wife and family. Ain Suwaimeh is close to the Dead

Sea. We feund it very hot here, and were glad to start early next morning for Zerka-Main.

"5th March.—Our path first led along the north-east end of the Dead Sea over blocks of sandstone and trap. We left at 8.5 a.m.; 9 a.m. passed Wady Ghuweir (stream of water); and at 9.25 arrived at Wady Menshallah, which is the name for a mass of wadies. Here we commenced our ascent. The path lay in the eyes of the Bedawin, and the steepness was very great. In one hour we had arrived at 1,450 ft. above the level of the Dead Sea, and at 11 a.m. got into the large Wady Menshallah. We now ascended more gently, and eventually arrived at a broken plain, with hills rising in front of us to the east, on the top of which is the ruin of Mineyeh. On our right was a cleft in the rock 200 ft. deep, and the bottom crowded with palm trees. The scenery was wild in the extreme. At noon we arrived at Wady Hamara, where there is a little water springing from the rocks. Here we encamped.

"We were now again in an unknown country which had not been visited for ages.

"In the afternoon we started for the Wady Zerka Main, which we understood had not been visited since Irby and Mangles were there in 1817. Our path lay over ravines and rocks for an hour, when we suddenly came upon the Zerka Main. The view was startling. A steep ravine, more than a thousand feet deep, the sides of the most varied hues — black, blue, scarlet, and yellow, every coloured sandstones; and at the bottom a stream winding among the palms and green shrubs; outside the ravine everything blue, and cold, and desolate. It took us only a short time to descend. At about one hundred feet from the bottom of the wady we came upon the hot spring, scalding water issuing from a cleft in the rock, and then disappearing again to come out at the bottom of the wady, and mingle with a cold spring which issues from a point a few yards more to the east. Going down the wady about two hundred yards from the junction of the hot and cold springs, the water was still too hot for the body to bear—167° Fahrenheit; at the point where it issues from the ground it must be near boiling—but our thermometers would not read so high. We looked about for the wonderful plant with pods spoken of by Josephus, but we could only find the young plants, the pods being about six inches to one foot long. The plant was, however, in flower, and the colour would fully justify his description of their looking like flames.

"We found a good deal of yellow stuff about the water, looking like sulphur, but none has been traced in it. The water tasted pure enough.

"These are the hot springs of Callirhoë, where Herod is supposed to have taken baths.

"It took us one hour and twenty minutes to ascend; the Bedawin in great wonder at our going down to such a place merely to come up again.

* * * * * *

"The valley of the Jordan has been described completely in many works, but it may be desirable to offer a few remarks on the subject. From the sea of Tiberias to the Dead Sea there is one deep depression, the hills from east and west nearly meeting in many places, but never joining. This depression is filled up to a certain level with an alluvial deposit, forming a vast plain called the Jordan valley or Ghôr (pronounced Rôr). This is the 'upper plain.' It varies in width, from one mile to twelve, and has a slope from Tiberias to the Dead Sea of about 600 ft. in the 60 miles.

"This plain, however, has not alone this southerly slope; it has also a slope from its lateral extremities to the line of its centre of about 5°, forming a very open V in section, at the lowest part of which runs the Jordan. The Jordan has cut out for itself a still lower plain—lower than the preceding by some 50 to 100 ft., and from a quarter to one mile wide. This is the 'lower plain.' Being itself only sixty yards wide, the river does not occupy the whole of this lower plain, but twists about in it, winding from side to side, and each day increasing the plain in width by undermining the banks on either side.

" The lower plain is inundated whenever there is a more than ordinary fall of rain in the hill country in the spring time.

"The banks between the upper and lower plain are not regular ; they are fretted away by the fervid sun, the strong winds and heavy rains, and are very ragged; in parts they are, during the rainy season, covered with the most beautiful verdure. In the lower portion of the Jordan valley the banks where the streams join the Jordan (Wadies Enwaimeh, Fasail, Kelt, and others) are broken up for miles, presenting a most curious appearance, forming, not a system of hills, but a system of valleys, the original plain being left standing every here and there, isolated and forlorn. At first sight it would appear impossible that such small streams could perform such a work; but it is the sun, wind, and rain completing what these small streams have begun ; and now there are to be seen these little streams, at best not three feet deep and six feet wide, winding through lofty banks, nearly 100 ft. high, whose irregularities exist perhaps a mile from the stream itself.

"The plains of the Jordan are only sterile at the

southern end for a few miles north of the Dead Sea, and
that only on the western side.   North of the Aujeh—that
is, about ten miles north of the Dead Sea, the soil is not
salt and will bear plentifully, provided there is water ;
so much so, that during the rainy season the Jordan plains
for miles are vast meadows abounding in grasses and
flowers.   Those who see the country after the sun has
burnt up all this pasturage may very well be led into the
idea that nothing will grow there, for when the hot winds
spring up in May the grasses, like tinder, are broken up
and blown away, and nothing remains but a barren waste.

"During January, February, and part of March, flocks
are brought down from the mountains to feed on the rich
pasturage of the plains ; they come down within a mile of
the Jordan."

LEBANON.

This journey was undertaken in July, 1869,
with a double object—first to recruit the health
of the party, who were all more or less worn out
with the hard work of the Jerusalem excavations,
and next to make an examination of the temples
and ruins of Cœle Syria.   The full journal of the
expedition, called "Our Summer in Lebanon,"
with detailed descriptions of the temples, was
found in the "Quarterly Statement" for April,
1870 (No. 5, First Series).   All the temples were
sketched and measured, and the drawings—two
of which were selected for publication—were sent
home.   Our limits do not allow us to quote any
portion of the journal.

The region of Cœle Syria, now called the Bukâ'a,

lies between the ranges of the Lebanon and the Anti-Lebanon. It is a great fertile plain, enclosed by hills, to which the inhabitants could retire for safety when attacked. The inhabitants of this district have from all time been under the influence of strange religious ideas. The worship of the sun lingered here long after it had died out everywhere else, and it was not till the year 420 that they gave up this idolatry, at the instigation of Simeon Stylites, and in the hope of being rid of wild beasts as a reward. It was at this date that the sun temples were destroyed. Later on, we find there the servants of the Sheikh of the Mountain (Assassins), "faithful to one another," says Benjamin of Tudela, "by the command of their old man." They, too, embraced that strange and wild religion of which the madman, Caliph Hakeem, was in some way the founder, and which still lingers in the sect of the Druses. At present, besides the Druses, Captain Warren tells us there are two sects of Moslems, several of Christians, and two sects of which very little is known. The old idea that Mount Hermon was a peculiarly sacred place to which the temples were turned, as to a *Kibleh*, is disproved by Captain Warren's examinations. First, the temples do not turn towards Hermon, but to the east; and, secondly, Hermon is not the site of a great preponderance of temples. They are not built on the summits of hills, nor on the plains; but generally, as if for the uses of the towns, on the hill-sides where the towns were built. Many of

them were examined, but only two have evidence
of having been used as Christian churches.   The
architecture is generally late Roman, and what
inscriptions were found were in Greek.

There is one peculiarity about some of these
temples which appears to distinguish them from
those of Europe.   They are mounted on stylo-
bates, and have no steps or staircase up to the
entrance, and the only method of entering is by
a small door opening from the side of the stylobate into the vaults underneath, and thence by
some means into the temple itself.   From this it
would appear, either that only the priests went
into the temple, or else that there was some
temporary wooden staircase up into the stylobate.

The small temples about Hermon appear to
be somewhat of more ancient date than those in
the Bukâ'a; they are of the Ionic order, and are
in antis.   They in some cases differ from the pure
Grecian style, in having similar designs on the
square capitals of the *antæ* to what there are on
those of the columns.   The friezes also bulge in
all; there are no dentals on the cornice nor
ornaments on the frieze; the *antæ* diminish in
width from bottom to top.

It would be interesting to collect the traditions
floating about among this people.   One of them
is given by Captain Warren.   "On our way," he
says, "we met a countryman, of whom I asked
some questions about ruins to south.   He said
there was only Nimrûd (described by De Saulcy).
On asking who Nimrûd was, he said he had been

a great man who used to shoot up in the air with blood-tipped arrows, and when they came down again he would show the blood on the ends, and say that he had wounded the gods. This provoked the gods, and they sent a mosquito, which ate up his nose and got into his brain, and he died in great pain."

Part of this legend is very similar to that given to Layard, at Nineveh. It seems odd in this nineteenth century to hear a man talking about "the gods."

But the collection of legends and traditions is a work of great time, and demands not only familiarity with the language, but also familiarity with the people. Captain Burton has done good service by his collection of Syrian proverbs, published in "Unexplored Syria," vol. i., p. 263, a valuable illustration of the mind of the people; but the collection of legends and traditions in Syria has hardly yet been even begun.

From the description given by Captain Warren of these temples, we make one selection only, which will be sufficient to show the architect the character of these monuments. We take that of Thelthatha, called also Neby Sufa :—

"A small village lying on the east side of the range separating the Hâsbâny from the Litâny. A few feet above the village is the site of the temple, whence can be seen a great portion of the Hermon range.

"The temple lies east and west, the entrance towards the east; the site bears due east (90°) by the compass,

R

TEMPLE OF THELTHATHA (تلثاثا) CALLED ALSO NEBY SÛFA. SCALE ⅟₅₀

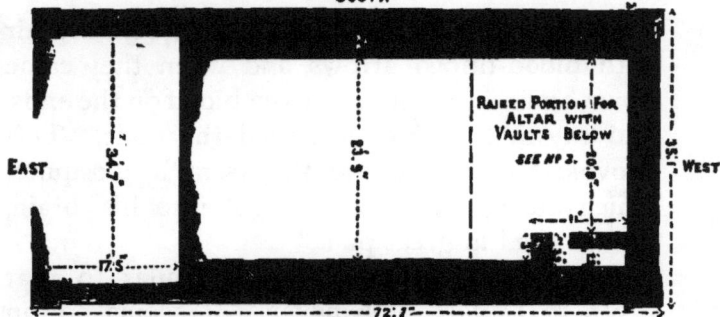

SOUTH

EAST

RAISED PORTION FOR ALTAR WITH VAULTS BELOW
SEE N° 3.

WEST

35·1"

34·7"

83·9"

17·5"

72·7

FIG. I.

NORTH

PLAN.

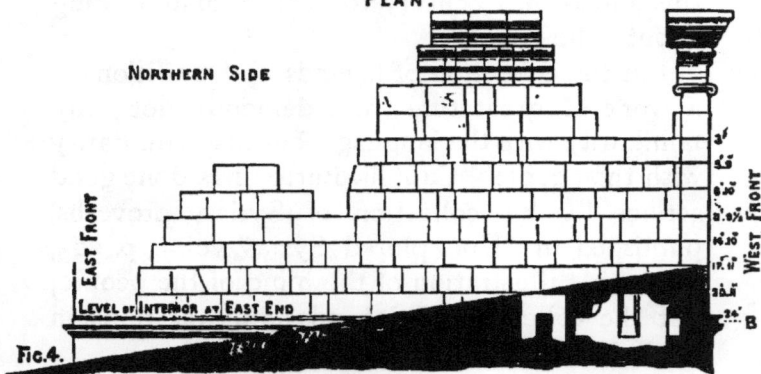

NORTHERN SIDE

EAST FRONT

WEST FRONT

LEVEL OF INTERIOR AT EAST END

FIG. 4.

ELEVATION.

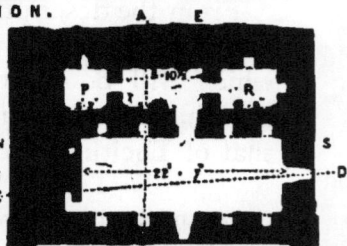

A   E

8·10½

22'·7

PLAN WESTERN END.

B

FIG. 2.

· FIG. 6.

EAST FRONT ⅟₅₀

N

S

D

5·0.25
C
1.75
10.75
13·6.75
16·1.76
18·7.76
21·2.25
23·9.75
26·4.75
29·0.75
31·6.75
34·3.75
36·9.75
38·4.76
39·11.75

CORBELS IN VAULT.
SCALE ⅟₅₀

FIG. 5.

LEVEL OF INTERIOR AT WEST END

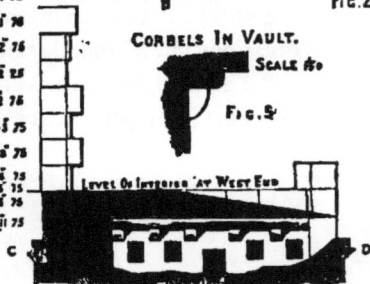

C

D

FIG. 3.   ELEVATION.

and a bearing to summit of Hermon gives 136°. Height above mean sea level, 3,780 ft.

"The temple is *in antis*, and measures (see Plate) in length 72 ft. 7 in., and in breadth 35 ft. 1 in., including the projections of the antæ. Height from cornice to stylobate, 34 ft. 4·75 in. The pronaos is 14 ft. 4 in. by 30 ft., the cella is about 48 ft. by 23 ft. 9 in., but the transverse wall between the pronaos and cella cannot readily be distinguished on its inner side. The cella is raised at its western end 6 ft. above the floor of the temple. This raised portion extends from western wall towards the east for about 19 ft., and below it are chambers.

"These chambers may have been used as store-rooms; they are furnished with niches, and one of them also appears to have acted as a passage to allow the priests to enter the temple secretly (*vide* 'Bel and the Dragon'). For this purpose there is a door on the south side of the temple in the stylobate at 7 ft. 7 in. from the western end: this opens through a wall 3 ft. 9 in. thick, into a chamber 22 ft. 7 in. long and 9 ft. wide. At the end of this chamber to the north is a staircase (now walled up) leading to the raised platform above: the side walls of the temple to east are then increased by 3 ft. to allow of the stairs. The side walls of the temple in other places are in thickness 5 ft. 7 in.

"In the centre of the west wall of this chamber is a window, formed like a loophole, 10 in. wide outside and 2 ft. 3 in. within. On either side of this window are two niches, 1 ft. 10 in. wide, 2 ft. 6 in. high, and 1 ft. 10 in. deep. Opposite to them on the east side of the chamber are two similar niches, and between them and opposite the window is an opening in the wall, leading into a chamber 8 ft. 10 in. by 5 ft. 1 in. From this on either side to north and south are other two chambers, 6 ft. 2 in. by 5 ft. 6 in.; in these latter are other niches. These small chambers (P.Q.R., Fig. 2) are covered over by great flat slabs. The silt or mud lies deep in these chambers, so that their height is uncertain; but it is probably not less than 7 ft. In the first and larger chamber, where the width is 9 ft., corbels are used for supporting the flat slabs for the roof (Fig. 3, 4, and 5). There is first a corbel 1 ft. 9½ in. high, and 1 ft. 4½ in. projecting out, and above it a smaller corbel 1 ft. 2 in. high, and projecting altogether 2 ft. 2½ in. from the side of the chamber; so that the space to be spanned by the slabs is only 4 ft. 7 in. wide. These slabs are probably not less than 9 ft. long; they vary in width from 4 ft. to 5 ft., and are perhaps 2 ft. 6 in. to 3 ft. in thickness. This description of these chambers is here given with some minuteness, because in most of the temples met with the arch is used instead of corbels and flat slabs.

" The temple is of the Ionic order (see restoration, Fig. 5). The antæ are 3 ft. 1 in. square near base, and diminish to 2 ft. 10 in. near capital; they project at base 4 in. beyond the pteromata: the bases are Attic; the capitals have two of their faces together uniform as in the Roman samples, there being volutes at three of the angles; but at the fourth angle the volute had been hollowed out, so as to form a sort of handle in appearance. There are nine courses between the entablature and stylobate, measuring exactly 27 ft. in height, and the courses themselves are individually each about 3 ft. in height (Fig. 6).

" Robinson says there are thirteen courses of stone; perhaps he included the stylobate. I only found nine courses. The entablature is in height 7 ft. 4·75 in.; the architrave and frieze are in one piece, measuring 4 ft. 4·5 in.; of this the frieze measures 16·5 in., and is cushioned. Nothing whatever could be found of ' the figures of a ram's head

and bull's head alternately' on the frieze, described in
' The Land of Israel,' though nearly every stone lying
near the temple was examined; but, on leaving, stones were
seen lower down the hill, and perhaps they may have been
on some of these. It does not, however, appear probable
that the heads were on the frieze, more likely at intervals
on the cornice; nothing, however, was seen of any heads
on the cornice. The upper mouldings of the architrave
are somewhat peculiar; the angle at the base of the pediment is about 21 deg. 30 min.

" The temple stands on a stylobate which projects very
slightly beyond the wall of the temple; to this there are
two cornices, but no base visible. It is in height altogether
5 ft. 6 in., and appears to have run right round the building,
so as to have admitted of no steps in front (see restoration,
Fig. 6); and as the height is too great to have allowed of
the people stepping on to it, it does not appear probable
that it was entered by the vulgar.

"No capitals or bases of columns could be found.
Several portions of the shafts were found lying about,
which measured 2 ft. 11 in. in diameter.

" There are no signs of any bevels (in the Jerusalem
nomenclature) on the stones, but they are each well
squared, and have a chamfer one quarter of an inch round
their edges. They are of the ordinary blue limestone.
This obtains by exposure a very blue colour, which gives to
the country such a cold appearance."

The summit of Mount Hermon is thus described:—

"At the top is a plateau, comparatively level; here are
two small peaks lying north and south, and about four
hundred yards from each other; situated to the west, and

separated by a ravine, at a distance of six hundred yards, is a third peak. The tops of these three are in altitude within a few feet of each other, and together they form the summit of Hermon.

"The plateau at top is of an irregular shape, and measures about five hundred yards in diameter: at its north-eastern end the ridge-bone of Hermon fines down to a sharp ledge, on which you can sit and look north and south. This ridge gradually falls to the north-east, until Hermon becomes lost in the minor hills of the Anti-Lebanon. The western peak is separated from the plateau by a ravine about one hundred feet deep, with gently sloping sides; from this peak the ridge-bone runs away to south-west at an angle of 210° with the magnetic meridian. It appears to fall for about a mile and a half, and then to rise again in a second culminating point, and after that to spread out into spurs; this second point appears to be lower than what is generally known as the summit.

"On the northern and western peaks no ruins could be found, or any sign that they had been used as places of worship; but on the southern peak there is a hole scooped out of the apex, the foot is surrounded by an oval of hewn stones, and at its southern end is a Sacellum, or temple, nearly destroyed: the latter appears to be of more recent date than the stone oval, and the mouldings on its cornice appear to be Roman.

"The oval is formed of well-dressed stones, from 2 ft. to 8 ft. in length, 2½ ft. in breadth, and 2 ft. thick; they are laid in a curved line on the uneven ground, their breadth being their height, and their ends touching each other. In some places it almost appears as though there had been two courses of these stones, one

on the other; many of them are still *in situ*, while
others are only just overturned; but in some places
to the west the stones have been completely removed,
and the position they occupied can only be ascertained
by the cutting in the rock made to receive them.

"These stones follow the inequalities of the ground;
where it is shingle they are let in two or three inches;
where it is rock there is just a level place cut down to
receive them. In one place, where the rock forms a small
natural scarp of 4 or 5 ft., the stones appear to have
broken their continuity and to have been laid at different
levels. On the south-eastern side the stones are lying
about, but no trace could be found of the site they
occupied. The oval appears to have been something of an
ellipse, its longer axis from north-west to south-east being
130 ft., its shorter axis being about 100 ft.; within, the peak
rises for about 18 ft., and the apex is a hole cut out like a
cauldron, 9 ft. in diameter and about 6 ft. deep; at the
bottom is shingle and rubbish, and the true bottom is
probably deeper. The rock is cut and scarped in several
places. To the south, and just outside the oval, is the
ruin of a rectangular building, whose entrance was to
the east, the angle of the side is 72°; it is 36 ft. 3 in.
long and 33 ft. 3 in. broad; the shorter sides being to
east and west. The rock is cut down to receive it; at the
north-east angle the rock has been scarped down so as to
leave a passage 2 ft. wide between it and the building;
at the north-west angle and west side the rock has been
cut down to afford room for the building, and part of the
lower portion of the wall appears to be cut out of the rock.
On the south side the rock falls away from the building;
the walls are about 2 ft. 6 in. thick. In some places two
courses still remain, but at the north-east angle and in

other parts the wall has quite disappeared. At the south-east angle the foundations appear to be produced for 2 ft. beyond the walls. On some of the stones a faint marginal draft is seen, but most of the stones are simply well squared ashlar. The ruins of the temple, for the most part, lie down the hill to the south-east.

"It is possible that there may have been columns at the entrance, which, if thrown down with the other *débris*, would most certainly have rolled down the gulley below for at least 2,000 ft.; but we could find no remains of columns either in the gulley or at the bottom of it. However, Dr. Porter (Murray's Handbook, page 430) mentions having seen a fragment of a column to north of ruins, and we found two columns at the entrance to a cavern to north-east, which may have belonged to the *Sacellum*. This cavern is hewn in the rock, and has its entrance to the east; it is irregular in shape, about 30 ft. in diameter, and is about 6 to 8 ft. in height; at the south-west end there is a rock-cut column to support the roof; at the entrance are the frusta of two columns, about 19 in. in diameter; a sloping ascent leads up to the surface; above is a level platform, sides 30 ft. by 26, south-western end cut out of the rock.

"The stone composing the oval and the buildings is of the same limestone as the mountain itself.

"To the north-west of the oval we found a stone, 4 ft. by 18 in. by 12 in., with a Greek inscription on the face very roughly cut; a squeeze was taken of this, and a *fac-simile* from it has been attempted: it is enclosed. This inscription does not appear to have been noticed by travellers before.

"The top of the mountain, when the rock does not crop out, is covered with a small shingle, possibly caused by the disintegrating influence of the frequent frosts and thaws on the summit; on the western slopes the same shingle is found, lying at an angle of 25° to 30°, so that it is just possible for a man to walk straight up the last one thousand feet; on the eastern side the rock is harder, and

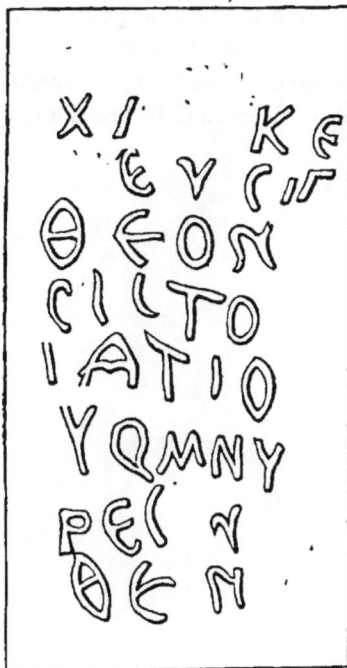

STONE ON SUMMIT OF MOUNT HERMON.

the shingle is only found in the narrow gulleys; the slope is also very steep, 45° and more, so that the stones and shingle must be continually on the move.

"In the winter time the snow appears to extend down the mountain side for about five thousand feet; it gradually melts away as the spring advances, until in September very little is left, and this only in the crevices where the sun is unable to penetrate. In November the snow begins to cover the mountain again.

"It is to be observed that the southern peak, where is the stone oval, cannot be seen from any point below except to the east, and the summit generally cannot be seen from the villages at the base of the mountain. From many of the villages there is a culminating point seen, but it is the side of the mountain, and not the true summit."

CHAPTER XII.

THE MOABITE STONE.

THE discovery of this memorable stone and the circumstances which led to its destruction are so well known that we may be content to pass over the history in a few words only. It was found at Dhibán (Aug. 19, 1868) by the Rev. F. A. Klein, a French clergyman employed by the English mission. By a most extraordinary and most unfortunate error of judgment, M. Klein communicated his discovery neither to his learned and zealous countryman, M. Clermont Ganneau, nor to his English employers of the mission, nor to Captain Warren, the English explorer; but he went secretly to Dr. Petermann, the Prussian Consul. Here was the grand mistake of the whole business.

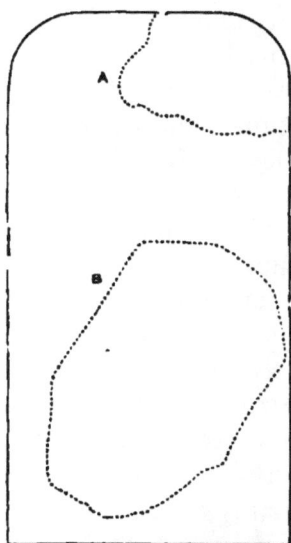

Either Captain Warren or M. Clermont Ganneau could have got up the stone, whole and uninjured, for a few Napoleons, because the Arabs *were wholly unacquainted with its value.* One or two attempts were secretly made by Dr. Petermann to get the stone by means of native agents. They failed, and doubly failed, because they taught the Arabs the value of the stone.* Then an appeal was made to the Turkish Government—the most fatal mistake of all; for the stone was in the possession of the Beni Humaydah (not the Beni Hamidah, as stated by error in the article on the Moabite Stone in the "Recovery of Jerusalem"), the wildest of the wild tribes to the east of Jordan. They were smarting, too, at the time from the effects of the "Belka Expedition," led by Rashid Pasha in person; and, says Captain Burton, "knowing what a *dragonnade* meant, they were in paroxysms of terror at the idea of another raid."

The secret by this time had oozed out, and was perfectly well known to Captain Warren, the Rev. Dr. Barclay, and M. Clermont Ganneau. It was decided by Captain Warren that it would be best at this point to leave the matter in the hands of Dr. Petermann. Observe that any interference on his part would have probably tended to complicate matters, and might have led to a still earlier destruction of the monument. In the spring of 1869, Captain Warren, with his party,

* The list of blunders perpetrated during the first attempts to get up the stone may be read in Burton and Drake's " Unexplored Syria," vol i., p. 335, *et seq.*

went to the Libanus. Dr. Petermann, too, left Jerusalem for Berlin, *after personally assuring M. Ganneau that the whole affair had fallen through.* Captain Warren away, and the Prussians having desisted from their endeavours, the coast was clear for M. Clermont Ganneau.

M. Ganneau got a squeeze of the whole—in rags, it is true, but still a squeeze. Then came the catastrophe. The wild Arabs, terrified at the prospect of another raid, angry at the probable loss of a stone which possessed super-natural powers in their eyes, lit a fire under the priceless relic, threw cold water on it when it was red-hot, and so smashed it into pieces. Captain Warren obtained squeezes of the two larger frag-ments; and then the work of decipherment, his-tory, controversy, and recrimination began. After all that has been said as to its history, one thing is clear: *the blame of its destruction rests neither with Captain Warren nor with M. Clermont Ganneau.* Had M. Klein gone openly in the first instance to the former, there is not the slightest doubt that this most invaluable monument would be now lying, intact and entire, in the British Museum, in the Louvre, or in Berlin. No matter where, provided only it had been saved.

For it is a monument which yields in im-portance to none yet found. It is a narrative by a Moabite king of his battles and conquests. It is like another page added to the Bible. It takes. us back to the time of King Omri and King Ahab; and it takes us nearer to the origin of

our own alphabet than any other document yet
discovered. In every way it is a gain. It has a
value historical, a value geographical, a value linguistic, a value theological, a value paleographic.
It has this value, mutilated as it is. It would be
priceless indeed, could we recover enough of the
upper surface to read it without doubt or hesitation. The number of letters on the monument
was a little over 1,000. The number preserved is
669. Subjoined is the translation given by M.
Clermont Ganneau, June, 1870:—

"I am Mesa, son of Chamosgad, King of Moab,
the Dibonite. | My father reigned thirty years,
and I have reigned after my father. | And I have
built this sanctuary for Chamos in Qarha [sanc-
tuary of salvation], for he has saved me from all
aggressors and has made me look upon all my
enemies with contempt. |

"Omri was King of Israel, and oppressed Moab
during many days, and Chamos was irritated at
his aggressions. | And his son succeeded him, and
he said, he also, 'I will oppress Moab.' | In
my days I said 'I will . . . him . . . . . and I
will visit him and his house.' | And Israel was
ruined, ruined for ever. Omri gained possession
of the land of Medeba. | And he dwelt there . . .
[Ahab] his son lived forty years, and Chamos
made him [perish] in my time. |

"Then I built Baal Meon and constructed
Qiriathaïm. |

"And the men of Gad dwelt in the country of
[Ataro]th from ancient times, and the King of

Israel had built the city of Ataroth. | I attacked the city and I took it, | and I killed all the people of the city, as a spectacle to Chamos and to Moab, | and I carried away from there the . . . and I dragged it to the ground before the face of Chamos at Qerioth, | and I brought there the men of Saron (or of Chofen) and the men of Maharouth (?).

"And Chamos said to me, 'Go; take Nebah from Israel.' | I went by night, and I fought against the city from the dawn to midday, | and I took it: and I killed all, seven thousand [men, and I carried away with me] the women and the young girls; for to Astar Chamos belongs the consecration of women; | and I brought from there the vessels of Jehovah, and I dragged them on the ground before the face of Chamos. |

"And the King of Israel had built Yahas, and resided there during his war with me. | And Chamos drove him from before my face: I took from Moab two hundred men in all; I made them go up to Yahas, and I took it to annex it to Dibon. |

"It is I who have built Qarha, the Wall of the Forests and the Wall of the Hill. | I have built its gates, and I have built its towers. | I have built the palace of the king, and have constructed the prisons of the . . . in the midst of the city. |

"And there were no wells in the interior of the city in Qarha: and I said to all the people, 'Make you every man a well in his house,' | and I dug cisterns for Qarha for . . . of Israel. |

"It is I who have built Aroer, and made the road of Arnon. |

"It is I who have built Beth Bamoth, which was destroyed. | It is I who have built Bosor which (is powerful) . . . Dibon of the military chiefs, for all Dibon was submissive. | And I have filled . . . with the cities which I have added to the land (of Moab). |

"And it is I who have built . Beth Diblathain, and Beth Baal Meon, and I have raised there the . . . the land. | And Horonaim, he resided there with . . . | And Chamos said to me, 'Go down and fight against Horonaim.' | . . . Chamos, in my day . . . the year . . . ."

At this point—viz., the publication by the Count de Vogüé of M. Clermont Ganneau's first reading—Mr. Deutsch urged strongly in the *Times* the desirability of waiting till further investigation should give us additional fragments, or confirm the readings already made. At the same time he pointed out some of the mistakes both of M. Ganneau's text and translation, and dwelt very strongly upon the general importance of the monument. His advice, the soundness of which has been proved by every subsequent addition to the Moabite Stone literature, has not been followed. So far from waiting for the promised complete and authentic text, treatise after treatise, edition after edition, have been published in England, France, Germany, and America, all based upon the squeezes of Captain Warren (the two large fragments), which were photographed

at very great expense by the Fund; while the
squeezes of the entire stone, from which "emen-
dated" edition after edition was successively published by M. Ganneau, have, up to this moment,
not been published to the world.

No doubt at all exists as to the general tenor
of the translation, and the discrepancies are such
as to interest chiefly the learned world. For the
general public, it will be sufficient to mention
that, after 3,000 years, there has come to light a
monument which is contemporary with King
Ahab, and refers to events which are recorded
in the book of Chronicles. After this, let no one
doubt the utility of Palestine research, or the
possibility of finding further illustrations of the
Bible in contemporary monuments.*

A word on one or two points brought out in
this monument. Mr. Deutsch states:—"It is un-
questionably, whatever the precise date of this
King Mesha, the very oldest Semitic lapidary
record of importance as yet discovered. . . . . It
illustrates, to a hitherto unheard-of degree, the
history of our own writing—I mean that which
we all use at this time. Nearly the whole of the
Greek alphabet is found here; not merely *similar*
to the 'Phœnician' shape, but as identical with it
as can well be. Not merely such letters as the·
Δ, P, M, N, Σ, E, O, Θ, X (Koppa),&c., . . . but even
the Ξ—one of the letters supposed to have been

* See Burton and Drake's "Unexplored Syria," vol. i.,
p. 318.

S

added during the Trojan war by Palamedes, because
not extant in the original 'Cadmean' alphabet—is
of constant recurrence here, as *Samech*. Further,
the knotty digamma question will receive a new
contribution, by the shape of the *vau* in this
monument, which is distinctly the Greek Υ,
another letter of supposed recent origin.   And
another thing will become clear—viz., that the
more primitive the characters the simpler they
become: not, as often supposed, the more complicated, as more in accordance with some pic-
torial prototype."

Professor Schlottman calls attention to the
word Astar Chamos, found in the seventeenth
line.   It is found, he explains, here for the first
time on Canaanitish soil.   It is the male name
corresponding to the female form Astarté: it is
identical with the Athtâr, or Athtôr, found on a
well-known Himyaritic inscription, and probably
also with the Estar of the Ninevitish cruciform
writings.   It is derived from a root signifying to
close together, to form an alliance with one
another; because in Astar and Astarté was placed
that power which holds creatures to one another,
and the world to the Godhead; and, in alliance
with this, the productive strength of nature.
"It is strange," he says, "that this bare name, on
the monument of a small nation of herdsfolk long
forgotten, should have even for classical archæology a many-sided interest.   It is the Canaanitish
original, now first found, of the Aphroditos mentioned by Aristophanes; of the name for Venus

Amathusia, represented as bearded, *eadem mas et femina*. The name Chamos has reference to his taming, compelling power. He is the fearful God who is appeased by human sacrifice. Any one not otherwise acquainted with the characteristics of Chamos might suppose from our inscription that he was only nominally different from Jehovah. Chamos is angry with his people: he delivers them into the hands of their enemies. He again looks mercifully on them. He drives Omri's enemies from before his face. He speaks in the same manner as Jehovah. But the wrath of Chamos was like his mercy, blind and fitful: not like the wrath of Jehovah, a symbol of that true divine energy by which an eternal moral order is preserved."

The date of the stone is probably about 900 B.C. It was engraved, according to the opinion of the Count de Vogüé, in the second year of the reign of Ahaz, · King of Israel. It is older than Homer, older than the famous inscription of Ashmunazar; and is in all likelihood written in the same characters as those used by David in the Psalms, and by Solomon in his correspondence with Hiram, King of Tyre.* From every point of view the stone is of the deepest importance and interest. Would that we could find others like it.

[NOTE I.—The most important papers published on the Moabite Stone are those in the

* "Unexplored Syria," vol. i., p. 318.

"Quarterly Statements" of our Society; the papers by Captain Burton ("Unexplored Syria," vol. i.), to which frequent reference has been made above; the treatises of Professor Schlottman, Noldeke, Rawlinson, and Wright, and that of Dr. Ginsburg. We must, of course, include the papers, on which all these rest, by M. Clermont Ganneau, together with Mr. Deutsch's letters in the *Times*, from which the above extract is taken.]

[NOTE II.—For Moab and its history, the reader may be referred to Mr. Grove's article on Moab in the "Bible Dictionary." The country is referred to repeatedly in the Bible. The most important references are—Numbers, xxi. 26, xxii., and xxiii.; Deut., ii. 9; Judges, iii. 17, xi. 15 *et seq.*; I Sam., xiv. 47; 2 Sam., viii. 2; 2 Kings, i. 1, iii. 4—27, xiii. 20, xxiv., li.; 2 Chron., xx.; Isaiah, xv., xvi.; Jer., xlviii.; Dan., xi. 41; Amos, ii. 1, 2.]

CHAPTER XIII.

THE SINAI SURVEY.

IT was not contemplated in the original prospectus of the Palestine
Exploration Fund to in-
clude the Peninsula of
Sinai in their survey.
This work, however, one
of equal interest with our
own, was greatly assisted
by the energy of the Rev.
F. W. Holland, one of
the Palestine Fund Hono-
rary Secretaries. He was
himself practically well-
fitted for taking part in
this expedition—which, through his exertions, was
enabled to start in the autumn of 1868—having
made no fewer than three separate visits to the
Peninsula, in 1861, 1865, and 1867. In the
brief account which is here given, we follow
Mr. Holland's own narrative as published in the
"Recovery of Jerusalem." It will be understood
at once that we insert this chapter on account of
its very great interest to biblical students, and

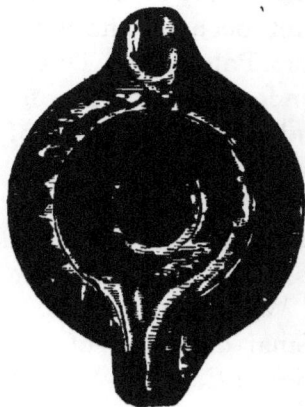

not in any way claiming credit for work done by others. The survey of the Sinai Peninsula is not part of "our work in Palestine." Not one penny of the subscribers' money was spent on it. The Committee had no voice in it. It was under the direction of Sir Henry James, the well-known Director General of the Ordnance Survey. Nevertheless, it had the cordial sympathy of every member of the Palestine Committee, and, no doubt, of every subscriber to the Palestine Exploration Fund. And it forms part of our work so far as this, that had it not been for the Sinai Survey the journey of Messrs. Palmer and Drake might never have been undertaken. For one thing leads to another, and the clearing up of one set of difficulties not only quickens the desire to clear up others, but often opens a way for exploration. Thus, the Ordnance Survey of Sinai led to Professor Palmer's exploration of the Desert of the Forty Years' Wandering.

The survey party of Sinai consisted of the Rev. F. W. Holland as guide; of Captains Wilson and Palmer, Royal Engineers; of Mr. E. H. Palmer as Arabic scholar; and Mr. Wyatt as naturalist. With them were four experienced non-commissioned officers. They started, with a caravan of forty-four camels and forty drivers, from Suez on November 11th, 1868. Their mode of travelling was on foot as much as possible— Mr. Palmer collecting the names of places as they went along, and the traditions which were connected with them. The depôt of stores and head-

quarters of the expedition were fixed at Jebel
Mûsa, which, from its central position, formed an
admirable starting-point for the work to be done.

The first thing done was a special survey 'of
Jebel Mûsa itself, and the surrounding mountains
and valleys, on a scale of six inches to the mile.
This included an area, altogether, of seventeen
square miles. This completed, while the non-
commissioned officers were engaged in the levelling and hill sketching, the general reconnaissance
survey was extended. Jebel Serbal, the rival site
of Sinai, received the same amount of attention
as Jebel Mûsa—a special survey, six inches to
the mile, being also made of this. The route and
reconnaissance surveys, with these several pieces
of work, brought the total amount of survey work
to 4,000 square miles of country—including, that
is, the whole amount of the country in the
Peninsula through which the Israelites must have
marched on their way from Egypt.

Here another vexatious doubt arises. How do
we know that the Peninsula, so called, of Sinai
is the real country through which the Israelites
marched? An attempt has been made to fix
Mount Sinai in Arabia, and to identify the Gulf
of Akaba with the Red Sea of the Bible. The
answer to the doubt has been furnished, at least
to the satisfaction of most, by Mr. Holland himself, from the work of this survey. He argues,
to sum up his evidence briefly, as follows:—

Goshen was to the north-east of Egypt, probably comprising that district now known as El

Wady, through which runs the fresh-water canal from the Nile to Ismailia. Now, from that valley to the head of the Gulf of Suez is three days' journey, the distance mentioned in the story of the Exodus; while the head of the Gulf of Akaba is 150 miles eastwards. Then, since the Children of Israel "encamped by the Red Sea," after five days' journey from the place of crossing it, we have another argument in favour of the Peninsula of Sinai; because in five days after crossing the Red Sea they could not even have reached the Gulf of Akaba. In fact, with the results of the survey before us, no reasonable doubt whatever seems to remain that the Peninsula of Sinai is actually the scene of the events recorded in the history of the Exodus.

This point cleared up, another remains. Which was the Mount of the Law? These points come out clearly (we are quoting Mr. Holland):—

1. It was a mountain easy of approach, and having before it an open space sufficiently large for the whole congregation to have been assembled there to receive the Law.

2. It was a prominent mountain, rising up abruptly from the plain before it, for (Deuteronomy, iv. 2) the people "stood under the mountain;" and it is described (Exodus, xix. 12—17) as a mountain which could be touched.

3. Its immediate neighbourhood must have afforded a plentiful supply of water and pasturage.

There are only two mountains in the limits of

the ground before us which can be considered at all. One of these is Jebel Serbal, the other Jebel Mûsa. Jebel Serbal is the most rugged and the boldest of the mountains in the Peninsula. It rises to the height of 6,300 ft. above the level of the sea; and, rising from a lower level, has a greater command than almost any other mountain over the surrounding country. Now, there are two valleys, Wady Aleyat and Wady Ajelah, which run from its base to Wady Feiran. The space between the two is a rugged chaos of mountains intersected by deep ravines. No camp could have been placed between the two. Further, the valleys themselves, from neither of which could a view of the highest peak be obtained, are a wild mass of boulders and torrent beds, with no possible place for a large encampment. It was the unanimous conclusion of every member of the survey party that Jebel Serbal *could not be the mountain from which the Law was given.*

This is negative evidence. What can be done with Jebel Mûsa?

Jebel Mûsa, including under this name Ras Sufsâfeh, consists, roughly speaking, of a central elevated basin, encircled by a ring of higher peaks, about two miles long from north to south, and one mile broad. The southern peak is its highest point, and to this the name of Jebel Mûsa is specially applied. On the north, east, and west it is separated from the surrounding mountains; on the south two smaller valleys separate it from the range of mountains which lies between the Wady Sebaiyeh and the Jebel Catharine. Now, sloping gradually from the watershed on the north to the foot of Ras Sufsâfeh is a plain, two miles long and half a mile broad,'called the plain of Er Râhah. About 300 yards from the actual base of the mountain there runs across the plain a low semicircular mound, which forms a kind of natural theatre; while farther distant, on either side of the plain, the slopes of the enclosing mountains would afford seats to an almost unlimited number of spectators. Not far off, on the Wady Leja, is an extensive recess, about a mile and a half long by three-quarters of a mile broad, which might be used as a very extensive addition to the camping ground. No spot on the whole Peninsula is so well supplied with water. There are four streams of running water, and there are numerous wells and springs. And there is no district in the whole Peninsula which has such excellent pasturage. Here, then, in the unanimous opinion of every member of the expedition, was the scene of the giving of the Law. From Ras Sufsâfeh the Law was proclaimed to the children of Israel, assembled in the plains of Er Râhah.

It will be remarked that the result of geographical explorations is not only to destroy untenable theories, but to build up new theories or support old ones by facts which are in themselves irrefragable. In illustration of this we may refer to the words of Lord Ossington at the

annual meeting of the Society of this year (1872).
He said:—

"I remember a remarkable instance which happened
in connection with this very Society not many years ago.
You may remember, perhaps, that there was a careful
examination made of Mount Sinai by officers of the Corps
of Engineers, and a part of the model made from that
survey now stands upon your table. A friend of mine who
was engaged in a learned and important work, having
read all the books of travels, and all the accounts he could
get, tried to fix upon the probable point upon which the
law was delivered on Mount Sinai; and he had, after great
pains and trouble, arrived at a certain conclusion. That
conclusion was that the real spot was at the south end of
the mountain; he thought that the majority of the authorities lay in that direction—always, I must take leave to say,
with the exception of a distinguished traveller, well known
in the neighbourhood of our Abbey, who now sits at my
left hand, and who had himself entertained a different view,
which I believe in the opinion of all now turns out to be
the correct one. My friend having studied all these books,
came to London, and he learnt that this survey made by
the Engineers was to be seen. He went to see it. It was
no doubt a painful thing for an author having made up his
mind, and having expressed a decided opinion, to find that
he certainly had been entirely wrong. He went to see
that very plan, or one on a larger scale, and satisfied himself that according to the description in the Bible of the
plain upon which the Israelites had been encamped, it was
impossible that it could have been on the rough uneven
ground such as these historians and narrators had fixed
upon, on the south extremity of the range; and that, on
the contrary, the north extremity possessed every requisite

for the encampment of a numerous host, a valley expand-
ing into a wide plain, extending itself from the very root
of the mountain."

Objections have been raised, based on the
present barrenness of the Peninsula, to the narrative of the Bible. They vanish before the results of
the survey. The barrenness of the Peninsula is
due to neglect. In former times it was more
richly wooded; the wadies were protected by walls
stretching across, which served as dams to resist
the force of the rushing waters; the mountains
were terraced, and clothed with gardens and groves.
This fertility lasted till modern times. The monks
—there was formerly a large Christian community
in the Peninsula—carried on the old traditions of
cultivation (traditions, perhaps, as old as the
Amalekites), and terraced, protected, and planted.
Then came the bad times of Mohammedan rule,
which let in the Bedawin to waste and destroy.
Then the protecting walls across the wady were
broken down; the green terraces along its sides
were destroyed; the trees were cut down or
carried away by the winter torrent. The whole
history of Sinai desolation seems embodied in one
scene witnessed by Mr. Holland in 1867, in Wady
Feiran. The wady had been dry. After two
hours' storm, the water rose so rapidly that this
dry course was turned into a raging torrent, 300
yards broad, 8 to 10 ft. deep, tearing down with
it tamarisks, palm trees, sheep, goats, camels,
donkeys, and even men, women, and children.

When the storm subsided, where had been trees and gardens, tamarisk wood, and groves of palm trees, were nothing but heaps of boulders, piled one upon another. In the old times, when men knew better how to struggle with the forces of nature, the wady would have been dammed—like the river Thames with its weirs—with walls to break the force of the rain stream; and what is now a curse would have been a blessing. Surely, we shall better understand the story of the Exodus when the old state of things is restored, and vegetation once more clothes the granite mountain sides.

And yet, in spite of neglect and desolation, it must not be supposed, says Professor Palmer, that no fertility is to be found in the Peninsula of Sinai. "There are no rivers; yet many a pleasant little rivulet, fringed with verdure, may be met with here and there, especially in the romantic glens of the granite district. At Wadies Nasb and Gharundel are perennial, though not continuous, streams, and large tracts of vegetation."

The celebrated Sinaitic inscriptions, on which so much stress has been laid, do not prove to be ancient or important. They have been read by Professor Palmer, and are, for the most part, proper names, with the usual Oriental introductory formulæ, such as "May he be remembered," "Peace be with him." They appear to be of the second or third century of our era.

We have not space to follow Mr. Holland's

observations on the wanderings of the Israelites, to which we shall have to recur in the next
chapter.   Let us, however, quote his concluding
words, worthy of note, as coming from one who
knows the Peninsula of Sinai, and its wadies and
mountains, as most of us know the streets of
London:—" Not a single member of the expedition," he says, " returned home without feeling
more firmly convinced than ever of the truth of
that sacred history, *which he found illustrated
and confirmed by the natural features of the
desert.*   The very mountains and valleys, the
very rocks, barren and sun-scorched as they now
are, seem to furnish evidence—which none who
behold them can gainsay—that this was the 'great
and terrible wilderness ' through which Moses,
under God's direction, led His people."

CHAPTER XIV.

THE DESERT OF THE EXODUS.

BETWEEN Palestine and Sinai lies stretched the vast Desert, "great and terrible," called the Desert of the Tíh. Historically, it is in interest surpassed only by the land north and the land south. The Law was given in Sinai; the history of the Israelites is chiefly occupied with Palestine proper; but it was in this region that the chosen people wandered for forty years; and in the hilly ground to the north-east were the flocks and herds of the Patriarchs.

If you look at any published map of the district, you will observe either a total blank, broken only by a few routes, or mountains put down "conventionally," as geographers call it — *i.e.*, marked as mountains, but with no certain contours, because the courses of the valleys have not been studied, nor the mountains themselves visited. The Desert itself is crossed by the Hajj,

T

or pilgrim's road to Mecca. Many travellers
have visited it from time to time. Among them
are Dr. Robinson, who describes his journey in
the "Biblical Researches," Mr. Rowlands and Mr.
George Williams, Canon Tristram, and others.
But the Desert has never yet been systematically
explored; and when, in the autumn of 1869, an
opportunity offered of visiting this country, the
Committee were glad to avail themselves of it,
and undertook the expense of an expedition, the
results of which, in the end, fully justified them.
Mr. E. H. Palmer—now Professor Palmer—
who had won his spurs in the Sinai survey, undertook to face the dangers of the country, and
to penetrate, off the beaten road, into some
of the secrets of the Desert and the adjacent
country. He was accompanied by Mr. C. F.
Tyrwhitt Drake, instructed by the University of
Cambridge to examine into the natural history
of the region.

It is not easy to explain the kind of country
into which our explorers went. This much,
however, was known before they went there.
Draw a line from Gaza to the south of the Dead
Sea; you will then have Palestine proper, with
all its existing towns and cultivated country, on
the north, and the Desert on the south. The
Desert has now no "fenced" cities, vineyards,
or cultivation. It is entirely and absolutely a
desert. It contains what was once the "Negeb,"
or "South country" of the Bible, with the pas-
tures of Gerar (Genesis, x. 19; xx. 1). South of

this lies the Desert proper, a vast limestone
plateau of irregular surface, projecting, wedge-
fashion, into the Peninsula of Sinai, just as Sinai
itself projects into the Red Sea. The hill country
terminates with the cliff Jebel Magrah, about
seventy miles south of Hebron. The southern
portion, Et Tíh, terminates in a long cliff or
escarpment, steep and abrupt on the south-
western side, gradually falling away towards the
south-east. It is drained by the Wady el Arish
on the west, and Wady el Teib (into the Dead
Sea) on the east. Wady el Arish is the "stream
of Egypt" (Isaiah, xxvii. 12) mentioned as forming part of the southern frontier of Palestine.

The country is nearly without water. Here
and there are a few springs in the wadies, where
water can be obtained by scraping little holes in
the ground, and baling it up with the hand.
Even when thus produced, it is a yellowish solution, which, when allowed to settle, produces a
cake of mud, about half its own bulk. The solid
ground is covered for the most part with a sort
of carpet of flints, worn and polished by the fine
detritus which is constantly blown upon them so
as to resemble pieces of black glass. Dry, however, as the ground is, there is a considerable
quantity of brown, parched herbage scattered over
it which makes admirable fuel for the camp fire.
It is dry and dead during the greater part of the
year, but bursts into fresh life with the approach of
spring. Only in the valleys is there to be found
vegetation during the whole year.

In the southern portion of the Desert of the Tíh there are no ruins of old towns; nothing to show that, within a historic period, the country was ever cultivated or inhabited. The traveller will, however, constantly come across stone circles and cairns, which testify to the former existence here of an extensive primæval population. To mark these, to collect what little notes in natural history may offer, and to determine as accurately as possible the course of the wadies and mountains, is all that an explorer has to do in the Tíh proper. There would be little importance, except from a geographical point of view, in exploring the region at all, were it not for the very important bearing which it has on the question of the wanderings of the Israelites. The notes of travellers in this Desert must be read by the light of the Pentateuch. From them alone can we ascertain, with any amount of precision, where were the stations of the Israelites.

It is after this dreary tract has been traversed that the country begins to grow really interesting. For then, ascending to the plateau called the Jebel el Magrah, we are in the hill country, the "South." Here we come upon the primæval stone remains of a pre-historic race, and on the *Hazeroth* or fenced enclosure of a pastoral people—probably the Amalekites, who lived here at the time of the Exodus; while in a steep ravine on the edge of the plateau is situate Ain Gadis—identified by Professor Palmer, though his conclusions have not been unanimously accepted, with Kadesh itself, the starting-point of the Forty Years' Wandering, the third resting-place of the Israelites beyond Sinai, the place where the people remained while the spies ascended by the South, and came unto Hebron, searching the land from the Wilderness of Zin unto Rehob; where Miriam died; where Moses smote the rock, and incurred the Divine displeasure; the starting-point from whence, after sojourning forty years in the Wilderness, the Israelites departed on their way to Canaan and came to Mount Hor, where Aaron died. Farther north we come to the ruins of once populous cities, the former seats of civilization, culture, and even Christianity. In the "South country," during that long and peaceful period between the last wild revolt under Bar Cochebas and the Persian invasion under Chosroes, a period of more than four centuries, there sprung up a flourishing Christian Church, having archbishops at Gaza and "Pharan or Cadis," and cathedrals in the chief towns, the ruins of which still exist. In all probability the churches were destroyed and the people dispersed when that great invasion by the Persian, Chosroes, took place; and not when, fifty years later, the Caliph Omar swept through the country. In the best of times, it could have been only by care and diligence that this country was kept fertile, and a very few years would suffice to reduce what had been a smiling plain to a scene of barrenness and desolation. The stopping-up of the wells, the destruction of

·the trees, the demolition of irrigation works, would naturally follow the capture of the towns; and very likely, when the Saracen hosts marched across the "hill country," there was nothing to show the former flourishing condition of the place more than what greeted the eyes of Professor Palmer when he stood upon the ruins of Sebaita and El Aujeh.

These towns are seldom named in Scripture: it is when we advance more northward—when we get beyond the wells of Rehoboth, Sitnah, and Beersheba, dug by Abraham and Isaac—that ruined cities and Scripture names occur in quick succession; and then the hills are no longer bleak and bare, the fields are no longer barren and uncultivated; trees are found, and corn, and vineyards, and we are among the mountains of Judæa.

In our version of the Bible, it might perhaps have been better to translate the word Negeb by "South country," rather than "the South," as has been done. By making this correction, a good deal of clearness will sometimes be given to the text. Thus, when the spies went up from Kadesh, we are told "they ascended *by the South*, and came to Hebron" (Numbers, xiii. 17, 22). Now, Hebron is north of Kadesh, wherever that be fixed; so that the verse, as it stands, does not convey a very clear idea of what is meant— viz., that they ascended to the plateau of the Jebel Magrah, and passed through the *South country* to Hebron. So, also, apply the same reading to Joshua, x. 40, 41; and to Numbers, xxi. 1.

The Arabs who now inhabit this region are among the wildest and most intractable of the Bedawin tribes. The worst of them are the Azazimeh, a tribe superstitious, violent, and jealous of intrusion to the last degree. If you produce a scientific instrument, they regard you as a sorcerer charged with the design of intercepting rain; if you ask the slightest question, you are supposed to be a spy. This agreeable tribe occupies the southernmost portion of the plateau. In the mountains to the north-west are the Saidiyeh and Dhallam; in the north-eastern corner are the Jelalín. The central portion of the Great Desert is occupied by the Teyáheh, a large and powerful tribe. They live by conveying the pilgrims on their camels across the Desert to Akabah, on their way to Mecca. They have no kind of agriculture, and procure grain from Gaza. Once in every year they despatch a party, sometimes mustering 1,000 guns, to pay their annual visit to their hereditary enemies and victims the Anazeh, who live round Palmyra and east of the Hauran. Their object is, of course, plunder. In a recent excursion of this kind, though it is a twenty days' journey, the Teyáheh brought back more than 600 head of cattle. Robbery is not, it may be remarked, at all a disgraceful thing among the Bedawin any more than it was when, in the days of Job, " the Chaldeans made out their bands and fell upon

the cattle, and carried them away, yea, and slew
the servants with the edge of the sword." Now,
as of old, a man "taketh his sword and goeth
his way to rob and steal" (Esdras, iv. 23) with
what Professor Palmer calls "a profound feeling
of conscious rectitude and respectability." The
neighbours of the Teyáheh are the Terabín,
whose territory extends from about forty miles
north-east of Suez, as far north as Gaza, and the
Haiwátt, who occupy the mountains west of
Akabah. Among these wild tribes, Professor
Palmer and Mr. Tyrwhitt Drake proposed to make
their way, unaided by any escort or protection. That they succeeded is a proof not only
of the greatest courage, patience, and tact, but
also of a singular power of speaking the language
and adapting themselves to the prejudices and
habits of the people.

The travellers emerged with no great love for
the Bedawin. To call them, we are told, "Sons of
the Desert" is to give them a misnomer. Half the
Desert has been made such by them. Many a
fertile plain has been deprived of its useful and industrious inhabitants, and converted into a barren
wilderness by them. They regard the man who
labours with unutterable scorn: they hate work,
and are entirely unscrupulous as to the means they
employ to live without it. "These qualities (which
also adorn and make the thief of civilization) the
Bedawi mistakes for evidences of thorough
breeding, and prides himself accordingly upon
being one of Nature's gentlemen."

Bitter Lakes

Suez

Jebel Rahah

Plateau about 2500 feet above the Sea

Wilderness of the Wandering
ET TIH

Bisher

Ayun Musa

Wilderness of Shur

Ain Suwarah

Jebel Tih

W. Ghurundel

W. Useit

Debbet er Ramleh

J. Ujmeh

J. Humr

W. Tayibeh

W. Shellal

El Markhah

W. Mukateb

W. Kenneh

el Akhdar

W. Feiran

Sük Eb Hena
El Watiyeh

W. Bibran

J. Abu Shäurne

GULF OF SUEZ

EL KAA

Ras Mohammed

Scale 25 Miles

J. Catherine   8537 f   J. Serbal   6735 f
J. Umm Shaumer 6450 f   J. Humum   1567 f
J. Musa   7375 f

Such are the people and such the country of
the Wilderness of the Forty Years' Wanderings.
Let us accompany our travellers in their adventurous journey, and note down a few of their
discoveries. It must be premised that, on their
return, an official report, full and detailed, though
concise, was drawn up by Mr. Palmer and presented to the Committee, by whom it was published, January and April, 1871. The whole edition of the January part (of 3,500 copies) was
speedily exhausted—a satisfactory fact, as showing the great interest felt in the subject. It was
followed, towards the close of the year, by the
appearance, in two volumes, of a much larger and
fuller work, called the "Desert of the Exodus,"
which comprises the work of the Sinai Survey
and that of the Tíh Desert. The book itself,
besides the immense amount of information it
affords on the country and the people, is a collection of anecdote, legend, and adventure, and
forms one of the most attractive volumes of
travel ever published. It is to be hoped that a
cheaper edition will bring the work more within
the range of the general public.

In the following brief *résumé* it is thought best
to use the words of Mr. Palmer himself whenever
possible.

The party consisted of Mr. Palmer and Mr.
Tyrwhitt Drake, absolutely alone. They had no
servants, not even a cook, and their only escort
consisted of the owners of the camels which carried their scanty camp furniture and provisions,

these being changed in passing from one tribe to another. They were dressed as Syrians, and carried arms, which, fortunately, they had no occasion to use.

As the Sinai Survey Expedition had left one little piece of the Peninsula unexplored—the district, viz., lying at the head of Wady Gharundel and that immediately beyond Ain Howharah— it was resolved to begin the journey by exploring this piece of country, which was accordingly done; and the geographical work here performed is included in the map of the Ordnance Survey of Sinai.   On the way they found numerous *nawámís*, with, in one place, a number of flint arrow-heads.   These *nawámís*, of which an illustration is given in the "Desert of the Exodus" (vol. ii., p. 317), are exceedingly curious.   The word itself is the plural form of "*namus*," a mosquito house, the tradition being that the Children of Israel built them as a protection against a plague of mosquitoes with which they were visited.   They are found in many places of the Peninsula of Sinai, and are of two kinds: first, circular houses about ten feet in diameter, built of unhewn stone, and covered with a carefully constructed dome-shaped roof, the top of which is closed by a large slab of stone, and the haunches, or sides, are weighted to prevent them from springing out; the entrance being by a low door, two feet high.   There can be no doubt about their having been human dwellings; indeed, in one, charred wood and linen were found on what had once been the hearth. They exactly resemble the *bothan* (shielings) of the Shetland Islands, and the chambers discovered in the large caverns at Clava, near Inverness. Some few had a spiral path running round the outside, and were almost identical in their construction with the *talayot*, or so-called ancient watch-towers found in the Balearic Islands.

The second, and perhaps more ancient, kind consists of large stone circles, some a hundred feet in diameter, having in the centre a cist covered with a heap of large boulders. In the cists were found human skeletons. Beside the sepulchral rings, or cairns, traces were found of the deserted buildings of the silent occupants of these tombs. They are a collection of circles, enclosed within rudely heaped walls—the stones employed being of precisely the same size and character as those used in the construction of the sepulchral rings. They were probably permanent camps of a pastoral people. Who and what they were it is impossible now to decide; but one or two facts seem certain enough—they must have existed in large numbers in the Peninsula; have buried in high places, and sacrificed at the tombs of the dead. "Who can say," asks the Professor, "that it was not on this very blackened earth before us that longing Israel was tempted to sin, and ate the offerings of the dead?" Most of their camps were found at the foot of Jebel el Éjmeh. The walls were not more than three feet high, composed of large boulders carefully packed to-

gether. Within was a series of very large circles
communicating with one another. The travellers
were a good deal puzzled to know what the circles meant, till the African experience of Mr.
Drake solved the difficulty. The Morocco Arabs
preserve many customs brought by them from
Arabia, which have since dropped out of use in
their mother country. To this day they construct
*exactly such camping grounds as the ruins now
standing under Jebel el Ejmeh*. There can be
little doubt that these are the *Hazeroth*, or field
enclosures, used by the pastoral people mentioned
in the Bible.

Before ascending Jebel el Ejmeh the travellers
paid a visit to a place visited by Mr. Palmer the
preceding year. It is called Erweis el Ebeirig,
and is a piece of elevated ground covered with
small enclosures of stone, *not like those previously
described*. On the summit of a small hill on the
right is an erection of rough stones, surmounted
by a conspicuous white block of pyramidal shape.
The remains of enclosures existed for miles round;
the small stones which then, as now, served for
hearth stones exhibited the action of fire. On
digging beneath the surface charcoal was found
in abundance, and outside the camp were a
number of stone heaps which could be nothing
but graves. The site, moreover, is a most commanding one, and admirably suited for the assem-
blage of a large concourse of people.

This is the evidence of the remains themselves.

We come next to that most important adjunct
—traditional evidence. It must be remembered
that tradition is valuable only as an adjunct. It
may be used to corroborate, never to originate.
Now, Arab tradition, our author informs us, de-
clares these remains to be "the relics of a large
pilgrim or Hajj caravan, who in remote ages
pitched their tents at this spot, on their way to Ain
Hudherah, and who were afterwards lost in the
Desert of the Tíh, and never heard of again."
Several observations may be made on this tradition. First, the caravan *lost its way*—the word
employed being that from which the name Tíh,
"Desert of the *Wanderings*," is derived. Then,
the people are described as a Hajj caravan, the
word Hajj being exclusively employed for the
pilgrimage to Mecca. But it owes its origin to
the Hebrew word *Hagg*, which signifies a festival,
and is used in Exodus (x. 9) to express the cere-
mony which the Children of Israel alleged as
their reason for wanting to leave Egypt—viz., "to
hold a *feast* unto the Lord" in the Wilderness.
No Moslem Hajj ever did or could pass this way.
Then, Arab legends are always related in exactly
the same words; so that one tradition is passed
down from generation to generation in an unde-
viating form. Lastly, the distance is exactly a
day's journey from Aín Hudherah. Put all these
facts together—remember, at the same time, the
mysterious graves outside the camp—then open
the Bible at the book of Numbers, xi. 33, 34, 35,

and read how the "wrath of God was kindled against the people, and the Lord smote the people with a very great plague. And he called the name of the place Kibroth-Hattaavah, because there they buried the people that lusted. And the people journeyed from Kibroth-Hattaavah unto Hazeroth, and abode at Hazeroth." And this, our explorers thought, can be nothing else but the scene of that Divine visitation. Who can say for certain? In the early ages "of faith," there would have been no doubt. The site, once suggested, would have been accepted without hesitation, and fresh legends would have grown up round it. The two modern travellers standing amid these mysterious remains—relics of some far distant encampment, some far distant disaster, so remote as to be long before the first beginnings of Islam—with the sacred narrative in their hands, with the shreds of evidence freshly gathered, come to a conclusion which strikes their minds with such force as to amount to a conviction. We, who only read, are bound at least to give their conclusions fair weight.

Near here they came upon a mountain called Jebel 'Arádeh, identified by them with Haradeh, one of the unidentified stations of the Israelites (Numbers, xxxiii. 24). Here they fell in with the Haiwátt Arabs, and experienced the usual suspicion and obloquy for having come into the country in order to stop the rain supply, the people firmly believing that rain is under the control of the Christians.

Climbing the Jebel el Ejmeh (the southern limit
of the Desert of Tíh) by a previously unknown
pass, they found themselves on a new scene
of their wanderings, and after a day's journey
over a monotonous country, they arrived at
Nakhl. This is a fort standing on the Hajj road
for the protection of the pilgrims, and garrisoned
by a few Egyptian soldiers.

Arrangements were here made, through the
Governor, with the Arabs for camels to cross the
Desert. Little occurred to mark the day's journey. On the first day, a long, low ridge near
the camp, covered with ancient sepulchral cairns,
was the only evidence in all that dreary expanse
of human handiwork. Among them was one
stone circle, which was dug into. Charcoal
and burnt earth, but no skeletons: the evidence,
therefore, of sacrifice only — perhaps offered
up by some Amalekite in memory of a departed friend. After this, day by day, monotonous plodding over flat, white gravel plains,
where the only incident to note was the appearance of a few shrubs, or some slight indication of
life.

The journal for one day contains nothing but
the following:—

" Monday. — Walked six hours. Saw two
beetles and a crow."

More cairns—this time recent. They are the .
graves of Bedawin who fell in a fight at this spot
between the Towarah and the Bení Wásil. The
Towarah still sing a song in honour of the hero

of the battle, Zewáid. You may read it in Mr. Palmer's book, beginning—

> " Like Israel's hosts, in days of yore,
> The trackless waste of Tíh we crossed:
> Both men and beasts were grieving sore,
> Both men and guides their way had lost."

Eight days of this marching brought them to the ruins of Contellet Garaiyah, on the hill of that name. There is on the summit a slight depression, surrounded by what at first appeared to be a natural parapet or rampart. On digging out the latter, it turned out to be composed of *débris*, covering up the foundations of an old wall composed of sun-dried bricks, and containing beams of wood, with signs of mortices, bolts, &c. At regular intervals were remains of amphoræ or jars, which had been built into the wall in sets of four, carefully packed in straw, and secured by a framework of wood. One jar was marked with a Phœnician *aleph*. If the wood was taken from the surrounding region, things must have very much changed for the worse; for there are now but two trees in the whole country, one at Nakhl and one in the Wady Fahdí.

The reader is begged, to save the trouble of description, to follow the route of the travellers in the map of the journey issued by the Fund. At the foot of Jebel 'Araif were found three circles (tombs), and at the mouth of the Wady Máyín the remains of what had once been a large collection of dwellings—a city that

has become quite literally "a desolate heap."
In the Wady Lussan were observed signs of
former cultivation, in the shape of dams constructed across the valley, while on the higher
slopes were long, low walls; the object being to
divide the enclosure into terraces. This, it will
be remarked, is exactly the same method—the
only one possible—as that employed in the
Sinai Peninsula. On the hill-side, too, were the
ruins of a dwelling-house, something like a Pom-
peian villa, with a cistern and a granary. It
seems probable, in the absence of any evidence,
that this may have been one of the farms with
which the wadies were studded previous to the
great overthrow by Chosroes the Persian. The
name suggests an identification with the ancient
Roman station of Lysa, mentioned in the Peutinger tables as being forty-eight Roman miles
distant from Eboda.

It is now many years since Dr. Rowlands, travelling with Mr. George Williams, suggested the
identification of Ain Gadìs with the disputed
Kadesh. Dr. Rowland, however, applied the
name wrongly to Ain el Gudeirat, situated a
few miles to the north. The place really called
Ain Gadìs consists of three springs or shallow
pools; one of these overflowing in the rainy
season, and producing a stream of water. They
are situated in lat. 31° 34′ N., and long. 40° 31′ E.,
three miles beyond the watershed of the valley,
at that part of the previously unexplored plateau
of the Azazimêh Mountains where they fall sud-

U

denly to a lower level; and, as was found on subsequently passing through it, is more open and
more easily approached from the direction of
Akaba. It is thus situated at what Mr. Palmer calls "one of the natural borders of the
country." What he means by a natural border
is very easily seen. From Northern Syria to
Sinai the country has certain natural divisions,
marked by the comparative fertility of each.
In Syria is a well watered and productive soil.
In Palestine the soil is much less fertile; but
must at some time, under better cultivation,
have been more productive than at present.
South of Palestine the Negeb extends over
what is now a barren waste, but was once a
blooming and fertile tract. Then comes the Tíh,
a country which, even when better watered, could
never have been more than a vast camping
ground, with pasture for flocks and camels, such
as the Israelites had with them. So that we
have four clearly defined districts, on an ascending scale of fertility: the Tíh, the Negeb,
Palestine, and Syria.

We are told that the spies went from Kadesh,
and returned, bringing grapes from Eshkol (Numbers, xiii. 23). Now, Eshkol has generally been
identified with Hebron; the principal reason for
this being that Hebron is the most southerly place
where grapes are found. But it was not always
so; for one of the most curious things discovered
by Messrs. Palmer and Drake was the existence
of miles upon miles of the small stone-heaps on

which, in former times, the vines were trained.
The spies would, therefore, be under no necessity of going so far as Hebron. But our travellers
would, in any case, put Eshkol some way south
of Hebron. Mr. Palmer rejects Dr. Robinson's
theory that Kadesh was at Ain el Weibeh, chiefly
for strategic reasons.

In the Wady Muweilíh is a spring which it has
been suggested is Hagar's Well, though the orthodox Mussulman traditions place it near
Mecca. Here are two caves, once the retreat of
some Christian hermit, in the days (A.D. 200 to
A.D. 600) when the whole of Palestine was a
nest of hermitages and monasteries. "Nothing,"
says Mr. Palmer, "affords me greater satisfaction
than the ruins of convents and hermitages. . . .
one feels that only a just and fit consummation
has been attained." The caves were marked by
Arab tribe marks, called by some travellers
"planetary signs." In point of fact, Mr. Palmer
was, we believe, the first to point out they are in
reality nothing but distorted Himyaritic letters.

On the three hills round Wady Muweilíh were
the relics of a primæval people, cairns and dwellings, with a new feature—a large number of
well-made heaps of stone, placed with regularity
along the edges of the cliffs, and facing the east.
Too small for tombs, too far apart to have been
a wall—what were they? It is supposed that
they are connected with the worship of Baal—
altars of the Sun God. The ruins evidence the
existence here of a very large and populous city.

Since it was destroyed, how many generations
have passed away? Was it a city of the Amalekites, or are we to go farther back still into these
pre-historic times, when the Amalekites themselves were strangers in the land?

Leaving Muweilíh, and passing more primæval remains, which here present a new feature—
pillars of stone accompanying the cairns on the
more prominent summits—the traveller is struck
with the increasing signs of former cultivation.
The hill-sides are covered with paths and walls,
the wadies are thickly set with dams, and the
hills themselves are covered with innumerable
stone remains; for we are passing across one
of the "natural borders" of the country, the
desert of the Tíh is behind us, and before us are
the borders of the "South country."

THE SOUTH COUNTRY.

Leaving, then, the Desert of the Tíh, we find
that we are still in presence of the mysterious
mounds, circles, and cairns of which we have
already seen so much. Arrived at Bircin, a large
number of Terabin and Azazimêh Arabs were
found encamped there, with their flocks and
herds, in mortal terror at the arrival of the
strangers, who were supposed to be Turkish military officers. Wady Bircin is described as a
broad valley, filled with vegetation, grass, as-
phodel, and *oshej* growing in profusion. Here,
besides the cairns and circles, are extensive ruins
of houses, among them being the foundations of

a square building and a tower, but no signs of
a church. Here, too, are two deep wells, one
of them yielding good water, and surrounded
with troughs for watering the flocks and herds.
The surrounding heights, too, are covered with
dilapidated cairns. The name and site suggested nothing to help in an identification; and
after a careful examination of these nameless
ruins, the travellers passed on to El Aujeh. On
the way, an incident is recorded, curious as
showing how names may be held back and
hidden from travellers. There is a broad, open
valley between Birein and El Aujeh, laid out,
with great industry, in terraces with strong em-
bankments. If an ordinary traveller asks the
name of the wady, he is told that it is the Wady
Hafir. Its real name, which has never before
been breathed to Christian ears, is the Wady
Hanein, and the reason of the secrecy is found
in an Arab superstition that should a *scil* (a
flood) come down the valley, there will be an
end to the prosperity of the country. To prevent
the Christians—everywhere believed to have control over the rain—from bringing down a flood,
the natives have given the place another name.

We come next to the ruins of El Aujeh. The
principal buildings—namely, the fort and the
church—stand upon the summit of a low hill,
round which sweeps the Wady Hanein. The
ruins of the town itself lie in the valley, and are
of considerable extent, though now little more
than a confused heap of broken walls and half-

filled fountains. Among them was discovered a
ruined church, the apse still standing, and some
of the columns lying broken in the *débris*. On
the slopes are innumerable rows of the grape
mounds spoken of above (p. 290). The church on
the hill is in the best state of preservation of all
the ruins. The wall in some parts is 23 ft. 6 in. in
height and 8 ft. thick; in others it is about 15 ft.
high. It is built of squared and dressed stones,
with a light cement like mud. The church is 122 ft.
long and 48 ft. wide, with three apses. There was
no trace of ornamentation, except on two fragments of stone, which bore a simple quatrefoil
pattern; nor any inscriptions, except scratches
of Greek letters. The walls were originally
plastered. The Orientation of the church is not
exact. No suggestion has been offered by Mr.
Palmer as to the ancient name of the city.

When, thirty years ago, Mr. George Williams
and Dr. Rowlands were travelling across the
Negeb, they heard of a site called Sebâta,
which Dr. Rowlands, in a letter published in
Williams's "Holy City" (vol. i., p. 463 *et seq.*), identifies with Zephath (Judges, i. 17). (Dr. Robinson's
Zephath is the Pass Es-Sufâ, by which the ascent
is made from the borders of the Arabah to the
higher level of the "South country.") Zephath
was the name of a Canaanite city destroyed by
the tribes of Judah and Simeon after the death
of Joshua. The city being destroyed, they called
it Hormah. After the visit of Dr. Rowlands—it
is not quite clear from his letter that he actually

saw the site—no traveller heard of Sebâta till Mr. Palmer discovered it anew, and was enabled to confirm his predecessor's statements, and to accept his theory.

On the way to the place, the travellers first came to a ruined fortress called El Meshrifeh, standing in a commanding position on the top of a hill. It consists of a walled enclosure protected by three large towers on the southern side, one on the eastern, and one on the western, with a series of escarpments and bastions on the southern and most precipitous cliff. Behind the first tier of escarpments the rocks are excavated into caves, fronted with masonry, so as to form a series of chambers in which sentinels or sharpshooters might be posted. The most westerly of them is of a ruder construction than the rest, and the wall in front is built of large unhewn stones, apparently of a much earlier date. The walls of the fort are strongly built, mostly of unhewn stones, and in the centre is a building 40 ft. square, with three chambers at the west end, and a large open space at the east. In front of this are three circles, built round with upright stones, and sunk a little below the surface, leading one into the other, and measuring respectively 50 ft., 25 ft., and 12 ft. in diameter, each being twice as great in diameter as the one that follows. These circles may possibly be traces of the primæval fort which existed here before the present building, allowed to remain through the reverence or superstition of the builders. The church, which resembles that of El Aujeh, measures 40 ft. by 30 ft., with a semi-circular apse at the east end. The towers are built in a series of tiers, with "pigeon holes" about 3½ ft. high—evidently a fortress of Roman times, if not of Roman architecture.

The country visible from the fort bears marks of very extensive and careful cultivation. Three miles and a half to the south stand the ruins of Sebaita—Dr. Rowlands's "Sebâta." The ruins of this place are more extensive than many others in the "South country." "Nothing," say the Arabs, "is grander than El Aujeh and El Abdeh, except Sebaita, which is grander than either." All round the city lie the gardens which once were covered with orchards of apples and pomegranates, and terraces of clustering vines. The city itself is marked by an expanse of ruins 500 yards long and from 200 to 300 yards wide; containing three churches, a tower, and two reservoirs for water. No timber is used in the building of the houses, the absence of wood being supplied by thick beams of stone.* Nearly every house had its well, about 2 ft. in diameter, and covered with square stone blocks having holes cut in them. The streets can still be traced, and the outer buildings are either walled in or strengthened with additional masonry, presenting a series of angles like a fortification.

* Compare this account with that by the Count de Vogüé, in the "Recovery of Jerusalem," of the buildings of the Hauran.

The churches are very interesting. The largest, which has three apses and a side chapel, like that of El Aujeh and El Meshrifeh, measures 49 by 21 yards wide, nearly half of this length being taken up by a building, apparently of later date, presumably part of a monastery. The interiors of the churches are similar to the ordinary Byzantine basilica type; but the outer walls have been gradually strengthened, till they are like fortresses. No inscriptions of any kind were found, and no ornamentation, except a few fragments of stone with the same quatrefoil pattern as that found at El Aujeh. On the side of the tower, however, is a small arched doorway, with a rudely sculptured design representing three circles with crosses between, and surmounted by an urn, from which a palm tree is growing, supported by a lion rampant, and a griffin standing upon the handles. This was ornamented with red and blue paint.

So much for the existing evidence. A hill fortress, and, three miles off, a large fortified city. Turn now to the Bible. There we read that the Israelites, when they attempted to force a passage into the hill country, were driven back and defeated by the Amalekites and the Canaanites, at a pass in the mountains near Hormah (see above, and Numbers, xiv. 40—45). Now, supposing Ain Gadis to be Kadesh, the fort of El Meshrifeh commands the only pass by which the plain where Sebaita, or Hormah, stands can be approached. It answers to the description in the

Bible.   The distance of Sebaita from Ain Gadis
is only twenty miles.   The names Dheigat el
Amerín (ravine of the Amorites), Rás Amir (a
chain of low mountains fifteen miles south-west·
of El Meshrifeh), and Sheikh el Amir (a place in
the immediate neighbourhood of El Meshrifeh),
all point to the identification of this region with the
hill country of the Amorites.   Thus the name, Sebaita, is etymologically identical with the Zephath
of the Bible.   Zephath means watch tower, and it
is remarkable that the fort El Meshrifeh exactly
corresponds both in situation and in name.   Mr.
Palmer suggests here that the city, though three
miles .distant from the fortress which protected
it, might yet well be called the City of the Watch
Tower; so that in El Meshrifeh we should have
the Zephath itself, and in Sebaita the city of the
Zephath.

The theory advanced by Professor Palmer is
opposed to that of Dr. Robinson; on the other
hand, the learned American explorer had not the
advantage of visiting Sebaita.   As has been
already explained, we give throughout the views
of our explorers, without at all pronouncing any
opinion on their value.

One remark, however, may be permitted.   If
Mr. Palmer is correct in his theory, is it not a
wonderful instance of the tenacity of names in
the Holy Land?   It is now 3,500 years since
"Judah, with Simeon, his brother," changed the
name of Zephath to that of Hormah.   The place
has been successively Jewish, Roman, Christian,

Mohammedan, Christian again, and Mohammedan again. No doubt the town has been frequently destroyed and rebuilt, with, perhaps, new names from every successive conqueror. Yet the first old name, which it had before the Bible mentions it, lingers yet in the name which the Arabs give it at this day.

Two days' march brought them to the ruins of another town, new to modern research. No traces of a church were found, and the ruins—those only of a small town—are little more than a collection of stone heaps. On the north-east side of the wady, opposite to that on which the ruins lie, is an ancient well, the troughs and other masonry, which still remain, being of immense proportions, and apparently of very great antiquity. One of the troughs is round, and the other circular, and cut in blocks 6 ft. by 5 ft. by 5 ft. Within a mile or two of these ruins lie those of Ruhaibeh, which is generally identified with Rehoboth. In Genesis, xxvi. 21, 22, we read that Isaac's servants dug two wells, of which they were deprived by the herdsmen of Gerar; whereupon he called the first well *Esek*, or *contortion;* and the second *Sitnah*, or *hatred;* and then removing to another place dug a third well, which he called *Rehoboth*, or *room*, saying—

" Now the Lord hath made room for us,
And we shall be fruitful in the land."

In Ruhaibeh itself, Dr. Robinson could not find a well at all; Dr. Stewart found it "regularly built, and 12 ft. in circumference;" Dr. Rowlands

found it "an ancient well of living and good
water." Mr. Palmer's account explains these conflicting accounts.   He and Mr. Drake could not at
first find any well ; then they found it was built
over and nearly filled with rubbish, its site being
marked by a piece of fallen masonry, apparently
the roof of a cupola, and strongly put together
with flat, brick-shaped stones and cement. There
is no other well than this in the Wady Ruhaibeh.
On the left of the wady is a small valley called
Shatneh er Ruhaibeh, in which we see the word
Sitnah, so that two of the three words are preserved.   It is a pity that no trace remains of the
third word, the well *Esek*.   Mr. Palmer suggests
that perhaps the great well of the Wady Sádi
may possibly be that of Isaac.

Khalasah, the Elusa laid down on the Peutinger
tables, lies in shapeless ruins in the Wady Aslúj,
not in the Wady El Kurn, as stated by Dr.
Robinson.   The people of Gaza, thirty miles
away, come over and remove the stones, taking
away even the foundations of the houses; so that
in time there will probably remain not even a
trace of the ancient town.   Here the worship of
Venus was formerly carried on, though it afterwards became an episcopal city.

Lastly, we arrive at Beersheba, the well of the
seven, or the well of the *oath* (Genesis, xxi. 31).
" There were seven wells," say the Arabs, " and
each well had seven tanks, and each tank had
seven troughs, and each trough had seven horses
drinking thereat."   Three wells remain, of which

two are filled with water, and one is dry: they are
built of fine solid masonry, and are in a tolerably
perfect condition. In the immediate neighbourhood are traces of the other four wells which once
existed here. The hill-side is covered with ruins,
now so confused that little can be made out.
Among them, however, was found the ground plan
of a perfect Greek church, with a semicircular apse.
Beersheba was once an episcopal city. But "the
cities of the South country shall be shut up and
none shall open them" (Jeremiah, xiii. 19); and
surely, in this journey from Jebel Maghrah to
Hebron, enough has been described to illustrate
the prophecy. After visiting Haurá, lying off the
road on the right, with its caves, cisterns, and
flint-built houses, they entered Palestine, and left,
for a time, the South country behind them.

Another ruined city, called now Dátraiyeh, was
discovered after leaving Haurá. It lies on the
left of the road, and consists of walls and houses
of solid masonry, some of the stones employed in
their construction being of immense size. The
basements are for the most part built in arches,
somewhat after the style of construction prevalent
at Sebaita. There is also a large system of wells
and excavated reservoirs. Farther on, the village
of Ed Dhahairiyeh was reached, where, according
to "Murray's Handbook," "there is nothing of
interest to detain the pilgrim." For once the
guide-book proved wrong; for the hill proved,
on further examination, a most interesting place.
It is covered with dwellings, consisting for the

most part of caves cut in the natural rock, some
of them having rude arches carved over the
doorways, and all of them being of great antiquity.
The spots selected for excavation are small ter
races on the hill-sides; these are walled round
with wood fences, and form a sort of courtyard in
front of the cave, where the dogs, goats, chickens,
children, and other members of the family take
the air. They are exactly like what the old
Horite dwellings must have been, and have doubtless been inhabited by generation after generation
since the days of that now forgotten race. The
village is evidently an ancient site; in the midst
of it is the basement of a building of massive
masonry, containing three arched apartments.
Old arches and other remains of antiquity appear
at every corner of the village.

After this, Hebron; and then, Jerusalem. Mr.
Palmer informs us, *en parenthèse,* that this part of
the journey, 600 miles, had been done wholly on
foot; that, besides the travelling, they had also
to perform for themselves all the menial and
domestic duties, as they had no servant; that
there was also the route sketching in the making
of plans, and other work; and that, finally, both
himself and Mr. Tyrwhitt Drake, who devoted
himself with equal energy to his own investigations and those of Mr. Palmer, seldom worked
less than from fourteen to sixteen hours a day.

After a little rest at Jerusalem, which was only
physical rest, because the time was entirely
given up to putting together their notes, they

started again for the South, this time taking a path—or rather, making a path—nearly parallel with the previous one, from ten to twenty miles east of it. This led them at first through the scenes of those eventful passages in David's life when he fled from the persecutions of Saul, and led the life of a robber chieftain on the borders of the wilderness of Paran. Ruined sites followed each other in quick succession, bearing nearly the same names now—Zif, Maîn, Kirmîl, and so on—as they bore in the time of David. Among these sites is one called Tel Arad. It is now nothing but a large white mound, marking the site of the city once ruled over by that Canaanitish king who, when "he heard tell that Israel came by the way of the spies, then he fought against Israel, and took some of them prisoners" (Numbers, xxi. 1). There is a considerable ruin at Kuseifeh, with the remains of a church; and at Tel Milh—where, according to Arab legend, Abraham dug wells and used to water his herds—are two wells of fine masonry. Milh is the Mount Moladah, mentioned in 1 Chronicles, iv. 28, and in Nehemiah, xi. 26. Ruins here, too; but too much injured by the hand of time and man for any plan of the city to be made out.

Next day, Wady Arárah was reached, the Aroer of Judah, one of the cities to which David, when he came to Ziklag, after his victory over the Amalekites, sent a share of the spoil. (1 Samuel, xxx. 28). A few walls only remain to mark the site of the city. And then—for we are getting south again—the face of the country begins to assume the character of a wilderness. Here and there, but at longer intervals, occur the vestiges of ancient habitations; but with the exception of a group of dismantled buildings— probably a wayside station on the old Roman road—no more ruins were found until Wady Rukhmeh was reached; nor, after that, till they came to the plain of El Jebail. And here we are in a place where no European traveller, so far as has been recorded, has yet set his foot— a wild, desolate place, where the Arabs are more suspicious than any before visited; but where there was a city they knew of—a city never before visited or heard of—the ruins of Abdeh. You will see it in the map, about seven miles to the south-east of Sebaita, at the head of the Wady Marreh, built like all these ruined cities, where the natural position afforded of itself means of defence. So was built Jerusalem, in the days when the Jebusites laughed at David's soldiers, and set their old and infirm upon the walls to mock his efforts at scaling their mountain fortress. The precipitous end of the plateau on which it stands is escarped, and the face furnished with an arrangement of chambers similar to those described as existing at Meshrifeh. The ruins consist of a fort, with a collection of buildings encompassed by a wall. A cross sculptured on one of the doors marks the architecture as Christian. To the south lie, in the valley, the ruins of a small town or village; so that, just as Sebaita was to Meshrifeh, so this low-lying town was to the fortress which protected it. Abdeh appears to be, beyond a doubt, the ancient Eboda.

We have spent so long a time over the South country that we must pass over a portion of Professor Palmer's narrative, and refer the reader to the abundant details to be found in the large work from which this narrative is condensed. We make no apology to Professor Palmer for using his own language in the descriptions; because in narrating "our work," we can do nothing better than present, as closely as is consistent with our space, the accounts given by the explorers themselves. A few of Mr. Palmer's closing remarks on the Negeb will be interesting. He calls attention to the fact that the Bible, besides speaking of the Negeb as applied generally to the whole district, gives it with other words indicating geographical or ethnological subdivision. The principal of these are the Negeb of the Cherethites, the Negeb of the Kenites, the Negeb of Judah, the Negeb of Caleb, the Negeb of Arad, and the Negeb of Jerahmeel. From a consideration of 1 Samuel, xxx. 14, 16, compared with Joshua, xxi. 11, 12, we learn that David made a raid upon the Negeb of the Cherethites and the Negeb of Caleb, but that the territory of Caleb was in the hill country of Judah, and consisted of "the fields of Hebron and the villages thereof." See also 1 Samuel xxv. 2, 3. Herein it appears that

X

the Negeb of Caleb was a subdivision of, if not identical with, the Negeb of Judah. The Negeb of the Kenites, again, may be placed in the neighbourhood of Tel Arad, because (Judges, i. 16) we learn that the Kenite, Jethro, went up "into the wilderness of Judah, which lieth in the Negeb of Arad." In Jebel Rukhmeh is found, by one who is linguist enough to see it, a reminiscence of the name of Jerahmeel, the name of the remaining portion of the Negeb. Since we are not all Arabic scholars, it is good to be informed that a similar process—the suppression of the Je—has taken place in the name Jericho, which has become in the modern Arabic, Rihá. Does not a little scrap of information like this teach us the vitality of names in Palestine, and the immense value of an explorer acquainted with Arabic ?

So that, after putting together all our information, linguistic and otherwise, we arrive at the following divisions of the South country:—

1. In the low country north and west of Beersheba we recognize the Negeb of the Cherethites.

2. South of Hebron, in the outposts of the hills of Judah, we can identify the Negeb of Judah, the ruined cities of Tel Zíf, Maín, and Kurmul, indicating the locality of the Negeb of Caleb.

3. Tel Arad and its adjacent plains form the Negeb of the Kenites, probably extending to the south-western end of the Dead Sea.

4. Between Wady Rukhmeh in the north, and Wadies El Abyadh, Marreh, and Maduah, in the

south, lay the Negeb of Jerahmeel. The mountains of the Azazimêh were not included in the Negeb.

As for the people who lived in this region, we are told (1 Samuel, xxvii. 8) that "the Amalekites were of old the inhabitants of the land as thou goest to Shur, even unto Egypt." Numbers, xiv. 25 and 45, speaks of both the Amalekites and Canaanites, in the former verse as occupying the valleys, and in the latter as dwelling in the hills. At first, an apparent contradiction. But no, because it helps us to identify the locality, which is described in Genesis, xiv. 7, as "the country of the Amalekites and the Ammonites." Now the word rendered country is *sádeh*, and might be exactly translated as *plateau*. "The division of territory," says Mr. Palmer, "between tribes living in the hills and others occupying the fertile regions at the lower level to which the seils and wadies debouch, precisely accords with our own experience of the present inhabitants; and the words of the Bible might be aptly applied to the Azazimêh, Terabin, and Teyáhah now, as they were to the Amalekites, Canaanites, and Amorites, in the time of the Patriarchs and the Judges."

In leaving the South territory, let us call attention once more to the map published by the Fund in January, 1870. The country to right and left of the route was carefully examined. Everywhere ruins; everywhere the remains of wells, aqueducts, reservoirs; everywhere the tokens of population, fertility, civilization, and prosperity. Christian

churches, where the people worshipped, as we worship now, for five centuries. Mountain forts, built
to resist the forays of the "Sons of the Desert."
Desolated gardens, once fair and luxuriant, lying
round the ruins. Valleys dammed to resist the
force of the torrent, and hill-sides laid out in terraces to receive the water. A land that awaits the
hand of industry to renew its youth; a soil which,
after two thousand years at least of varying
fortune but constant cultivation, has lain fallow
for twelve hundred years, till the toiler should
come once more. Surely, thinking of the words
of the Prophet, there was room here for the
"strange and solemn thoughts" which fell upon
our travellers when they looked back upon the
work they had accomplished.

EDOM.

Leaving the country of the Azazimêh, and
now descending into the Arabah (see the map),
we find ourselves in the ancient country of
Edom—the "Red country"—or the "country of
Esau the Red," formerly called Mount Seir, the
Rugged. Before the land was taken by the descendants of Esau—according to the promise—it
was inhabited by the Horites, a nation of cave-
dwellers. It extends from the Dead Sea to the
Gulf of Akaba, where once stood the seaport
Elath. It is a singularly fertile country; the
valleys and flat terraces on the mountain sides
abounding with trees, shrubs, and flowers, reminding us of Isaac's prophecy to Esau: "Thy

dwelling shall be the fatness of the earth."
"With a peaceful and industrious population, it
might become," says Mr. Palmer, "one of the
wealthiest—as it is one of the most picturesque
—countries in the world." But the gifts of nature are lavished in vain; and what little crops
the Fellahín can rear serve for very little other
purpose than to excite the cupidity of the Bedawin, and to keep alive perpetual wars and
feuds. The northern part of Edom is called El
Jebál (formerly Gebal), in which are the villages
of Tufílch, Buserah, and Shobek. The northern
portion is called Es Sherah. The country is inhabited by Fellahín (chiefly in the north), the
Hejáyah Bedawin, the Haweitát, and the Ammarín; the latter being described by our traveller as so poor and degraded as not even to
have the Bedawi virtue of keeping their word.
In the immediate neighbourhood of Wady Músa
are a tribe of Fellahín called the Liyátheneh.
This curious people possesses so marked a Jewish
type of countenance that some travellers have
imagined them to be the descendants of those
Simeonites who settled in Edom. But Mr. Palmer has ascertained this view to be erroneous,
and has given them an origin equally interesting.
They came into the country at the time of the
Mohammedan conquest, and are a branch of
the Kheibari Jews, who resided near Mecca, and
played an important part in the early history of
Islám. The Kheibari are still found in large
numbers in Mecca and Medina, and enjoy the

reputation of robbing and murdering stragglers from the Hajj caravans. Dr. Wolff identifies them with the Rechabites mentioned in Jeremiah (xxxv. 6, 7):—" They said, We will drink no wine, for Jonadab, the son of Rechab, our father commanded us, saying, Ye shall drink no wine, neither ye, nor your sons for ever. Neither shall ye build houses, nor sow seed, nor plant vineyard, nor have any; but all your days ye shall dwell in tents, that ye may live many days in the land where ye be strangers."

The Liyáthench profess to be Mohammedans, but their morals are much more lax than those of the Bedawin. They retain not only the distinctive physiognomy, but also many of the customs of the Jews; such as wearing the Pharisaic love-locks.

On approaching Petra, Messrs. Palmer and Drake were met with the news that the Arab tribes were at war, and that the place was closed to travellers. Trusting, however, to their small and unpretending cortége, and to their own knowledge of native character and customs, they determined to keep on at all risks. Accordingly, they entered the mountains of Edom, meeting at first with no molestation, and pitched their tent on the top of a pass to the north-west of Mount Hor (Jebel Hárún), on the top of which is the reputed tomb of Aaron. But they were not destined to examine the tomb unmolested. Just as they reached the base of the highest peak, a boy who was herding goats saw them, and began shrieking wildly to the Arabs below in the wady. Let us describe the scene in Mr. Palmer's own words:—"His cry was soon answered by a loud report in the valley below, and in a few minutes the rocks around echoed with the firing of alarm guns, and an ominous din was heard coming from the direction of Petra itself. The first thing which met our eyes when we stepped upon the small plateau, immediately below the summit, was a heap of ruins, and, beside the rock, a huge black cauldron, used for boiling the sheep which were there sacrificed to the 'Prophet Aaron.' A flight of steps, cut out in the rock, leads up a steep precipice to the tomb itself; and about half-way up those steps is a large cistern or chamber covered in with arches, over which the staircase is built. The door of the tomb, which is an ordinary Moslem *well*, was locked at the time; but we contrived to look inside, and saw that the roof was decorated with ostrich shells and similar ornaments. Over the door is an inscription, stating that the building was restored by Es Shim'ani, the son of Mohammed Calaín, Sultan of Egypt, by his father's orders, in the year 739 of the Hijrah."

The so-called tomb itself, which has been described by previous travellers, is a square building, of rude stones and old materials, measuring inside 28 ft. by 33. The interior of the chapel consists of two chambers, one below the other. The upper one has four large pillars and a stone chest, at the head of which sacrifices are made.

Steps lead down to the lower chamber, which is
partly in the rock, partly plastered.   It is dark;
and at the end, apparently under the stone chest
above, is a recess, guarded by a grating.   Within
this is a rude protuberance, whether of stone or
plaster is unknown, resting on wood, and covered
by a ragged pall.   In one of the walls of the
upper chamber is a round polished black stone,
like the Kaaba of Mecca.*   Mr. Palmer was unable to penetrate to the interior, for "in the
meanwhile the noise in the valley grew louder
than ever, and we judged it time to descend;
for to have been surprised on the sacred mountain would inevitably have led to serious con-
sequences.   So, having stayed long enough to
boil the thermometer, read the aneroids, and
enable Drake to make a sketch of the magnificent mountain landscape which the summit
commands, we came down the steep sides of
Mount Hor rather quicker than ever I descended
a mountain either before or since.   We luckily
came across our own camels as soon as we reached
the valley; but immediately afterwards we were
set upon by a very unprepossessing gang of half
naked savages, who turned out to be Arabs of
the Maàzah tribe.   They accused us of having
'visited the Prophet' by stealth, swore they
would confiscate one of our camels, and otherwise
made themselves objectionable; but our Jelalín
camel drivers—especially the one who had accom-

* See "Dictionary of the Bible," vol. i., p. 825.

panied us in our somewhat perilous attempt—
swore that we had not done so, and by judiciously
bestowing a few piastres we got rid of them.
We then made for our camping-place, and were
approaching the solitary pillar called Zibb Farún,
when a furious shout was heard in the valley, and
about twenty or thirty armed men were seen
rushing upon us. We were quite prepared for a
scene and a row; but as we were dressed in native
costume, and very dirty, they were thrown off
their guard by our appearance, met us with
friendly demonstrations, and rushed off shouting
as before, declaring that the enemy were upon.
them."

These difficulties being got through, there was
nothing to prevent a quiet examination of Petra.
The reader may refer to Mr. Palmer's book for
his description of this, perhaps the most curious
and interesting city in the world. It is exces-
sively ancient, having been first—*i.e.*, historically
first—known as Selah, and is mentioned twice in
the Old Testament—once in 2 Kings, xiv. 7, when
Amaziah "slew of Edom in the valley of salt
ten thousand, and took Selah by war;" and once
when Isaiah tells the Moabites (xvi. 1) to send
"to the lamb the ruler of the land from Selah to
the wilderness, unto the mount of the daughter
of Zion."

The city, which became the capital of the Na-
batheans about the fourth century before Christ,
is briefly but accurately described by Strabo. It
is mentioned by Pliny, Josephus, Eusebius, and

Justinian, and became an episcopal city before its conquest by the Mohammedans. After that, it was absolutely unknown until, in 1807, Seetzen collected and published reports of wondrous remains in the Wady Músa, and Burckhardt visited the place in 1812. In 1818 it was visited by Messrs. Irby, Mangles, Banks, and Legh. In 1828, Messrs. Laborde and Laurent spent eight days here, sketching and copying. Since then, travellers in great numbers have visited the city, and descriptions of the ruins, with photographs and sketches, have been repeatedly published. To those who have read accounts of Petra, or who have seen the place, one observation of Mr. Palmer's will prove of interest. They will remember the Khazneh, the "Treasure," that exquisite work of art which, "in grandeur of situation, in richness of natural colouring, and in singularity of construction, stands unrivalled in the world."* Many theories have been propounded as to what it was intended for. Mr. Palmer's will be accepted, at least, as the latest and most original. He says:—

"The façade of the temple consists of a portico, originally of six columns, but one of them has now broken away. The four middle pillars support a pediment. On the apex of this is an ornament which has been variously described, but which a more careful inspection proved to be a lyre. Above the whole is a very curious piece

* "Murray's Handbook," p. 46.

of ornamentation. A second pediment, the width
of the whole façade, is supported by two pilasters at either end. The pediment has thus been
cut through on each side of the centre, and the
block so left has been fashioned into a cylindrical
ornament surmounted by an urn. The cylinder
and the recess thus formed have been then furnished with pilasters, and dressed to correspond
with the front portions. This pediment, which is
thus divided into three portions, forms nine
faces of rock, each having a pilaster on either
side, and in them are sculptured female figures
with flowing drapery. The curious device was
in all probability adopted to admit of the sym-
metrical arrangement of nine figures—those, I
take it, of the Nine Muses. The lyre, the emblem
of Apollo, being also introduced, lends colour
to the supposition that it was dedicated to these
divinities. The mysterious excavation, then, is
nothing but the Museum of Petra—not what the
Turks would call an 'Antiquity House,' but the
Philharmonic Institution of the place."

Getting away from Petra was a process far
more difficult than getting into it, on account of
the anxiety of the Liyátheneh not to let their
visitors go until the last bit of possible plunder
was extracted from them. It was effected, however, by playing off the Ammarín Arabs against
the Liyátheneh, and by preserving in the midst
of the general "row" an unconcerned demeanour,
which the natives construed into reliance on some
unseen resources of which they were ignorant,

possibly Turkish soldiers. The travellers had
now resolved upon taking the extremely dangerous route up the Arabah, to the south of the Dead
Sea, and so along its eastern shores into Moab,
where it was hoped some new inscriptions would
be found. In this hope, as will be seen, they were
disappointed. A few miles north of Petra they
had the good fortune to discover two ruined cities,
named respectively El Beidha and El Barid. The
latter, a sort of smaller Petra, is approached by a
small ravine, so narrow that it has once been closed
by gates, the sockets being still distinctly visible.
Then the ravine widens out, and you "enter a
street of dwellings, temples, and cisterns all cut
out of the rock, not so elaborate as those of Petra,
and wanting the beautiful colouring of the latter,
but still very pretty. At every point are stair-
cases made in the small clefts, and sometimes in
the face of the rock, most of them leading to
platforms in 'high places,' designed, perhaps, for
sacrificial purposes. Some of the temples have
plaster on the interior walls, and this is rudely
painted to represent stones. One has a very
elaborately painted ceiling, containing a pretty
design of flowers, festoons of grape vines, and
convolvuli, with Cupids playing about in the
branches, and some of them holding drawn bows."
The whole ravine is full of oleanders, and carpeted
with the softest grass; it terminates abruptly in
a narrow cleft, at the top of which is a temple,
the façade of which has fallen down, and blocked
up the way. The city was evidently Horite in

its origin—as all the caves were evidently used as dwellings—but has been occupied by later peoples. The Arabs have a certain tradition, to the effect that the former inhabitants of the city found a door in the rock, leading to a rich and fertile subterranean land, with which they were so pleased that they all went into it, closing the door behind them.

Who, asks our author, that passes through this goodly but desolate land and regards the vestiges of perished grandeur in these rock-hewn cities, can recall without emotion the solemn words of prophecy?—"Thy terribleness hath deceived thee, and the pride of thine heart, *O thou that dwellest in the clefts of the rock, that holdest the height of the hill:* though thou shouldest make thy nest as high as the eagle, I will bring thee down from thence, saith the Lord. Also Edom shall be a desolation: every one that goeth by it shall be astonished, and shall hiss at all the plagues thereof."—Jeremiah, xlix. 16, 17.

Two more days brought them to the Ghor, with its tropical vegetation and its almost tropical climate, and they found themselves on the shores of the Dead Sea. "The sky was overcast with clouds, and a dense haze, obscuring the mountains, made the landscape as dreary and monotonous as it could be. In an aspect such as this, the Dead Sea seemed more than ever to deserve its name. Not a sign of life was there—not even any motion, save a dull, mechanical surging of the water. The barren shore was covered with a thick incrustation of salt, relieved only by occasional patches of black, rotting mud, or by stagnant pools of brine. All along the dismal beach large quantities of drift-wood are thickly strewn, and amongst them might be detected the blackened trunks of palms."

Keeping along this mournful shore, they reached the ruins called N'meirah, which is probably identical with "the waters of Nimrim," mentioned by Isaiah, chap. xv.:—"My heart shall cry out for Moab . . . . for the waters of Nimrim shall be desolate: for the hay is withered away, the grass faileth, there is no green thing."

Descriptions of the Dead Sea are found in every book on Palestine. The admirable work done by Lieutenant Lynch, of the American navy, in the year 1848 (see "Narrative of the United States Expedition to the River Jordan and the Dead Sea." Bentley: 1850), has been followed up by the researches of M. Lartet, Dr. Tristram, and others; so that there would appear at first as if there was nothing left to explore. But the work of minute exploration is very long, and takes many such expeditions as are generally made in Palestine. Thus the Lisan, "the Tongue," the broad promontory extending northwards from the south-east corner of the Dead Sea, had only been visited before by the Duc de Luynes and Lieutenant Lynch; so that Messrs. Palmer and Drake may claim the credit of being the first to explore thoroughly this curious spot. Mr. Palmer describes it as a plateau of soft chalk

or marl, encrusted with salt, and containing large
quantities of sulphur in a very pure form. "The
surface is for the most part perfectly flat, but a
few little plateaus rise up here and there upon
it. The strip of land which connects it with the
shore is lower than the rest; and the impression
conveyed to our minds was that this isthmus had
been under water, and that the main body of the
promontory had formed an island at some period
when the level of the sea was higher than it is at
present. That such was once the case, we were
able to ascertain on subsequently visiting the
coast farther to the north from Moab. Here
the rocks come down precipitously almost to the
water's edge, and former water-lines can be
plainly detected upon the lower portion of the
cliffs. The south-eastern edge—that adjoining
the isthmus—is cut up into deep wadies, which,
however, run only for a short distance, and then
stop abruptly, as the soil is too absorbent to
admit of a long flow of water. It was by one of
these valleys, called El Meraïkh, that we entered
the Lisan, and proceeding a short distance down
it, we came upon the ruins of a tower built of
solid masonry, and a small reservoir. The tower
stood upon a hill, the side of which had been
strengthened in a very ingenious manner by
facing it with masonry composed of brick-shaped
stones, in order to counteract the crumbling
nature of the soil. On the site were some broken
columns of considerable architectural pretensions,
and many pieces of glass and pottery lying in

the ash-heap contiguous to the ruins; but we could find nothing to indicate the date. Making a circuit of the promontory, we came to a depression called Aril, situated at the south end of the bay which separates the mainland from the eastern edge of the Lisan. In this hollow, water collects during the rainy season, and it consequently shows some signs of fertility, containing a few shrubs and a fine spreading tree."

And now we have left Edom behind us, and are in the land of Moab.

MOAB.

The Land of Moab is a country about fifty miles long and twenty broad, including the table land east of Jordan, and that part of the Ghor lying on the eastern bank of the Jordan, opposite Jericho. It has been repeatedly visited, and its general features described (especially by Dr. Tristram); but, like all the rest of the country, never completely explored. The survey of Moab, when once undertaken, is certain to lead to results of the very greatest interest and importance. It will be the special work of the American Exploration Society, and we look forward with great hopes of hearing of new inscribed stones, when excavations can be conducted among the principal ruins. They are those of Rabbath, Moab, Kerak, Dibon, Medeba, Maín, and Umm Rasás. Of these, the most important are those of Kerak, the Kir Hareseth of the Bible. The entrance to this place is by a

natural arched tunnel, out of which the traveller emerges into the city, old and strong. Its
fortifications are of three distinct periods—
ancient, *i.e.*, perhaps of Jewish date—"for the
foundations of Kir Hareseth shall ye mourn"
(Isaiah, xvi. 7); those of Roman date; and,
lastly, of Crusading times. It was here that
Renaud de Chatillon, Seigneur or Marquis of
Kerak, strong in the possession of the fortress
and in the assistance of the Templars, defied the
authority of King Baldwin the Leper, and broke
the treaty with Saladin. It was a fatal treachery,
for it led to the fall of the Christian kingdom of
Jerusalem; though, perhaps, only a few years before
it would have fallen to pieces by its own corruption
and vices. Professor Palmer discovered the real
meaning of its old name—Kir Hareseth—which
has hitherto puzzled everybody. The fortress is
placed on the top of a steep hill, surrounded on
all sides by a deep and narrow valley. Now,
when, at Dhibán, Mr. Palmer asked an Arab
where the Moabite Stone was found, he was told
"between the *harithein*"—*i.e.*, between the two
hariths. It lay, in fact, between two hills; and
in Moab the Arabs call every hill a *harith*. But
the word *harith* is identical with the word *haresh*,
or *hareseth*, so that we have at once the meaning
of the name. Kir Hareseth is the *City of the Hill*
—emphatically so, because it is placed on the
most decided hill in the whole country. "Thus,"
says our author, " in an apparently insignificant
idiom, we have a confirmation of the accuracy

Y

of the Bible in topographical details, an additional reason for identifying the modern with the ancient site, and the interesting discovery of a local Moabite word handed down from the time of Jehoram, the son of Ahab, to the present day."

Everything in Moab speaks of its former wealth and cultivation. Even yet, though the soil is badly tended by the few Arab tribes who inhabit it, large tracts of pasture land and extensive corn fields meet the eye at every turn. Ruined cottages and towers, broken walls that once enclosed gardens and vineyards, remains of ancient roads, meet the traveller at every step. The thing to do, however, was obviously to find, if possible, another Moabite stone. The Arabs were asked everywhere for inscribed monuments; and the rumour spreading over the country, they had many a journey, undertaken from a message that in such a place an inscription was to be seen, only to find a stone covered with old tribe marks, natural veins, or, at the best, a fragmentary Nabathæan inscription. They were told of men who had buried stones, "the exact counterpart of the celebrated one;" of mysterious monuments in out-of-the-way places; but all to no result, and they left the country with a conviction that there does not remain *above ground* a single inscribed stone of any importance.

Among the rumours that reached them was one of an extraordinary "statue," called "Lot's

Wife;" and they resolved upon investigating the truth of the reports. Among the men employed in this little expedition was one who bore the name of *Fair*, a name not Mohammedan, nor even Arabic, but the literal representation of the old Moabitish idol, Baal Peor. Is not this a curious vestige of old local tradition?

The statue was found at the edge of the Dead Sea, in a plateau 1,000 ft. above its level. " It is a tall, isolated needle of rock, which really does bear a curious resemblance to an Arab woman with a child upon her shoulders. The Arab legend of Lot's wife differs from the Bible account only in the addition of a few frivolous details. They say that there were seven cities of the plain, and that they were all miraculously overwhelmed by the Dead Sea as a punishment for their crimes. The prophet Lot and his family alone escaped the general destruction. He was divinely warned to take all that he had and flee eastward, a strict injunction being given that they should not look behind them. Lot's wife, who had on previous occasions ridiculed her husband's prophetic office, disobeyed the command, and, turning to gaze upon the scene of the disaster, was changed into the pillar of rock."

Travellers in all ages have discovered a "Lot's Wife" in the pillars which atmospheric influences are constantly detaching from the great masses of mineral salt at the northern end of the Dead Sea; but these are all accidental and transient. The rock discovered by us does not

Y 2

fulfil the requirements of the Scriptural story; but there can be no doubt that it is the object which has served to keep alive for so many years the local tradition of the coast.

"The sun was just setting as we reached the spot; and the reddening orb sank down behind the western hills, throwing a bridge of sheeny light across the calm surface of the mysterious lake. As we gazed on the strange, statue-like outline of the rock—at first brought out into strong relief against the soft yet glowing hues of the surrounding landscape, and then mingled with the deepening shadows, and lost amid the general gloom as night came quickly on—we yielded insensibly to the influence of the wild Arab tale, and could almost believe that we had seen the form of the prophet's wife peering sadly after her perished home in the unknown depths of that accursed sea."

Mr. Palmer entirely agrees with Captain Wilson in placing the site of Sodom and Gomorrah at the northern extremity of the lake. Leaving the "Bint Sheikh Lot," the travellers proceeded on their journey to Shihan, the ancient Sihon, where they found little left but a few rude forts and dwellings, and, on the crest of the hill, a Roman temple, with some pieces of broken columns. Not far from Shihan is a square building, with a series of chambers built against the interior wall and an open courtyard in the centre, containing a tomb 26 ft. long, about which the Arabs dispute, some saying that it is the tomb

of David, and others that of Solomon. It is, of
course, a very sacred place; and numerous offerings, such as beads, buckles, coins, &c., have been
deposited by the Bedawin. Among them were
many of the curious worked goads with which
they drive their camels, the type for the sceptres
carried by the Kings of Egypt and Assyria.
The Arabs of Moab, like the ancient people whose
lands they occupy, are an essentially pastoral
people, their encampments being chosen entirely
for the sake of the cattle, and sometimes far
away from any fresh water. Sour or fresh milk
takes its place; and Mr. Palmer often found, in
asking for a drink of water, that none had been
in the encampment for days. He says that the
reception you meet with in the tents of the
Moabite Arabs reminds him often of the reception of Sisera by Jael, the wife of Heber the
Kenite. "And when he had turned in unto her
into the tent, she covered him with a mantle.
And he said unto her, Give me, I pray thee, a
little water to drink; for I am thirsty. And she
opened a bottle of milk, and gave him drink, and
covered him." King Mesha, as we know, was
a sheep-master, and "rendered unto the King
of Israel an hundred thousand lambs and an
hundred thousand rams with the wool."

Dhiban, the ancient Dibon, where the Moabite
Stone was found, shows traces of having once
been a flourishing town, though the ruins that
remain are all of Roman date. Some of the
fragments of the unfortunate stone—but, un-

luckily, none of the inscribed portions — are
still lying about. A wall runs round the
town; and near the gate of this, at the point
where the high road comes in, the stone was
found. Its preservation is apparently, therefore,
due to the fact of the later occupants of the
site having made use of it in constructing the
foundations of the city wall. When this, in
turn, had yielded to the destructive influence of
time, and the earth of the hill-side had also fallen
away, the stone rolled down into the valley, and
was once more brought forth into the light of
day.*

From Dhiban the explorers proceeded to
Umm Rasás, in search of another inscription,
which turned out to be nothing but a rude
Nabathæan sepulchral monument, of which a
squeeze had already been sent to Jerusalem.
The town contains two large churches of
the Byzantine period, and a tower about 50 ft.
high, with a curious legend attached to it
(see "Desert of the Exodus," p. 499). Mr.
Palmer thinks, from the meaning of its name,
"Mother of Lead," that it may be identified with
an episcopal town called Μέρων, or Μέρου.

And now the journey was drawing to a close.
They stood at last—a fitting end to wanderings
which had led them over the very ground trodden
by the Israelites—on that mountain where Moses

---

* See Appendix, which shows how one stone, at least,
of Herod's Temple was preserved in a precisely similar
manner.

gazed for the first time upon the Promised Land, and looked his last upon the world. "The hills of Palestine rose up before us. At our feet the Jordan meandered along its noble valley to the calm blue waters of the Dead Sea. And as we meditated on the scene, the solemn words of Deuteronomy (xxxiv. 4) came to our minds with a reality which they had never before assumed: 'This is the land which I sware unto Abraham, unto Isaac, and unto Jacob, saying, I will give it unto thy seed: I have caused thee to see it with thine eyes.'"

And here let us leave them. Those of our readers who have followed us so far, who would like to go farther, may read the full account given by Mr. Palmer in his "Desert of the Exodus." We have, as far as possible, used his own words in compiling this brief narrative; but we have not had space enough to give to our details the brightness of colouring, the high spirits, the deep earnestness and reverence which are in his two volumes. So far as any brightness is found, we are plagiarists.

One word more. After this expedition, which may be considered to a certain degree preliminary, we—the Committee of the English Society —made an arrangement with our friends in America by which we have left them the east of Jordan, and reserved to ourselves the west. It is fair that the two great Anglo-Saxon peoples who, above any other race, read and delight in the Bible, should share this work between them. And to those who propose to raise any private expedition, we would say—*wait*. A few discoveries will, doubtless, be made; but what is wanted is a complete and scientific survey, such as we are doing in Palestine. Backed up with ample funds, prepared to excavate, to search properly, to remain long in one spot if necessary, Mr. Palmer and Mr. Drake have shown us what ought to be done. To attempt to do piecemeal, and with inadequate funds, what ought to be done by a large and well-organized party, is to fritter away money in paltry nibblings, to raise prices, to make exorbitant tribes still more exorbitant, and to add here and there, perhaps, a little bit to geographical and archæological knowledge. But this is not what we mean by the exploration of the Holy Land.

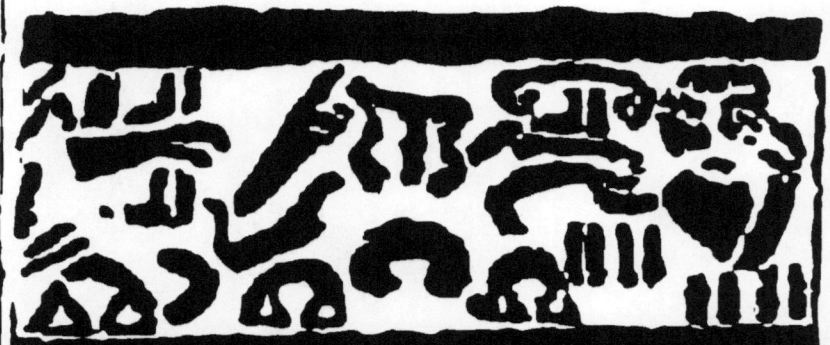

CHAPTER XV.

THE HAMATH INSCRIPTIONS.

IT was in the year 1812, sixty years ago, that the singular inscriptions that are now occupying the attention of so many *savans* were first discovered* by that indefatigable traveller Burckhardt, who found one of them, and describes it as a stone "with a number of small figures and signs which appear to be a kind of hieroglyphical writing, though it does not resemble that of Egypt." No one seems to have noticed the stones again until, in the year 1870, Mr. J. Augustus Johnson, the American Consul-General at Beyrout, travelling with the Rev. P. Jessup, rediscovered them. They first endeavoured to get squeezes of the one in the Bazaar, but failed through the interference of certain Moslem fanatics; and were, finally, obliged to content themselves with such

* See Burton and Drake's "Unexplored Syria," vol. i., pp. 332 *et seq.*; Palestine Exploration Fund "Quarterly Statement," New Series, p. 173.

copies of this and the other stones as could be obtained through the agency of a native painter. Mr. Jessup also endeavoured to purchase one of them; but, unfortunately, it is believed to be a certain cure in cases of deformity and spinal diseases, and is too valuable to its owner to be sold for anything like a moderate sum.* Copies of the tracings thus obtained were sent to America and to England, Mr. Deutsch having received copies. They were seen by Professor Palmer and Mr. C. F. Tyrwhitt Drake on their return from the Tíh expedition; and when Mr. Drake went out to Syria again in the following year, he went to Hamath himself for the Fund, and obtained a valuable set of squeezes. He also tried to photograph them, but with no great success. The squeezes themselves have since been photographed. They lie at the office of the Fund, and can be seen by any one desirous of studying them.

No attempt at deciphering them has as yet been successful, but there seems to be no doubt in any one's mind about their very great antiquity. Mr. Drake discovered another stone with similar characters at Aleppo, and we may fairly hope to find more as we extend our researches in this little known region. " May it not be," asks Mr. Johnson in his paper on the subject, "·that in these Hamath inscriptions·we have fallen upon a transition period, when the Phœnicians, or their predecessors in the land, were using the elements

* Captain Burton heard nothing of this superstition.

of writing then in existence, and before the regular and simple Phœnician alphabet had been perfected?"

The British Museum possesses several seals engraved with similar characters, and there are also certain imperfect copies of the stones in the University Library at Cambridge, discovered by Professor Palmer in a Syriac volume presented to the Library by the Rev. George Williams.

There are, in all, four inscribed stones. The material is compact black basalt, polished as if by hand rubbing. The characters are not incised, but "in cameo, raised from two to four lines, separated by horizontal framing, also in relief" (we are following the account given by Captain Burton). "They are sharply and well cut. The first thing which strikes the observer is that they must date from the metal age, and that they are the work of a civilized race."

The first stone has three lines. It is in the Christian quarter, in the house of Khwajah Jubbúr el Nasrani. "The stone stands, or rather lies, on its side in the eastern wall facing the front impasse; it is close to the left jamb of the doorway to one coming out of the tenement, and the height of the lower margin is 5 ft. from the ground. Under the three lines is a plain surface. . . . . .

"No. 2, which has two lines, lies in the lane called Daib Tak el Tahun, that runs south of the same garden.

"No. 3 is in the orchard of Sayyid Umar bin Hajj Hassan, a little to the west of the ruined

Bab el Jisr, the gate at the southern end of the
third bridge that spans the Orontes, the whole
number being four. This tablet is built up with
common stones around it, close to the ground, in
the northern face of the southern wall, whose
upper part is of unbaked brick. It is remarkably
well and sharply cut, with long raised lines separating, as in No. 1, the three rows of writing.

"No. 4 (total, nine lines) is at the north-west
corner of a little shop belonging to Mohammed
Ali Effendi. . . . . . Its site is the dwarf Bazaar,
a few paces from the west end of the Jisr el
Tayyarah, also called Jisr el Shaykh, the second
of the four bridges, beginning from the south.
. . . . . This stone, unlike the others, shows two
inscribed faces. To the north, where its breadth
is least, appears inscription No. 4 (four lines), with
the upper part plain. . . . . The other inscription
(in five lines) is upon the western side of the wall;
it is immensely larger than the other."

Captain Burton thinks that the Hamath inscriptions form a link between picture writing
and alphabetic character, and suggests a comparison with the Wasúm, or tribe marks of the
Bedawin. Mr. Hyde Clarke has made a careful
examination of the signs, and thinks that the bulk
of them are not hieroglyphs, but characters. Mr.
Dunbar Heath thinks they are hieroglyphs peculiar to Hamáh, but finds upon them the name of
Thothmes III., who successfully invaded Syria
about 1500 B.C.

The town of Hamáh is on the site of the old
Hamath, which appears to have been the principal

city of Upper Syria from the time of the Exodus
to that of the prophet Amos. The Hamathites
were descendants of Canaan, and were closely
akin to the Hittites. Hamath is mentioned from
time to time in the Bible. When David defeated
the King of Zobah, Toi, King of Hamath, sent
him his congratulations. Solomon built "cities"
here (2 Chronicles, viii. 4). In the Assyrian irrup-
tion of Ahab's reign it is mentioned as an independent power. Jeroboam II. recovered and dismantled the town. Antiochus Epiphanus called
it Epiphaneia; but the natives, probably, very
soon reverted to the old name.

One of the most striking features of Hamáh,
Mr. Drake tells us, "are the Ná'úrahs, water-
wheels from 20 to 75 ft. in diameter, intricate
edifices of timber, which, by means of boxes
round the edge, throw the water into, aqueducts, which irrigate the gardens. Each Ná-
'úrah belongs to a company, who keep it in
repair. The creaking of these huge machines,
which spill as much water as they lift, is cease-
less and monotonously discordant. In all, there
are about twenty of them; the principal one is
the Mohammedíyeh, to the west of the Kala. El
Khudúrah is also large. To the south-east of
the Kala are El Jisriyeh on the north-east, and
El Mamúríyeh on the south-west bank. The
current of the Orontes is strong and very deep.
Fish are plentiful.

El Jami'a el Kibír (the great mosque) was
originally a Christian church. There is a Greek
inscription over one of the windows (seemingly

a sister one to that which now forms the altar of
St. Michael in the Greek church of the Blessed
Virgin), and another long inscription is said to
be covered with plaster in the interior of the
building. The mosque has two rows of four
pillars each; the nave has three domes, and
there is another over the Mihrab; the aisles and
. ends of the nave are vaulted. On the outside a
flat projecting cornice is supported by heavy
corbels. In the courtyard there is a small dome
(similar to that which contains the books in the
great mosque at Damascus), supported on eight
pillars, with acanthus capitals.

Many of the mosque towers are in good
taste; the reddish yellow limestone and black
basalt are well contrasted in artistic patterns.

The Greek orthodox Christians here number
about 200 men (*i.e.*, houses), and there are a few
Jacobites. The churches contain little of interest.
The colony of Jews was driven out some fifty or
sixty years ago, on account of the disappearance
of a Turkish girl in their quarter, and have never
been allowed to return. Mr. Drake visited their
cemetery, and copied the solitary inscription there,
which seems to have been over the entrance to
an excavated place of burial. This cemetery,
Kabúr el Yehúd, lies about one mile north-west
of the town on the plateau. The cliffs between
it and the town are full of caves, now used as
dwellings and storehouses. All that were seen
seemed originally made for those purposes, and
not for sepulchres.

CHAPTER XVI.

THE SURVEY OF PALESTINE.

·AFTER the work at Jerusalem had terminated by Captain Warren's return, it was resolved to proceed, as soon as circumstances permitted, with the survey of the whole country. The establishment of an association in America having exactly the same objects as ourselves, willing and anxious to work in perfect friendship with us, gave an opportunity for the division of labour which was not neglected. The river Jordan will divide our work. America takes Moab and all the country to the east, including the Hauran and the Belka—a hitherto unexplored region—where there is a far greater probability of finding treasures, in the shape of inscriptions and coins, than in Palestine proper, which is now being surveyed by ourselves.

The expedition, which was delayed by various hindrances—the war of 1870 being one of the greatest—was started in the autumn of last year. It consisted of Captain R. W. Stewart, R.E., who resigned his work on the Ordnance Survey of England to take this, and two non-commissioned officers, Sergeant Black and Corporal

Armstrong, both experienced surveyors, having been employed for many years in this especial work. They were joined in Palestine by Mr. C. F. Tyrwhitt Drake, who very kindly offered his services in the capacity of Arabic scholar, interpreter, naturalist, and archæologist. His previous experience in the East, as fellow-traveller with Professor E. H. Palmer, and in the Hauran, Lebanon, Cœle Syria, and Hamath, with Captain Burton, made him the most valuable colleague that it was possible for Captain Stewart to have. No time was lost, and proceedings were commenced by the measurement of a base-line, four miles long, near Ramleh, at the close of the year. The base-line measured, the triangulation was carried on vigorously. But here a misfortune occurred. Captain Stewart was seized with an attack of congestion of the liver, which first disabled him, and, after a few weeks of struggle and suffering, sent him home in a prostrate condition. Greatly to his own disappointment and regret, greatly to the disappointment and regret of the Committee, he found himself obliged to resign his appointment. It must, however, always be remembered, when our great map of Palestine is completed and published, a κτῆμα ἐς ἀεί for the whole world—a work never to be done again—that it was begun by Captain Stewart.

Mr. Tyrwhitt Drake, in his absence, assumed charge of the survey for a space of eight months, during which it went on vigorously and well.

Several towns have been identified, and sketches of the ruins made, while the map work has up to the present date (October 17, 1872) extended over upwards of 880 square miles, the scale being one inch to the mile.

The officer selected by the Committee to replace Captain Stewart is Lieutenant Claude R. Conder, R.E. He has now joined Mr. Drake in Jerusalem. Mr. Conder possesses, besides the technical knowledge requisite for map work, a knowledge of Jerusalem based on some years' study. He has followed the work of Captain Wilson and Captain Warren with the deepest attention from the beginning, and is conversant with those works (of Messrs. Robinson, George Williams, Fergusson, Lewin, Thrupp, and others) which have been written on the Jerusalem question. He is also an accomplished artist. We hope the very best from the zeal and activity of Lieutenant Conder and Mr. C. F. Tyrwhitt Drake.

And here we lay down the pen. You, who have followed us so far, know now that our aims are neither visionary, sentimental, nor denominational. We said at the beginning of the work what we say now. There is no country so interesting as Palestine, no city so interesting as Jerusalem. The words that move our hearts, the hopes that nerve our hands, the faith that heals our sorrows—these are all associated with those barren hills, those ruined heaps of stones and rubbish, those dry watercourses of the Holy

Land.   Take the Bible in your hand, and as you
light upon some passage which is cleared up and
illustrated by some of those who have gone
before us in research, confess that the aims of
an Association which only exists by reason of
its love for the Bible, and of its general desire to
do all it can for the illustration of GOD'S word,
are noble indeed.   Help us, you who can.   Wish
us God speed, you who can do us no other
service.

APPENDIX.

M. Clermont Ganneau.

It is now three years since the name of this learned and diligent explorer first became generally known as the possessor of two large fragments of the Moabite Stone. He was then "*Drogman-Chancelier*" of the French Consulate at Jerusalem, and had acquired, by means of his perfect familiarity with Arabic, the keenness of his observations, and the minute care with which he was accustomed to investigate every house into which he entered and every street along which he passed, a knowledge of Jerusalem and its ancient monuments possessed by few, if any, of its residents.

We subjoin some of the results of his investigations. Most of them have been already noticed in the "Quarterly Statement." The first in our list is his note on the Stone of Zoheleth.

It will be remembered that it was at this stone, "which is by En Rogel," that Adonijah "slew sheep and oxen and fat cattle" when he purposed to seize the kingdom in his father's extreme old age. So that if we can identify the Stone of Zoheleth, we are not far from En Rogel, a fountain which lay on the boundary line between Judah and Benjamin (Joshua, xv. 7, and xviii. 16). It was, too, the point next to Jerusalem, and lower down than the city. Modern tradition identifies it with the Bîr Eyub. The name En Rogel means "the spring of the fuller." Now, Bîr Eyub is not a spring, but a well. Bîr Eyub appears to be too far south to be on the frontier line. Now, M. Clermont Ganneau finds in the village of Siloam a rocky plateau, its western face cut perpendicularly, with rude steps up the face, which the natives call *Ez Zehweile*—a name exactly similar to Zoheleth.

The Stone Bohan.—Another monument previously unidentified is the *Stone Bohan*, mentioned in Joshua, xvi. 6, and xviii. 17; it is on the frontier of Judah and Benjamin, between Beth-arabah and Beth-hogla in the east and Adummim and En-shemesh in the west. M. Clermont Ganneau considers that the translation of the authorized version, "Bohan the son of Reuben," is erroneous; and he identifies Bohan, the *Stone of the Thumb*, with the *Hajar-el-asbah*, *Stone of the Finger*, of the Bedawin, close by where the Wady Daber enters into the narrow plain which separates it from the Dead Sea.

Inscribed Stone from King Herod's Temple.—This is, perhaps, the most interesting, next to the Moabite Stone, of all the discoveries connected with the name of M. Clermont Ganneau. There lies close to the Via Dolorosa, and not far from the north-west angle of the Haram (it is on the left-hand side of the Via Dolorosa, opposite the *Bab el Aksa*), a small Moslem cemetery, where lie the remains of certain Sheikhs who have from time to time died in the odour of sanctity. Here is a gateway. While examining the walls, step by step, M. Ganneau observed two or three Greek characters on a block forming the .angle of the wall, on which was built a small arch. The characters were close to the surface of the ground. M. Ganneau proceeded to scrape away the soil, in hopes of finding them continued. More characters appeared, and when the stone was finally cleared, the discoverer had the gratification of reading the following inscription in Greek, in seven lines:—

ΜΗΘΕΝΑ ΑΛΛΟΓΕΝΙΙ ΕΙΣΠΟΡΕΤΕΣΘΑΙ ΕΝΤΟΣ ΤΟΥ ΠΕΡΙ
ΤΟ ΙΕΡΟΝ ΤΡΥΨΑΚΤΟΥ ΚΑΙ ΠΕΡΙΒΟΛΟΥ ΟΣΔΑΝ ΛΗΨΘΗ
ΕΑΥΤΩΙ ΑΙΤΙΟΣ ΕΣΤΑΙ ΔΙΑ ΤΟ ΕΞΑΚΟΛΟΥΘΕΙΝ ΘΑΝΑΤΟΝ.

The characters are monumental in size, and present the appearance which one would expect in an inscription of the period.

The translation is:—

"No stranger is to enter within the balustrade ($\tau\rho\upsilon\varphi\alpha\kappa\tau\sigma\varsigma$) round the temple and enclosure. Whoever is caught will be responsible to himself for his death, which will ensue."

Josephus says as follows:—

"When you go through these first cloisters unto the second (court of the seven temples), there was a partition ($\delta\rho\upsilon\varphi\alpha\kappa\tau\sigma\varsigma$) made of stone all round, whose height was three cubits; its construction was very elegant. Upon it stood pillars at equal distances from one another, declaring the laws of purity, some in Greek, and some in Roman letters, that no 'foreigner should go within that sanctuary.'"

We may boldly affirm that this Greek inscription is

not only the most ancient, but also the most interesting, in all its bearings, which Jerusalem has yet produced. *Bahurim* (2 Sam., xvii. 18; 1 Kings, ii. 8), where dwelt Shimei, is another place which has baffled students. Mr. Grove says that it "must have been very near the south boundary of Benjamin, but it is not mentioned in the list in Joshua; nor is any explanation given of its being Benjamite, as, from Shimei's residing there, we may conclude it was." M. Ganneau has discovered a point which he thinks exactly corresponds to the Biblical requirements, and at the same time is etymologically identical. It is *Fakhoury*, a place which corresponds letter by letter to Bahurim, without the plural termination. It is an uninhabited locality, situated between the Mount of Olives, Siloam, Bethany, and Abou Dis. Do not look for it in the map, because it is not marked in any.

The Count de Vogüé.

Hardly any part of the Holy Land is more interesting than the remote and little visited region, now known as the Hauran, which in the Bible we find called Argob, " a heap of stones." Here were formerly great cities, with walls and brazen bars; this was the kingdom of King Og—" the region of Argob, with all Bashan, called the land of giants," was given to the half tribe of Manasseh; it was the retreat of the Geshurites, who "dwell among the Israelites to this day" (Joshua, xiii. 13), and furnished a wife to King David, in the person of " Maacah, the daughter of Talmai, King of Geshur," and mother of Absalom. The country has been visited and described by Dr. Porter, Captain Burton, Mr. Freshfield, and other recent travellers, whose accounts may be consulted by readers desirous of further information. We are indebted to the Count de Vogüé for a very careful and valuable paper on its architecture and natural features, originally published in the " Recovery of Jerusalem," and to Mr. Waddington for a collection of Greek inscriptions found here by himself and M. de Vogüé; these have been recently supplemented by others found by Captain Burton.

Mr. Macgregor.

Mr. Macgregor's journey with his canoe to the Jordan need only here be alluded to from its geographical aspect. His discoveries at the Lake Huleh—waters of Merom—

and at the lakes near Damascus, have considerably modified the maps in that place. In his book ("Rob Roy on the Jordan") may be read accounts of the Lake of Galilee, Castle of Banias, and many other places of which we have had to speak. The Palestine Exploration Fund is also indebted to him for a most vivid and eloquent account of a visit to Captain Warren's shafts.

CAPTAIN BURTON AND MR. TYRWHITT DRAKE.

In two valuable and interesting volumes very recently published, called "Unexplored Syria," we have the principal results of Captain Burton's stay in Damascus as our Consul, and of his wanderings with Mr. Drake. Captain Burton's unparalleled experience as a traveller, his extraordinary linguistic attainments, his clear faculty of observation, his scholarship, and retentive memory, all make him one of the foremost in the long roll of England's travellers. The two volumes just published, to which we refer our readers, contain accounts of journeys in Lebanon, the Hauran, in the Anti-Lebanon, and in the Alah, or Highlands of Syria. There are also a collection of Syrian proverbs—Captain Burton has before this issued a collection of West African proverbs—and *fac-similes* of the Hamath stones, with other important matter.

DR. TRISTRAM.

A sum of £100 was voted by the British Association in 1870 towards the exploration of Moab. The money was not spent in that year; nor was it till the autumn of 1871 that an expedition was undertaken by the Rev. Canon Tristram, Mr. C. Louis Buxton, and Mr. B. C. Johnson. The geographical results of the expedition, as described in the papers read before the British Association, appear to consist chiefly in the discovery of certain ancient cities previously unvisited in the country east of Moab. Archæologically, the expedition discovered a most curious and interesting ruin, a few miles east of Ziza (formerly the head-quarters of the Dalmatio-Illyrian Cavalry). The ruin is of a magnificent palace, probably of the time of Chosroes the Second, the invader of Palestine. Survey work is also spoken of; but until a full account of the work done is published we cannot speak of its value.

FROM A LETTER BY MR. DEUTSCH ON THE MARKS AT
THE SOUTH-EAST ANGLE (*see p.* 122).

"I must now speak somewhat fully on a subject which
has engaged public attention for some time, and has
already given rise to many conjectures — namely, the
'Writings,' either painted on, or cut into, the stones, discovered lately on the bottom rows of the wall at the south-
east corner of the Haram, at a depth of about 90 ft., there
where the foundations lie on the live rock itself. I have
examined them carefully in their places—by no means an
easy task.

"I have come to the following conclusions:—1, The
signs cut or painted were on the stones when they were
first laid in their present places; 2, they do not represent
any Inscription; 3, they are Phœnician.

"I consider them to be partly letters, partly numerals,
and partly special masons' or quarry signs. Some of
them were recognizable at once as well-known Phœnician
characters; others, hitherto unknown in Phœnician epi-
graphy, I had the rare satisfaction of being able to identify on absolutely undoubted antique Phœnician structures
in Syria; such as the primitive substructures of the har-
bour at Sidon. No less did I observe them on the
'bevelled' stones taken from ancient edifices, and built
into later work throughout Phœnicia. For a most striking
and obvious instance of this I would point to the ruined
citadel standing above Saida, the stones of which—old
Phœnician stones to wit, immured in their present place
at subsequent periods—teem with peculiar marks ('Fan-
tasias') identical with those at Jerusalem. These signs
have, to my knowledge, never been noticed before, as, indeed, I was the first to point them out to the very exca-
vator of the famous Ashmunazar Sarcophagus himself—
a Syrian gentleman resident at Saida, and well acquainted
with all the extant remains."

THE END.

LIST OF BOOKS PRINCIPALLY REFERRED TO
IN PRECEDING PAGES.

RECOVERY OF JERUSALEM. *Bentley and Son,* 1872. One Guinea.

QUARTERLY STATEMENTS OF THE PALESTINE EXPLORATION FUND. *Bentley and Son,* 1869—1872.

SMITH'S BIBLE DICTIONARY.

ORDNANCE SURVEY OF JERUSALEM, WITH NOTES, PLANS, SKETCHES, AND PHOTOGRAPHS. 1865. *Agent, Mr. Stanford, 6, Charing-cross.*

ORDNANCE SURVEY OF SINAI, WITH NOTES, PLANS, &c. 1872. *Agent, Mr. Stanford, 6, Charing-cross.*

PALMER'S DESERT OF THE EXODUS, 1871. *London: Bell and Daldy; and New York: Harper.* Twenty-eight Shillings.

BESANT AND PALMER'S HISTORY OF JERUSALEM, FROM TITUS TO THE PRESENT DAY. *Bentley and Son,* 1872. Six Shillings.

MURRAY'S HANDBOOK TO SYRIA AND PALESTINE.

ROBINSON'S BIBLICAL RESEARCHES.

WILLIAMS'S HOLY CITY.

FERGUSSON'S JERUSALEM.

THRUPP'S ANCIENT JERUSALEM.

LEWIN'S SIEGE OF JERUSALEM.

&c.   &c.   &c.